Babylon

Words & Music by David Gray

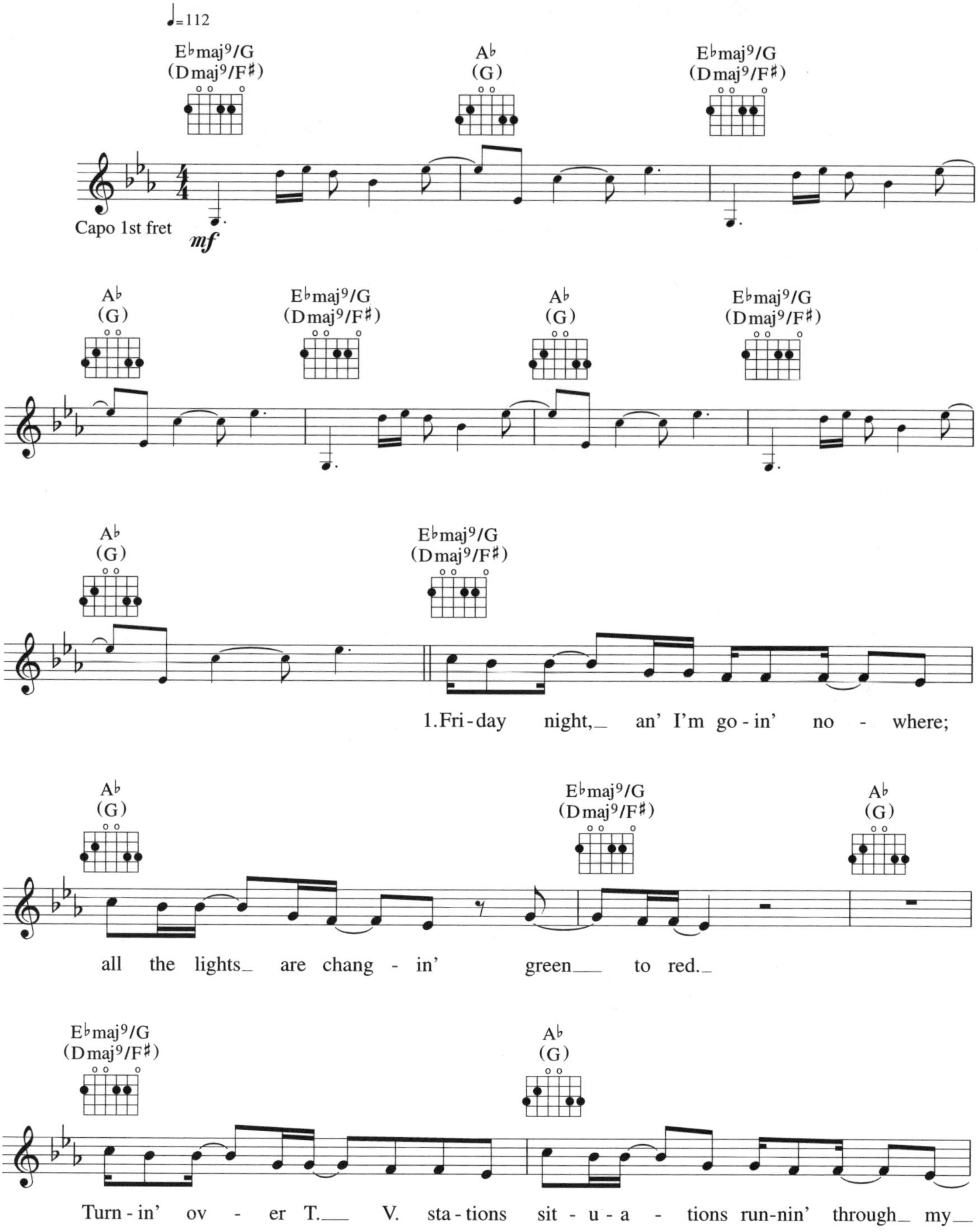

♩=112

E♭maj⁹/G (Dmaj⁹/F♯) A♭ (G) E♭maj⁹/G (Dmaj⁹/F♯)

Capo 1st fret

mf

A♭ (G) E♭maj⁹/G (Dmaj⁹/F♯) A♭ (G) E♭maj⁹/G (Dmaj⁹/F♯)

A♭ (G) E♭maj⁹/G (Dmaj⁹/F♯)

1.Fri-day night,_ an' I'm go-in' no - where;

A♭ (G) E♭maj⁹/G (Dmaj⁹/F♯) A♭ (G)

all the lights_ are chang - in' green__ to red._

E♭maj⁹/G (Dmaj⁹/F♯) A♭ (G)

Turn-in' ov - er T.__ V. sta-tions sit - u - a - tions run-nin' through_ my_

E♭maj9/G (Dmaj9/F♯) A♭ (G) E♭maj9/G (Dmaj9/F♯)
head. Look-in' back through time, you know it's clear
A♭ (G) E♭maj9/G (Dmaj9/F♯)
that I've been blind I've been a fool.
A♭ (G) E♭maj9/G (Dmaj9/F♯)
To op - en up my heart to all that
A♭ (G) E♭maj9/G (Dmaj9/F♯) A♭ (G)
jea-lous-y that bit-ter-ness, that rid-i-cule.
Fm (Em) E♭maj9/G (Dmaj9/F♯)
2. Sat-ur-day I'm run-nin' wild, an' all
3. Sun-day all the lights in Lon-don
A♭ (G) E♭maj9/G (Dmaj9/F♯) A♭ (G)
the lights are chang-in' red to green.
shin-ing sky is fad-ing red to blue.

90's Hits for Buskers

Wise Publications
London/New York/Sydney/Paris/Copenhagen/Berlin/Madrid/Tokyo

Exclusive distributors:
Music Sales Limited
8/9 Frith Street,
London W1D 3JB, England.
Music Sales Pty Limited
120 Rothschild Avenue
Rosebery, NSW 2018,
Australia.

Order No. AM959354
ISBN 0-7119-7439-X

Music arranged by James Dean
Music processed by Andrew Shiels
Cover design by Chloë Alexander

Printed in the United Kingdom by
Printwise (Haverhill) Limited, Suffolk.

Your Guarantee of Quality
As publishers, we strive to produce every book to the highest commercial standards. The music has been freshly engraved and the book has been carefully designed to minimise awkward page turns and to make playing from it a real pleasure.
Particular care has been given to specifying acid-free, neutral-sized paper made from pulps which have not been elemental chlorine bleached. This pulp is from farmed sustainable forests and was produced with special regard for the environment.
Throughout, the printing and binding have been planned to ensure a sturdy, attractive publication which should give years of enjoyment. If your copy fails to meet our high standards, please inform us and we will gladly replace it.

E♭maj9/G
(Dmaj9/F♯)
Mov - in' through the crowds, I'm push - in'
Kick - ing through the au - tumn leaves an'
A♭
(G)
E♭maj9/G
(Dmaj9/F♯)
chem - i - cals are rush - in' in my blood-stream.
won - derin' where it is you might be go - ing to.
A♭
(G)
E♭maj9/G
(Dmaj9/F♯)
On-ly wish that you were here, you know I'm seein'
Turn-in' back for home you know I'm feel -
A♭
(G)
E♭maj9/G
(Dmaj9/F♯)
it so clear, I've been a - fraid.
- ing so a - lone I can't be - lieve.
A♭
(G)
E♭maj9/G
(Dmaj9/F♯)
To show you how I real - ly feel, ad - mit
Climb - in' on the stair I turn a - round
A♭
(G)
E♭maj9/G
(Dmaj9/F♯)
A♭
(G)
to some of those bad mis - takes I've made.
to see you smil-ing there in front of me.

E♭maj9/G
(Dmaj9/F♯)
B♭
(A)
And if you want it come an' get it,
Fm
(Em)
Gm11
(F♯m11)
for cry - in' out loud.
E♭maj9/G
(Dmaj9/F♯)
B♭
(A)
The love that I was giv - in' you was
Fm
(Em)
A♭
(G)
E♭maj9/G
(Dmaj9/F♯)
3
nev - er in doubt.
Let go your heart
B♭
(A)
Fm
(Em)
B♭
(A)
let go your head and feel it now.
E♭maj9/G
(Dmaj9/F♯)
B♭
(A)
Fm
(Em)
To Coda
Let go your heart let go your head, and feel it
1.
B♭
(A)
E♭maj9/G
(Dmaj9/F♯)
now, Ba - by - lon,

1. cont.
Ab (G)
Ebmaj9/G (Dmaj9/F#)
Ba - by - lon,
Ba - by - lon.
1. cont.
2. Bb (A)
D.S. al Coda
now.
Coda
now,
Ba - by - lon,
Ba - by - lon.
Ba - by - lon,
Ba - by - lon,
Ba - by - lon,
ah.

Angels

Words & Music by Robbie Williams & Guy Chambers

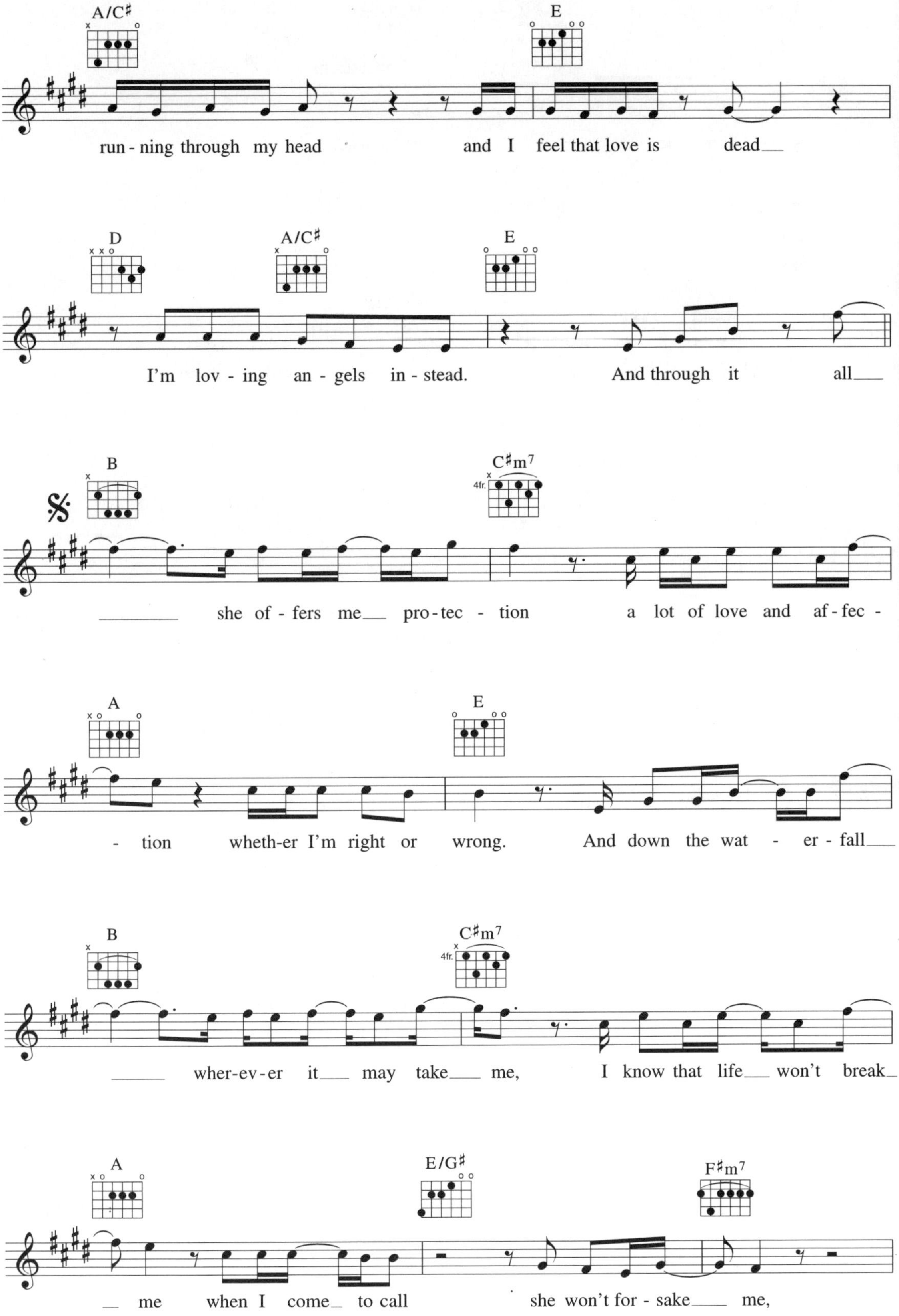

A/C♯ E

run - ning through my head and I feel that love is dead__

D A/C♯ E

I'm lov - ing an - gels in - stead. And through it all__

B C♯m7

______ she of - fers me__ pro - tec - tion a lot of love and af - fec -

A E

- tion wheth-er I'm right or wrong. And down the wat - er - fall__

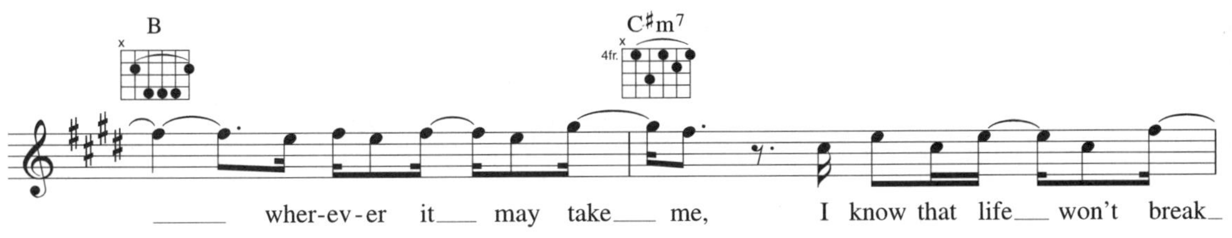

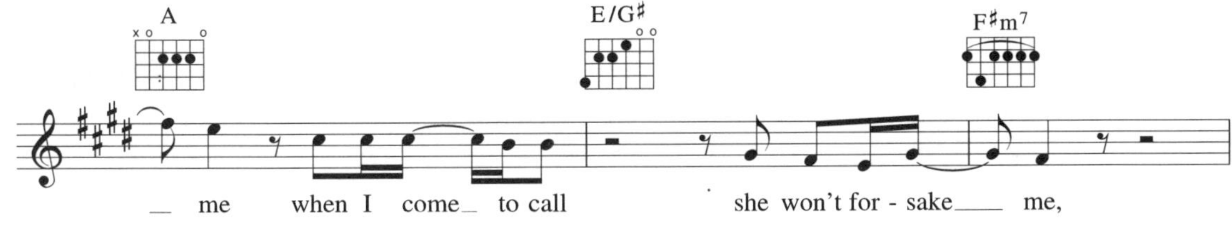

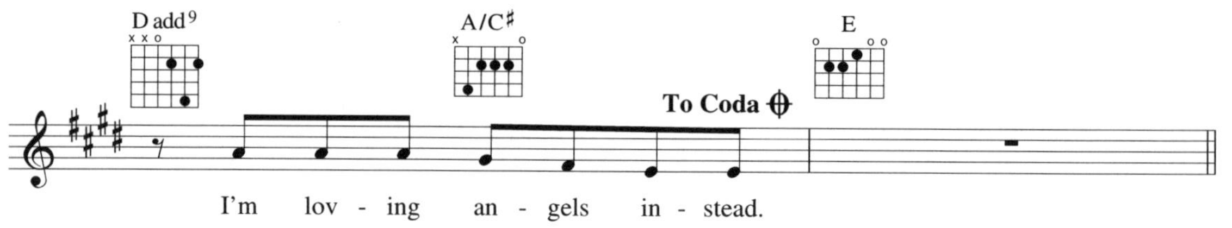
D add9
A/C♯
E
To Coda
I'm lov - ing an - gels in - stead.

E
2.When I'm feel-ing weak and my pain walks down a one -

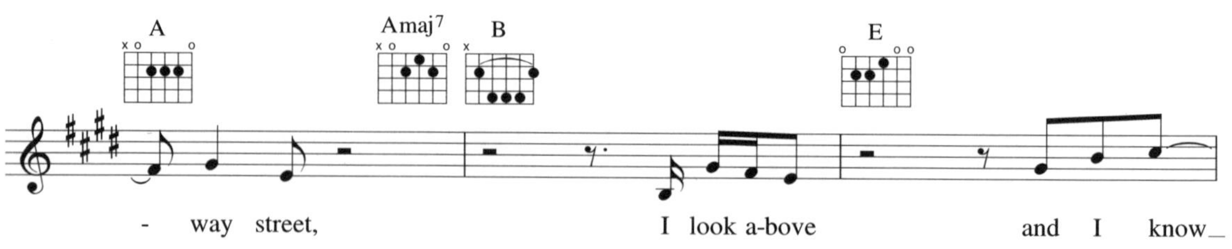
A
Amaj7
B
E
- way street, I look a-bove and I know

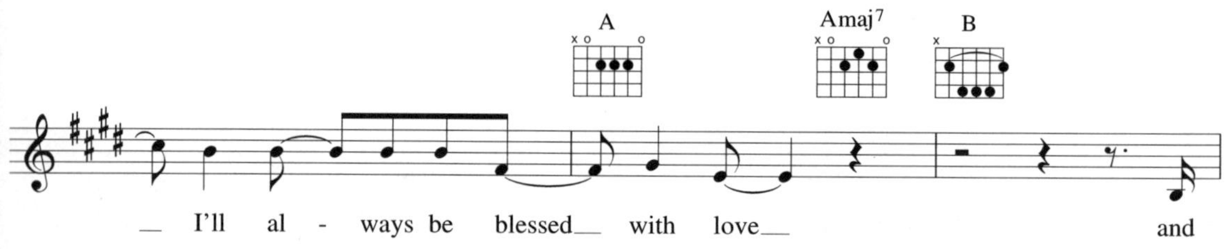
A
Amaj7
B
I'll al - ways be blessed with love and

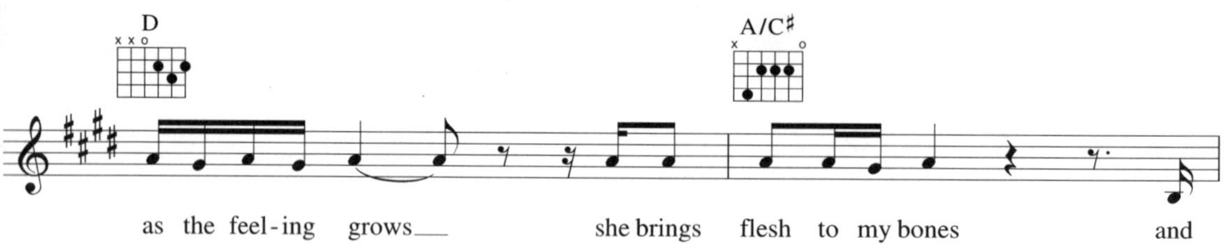
D
A/C♯
as the feel-ing grows she brings flesh to my bones and

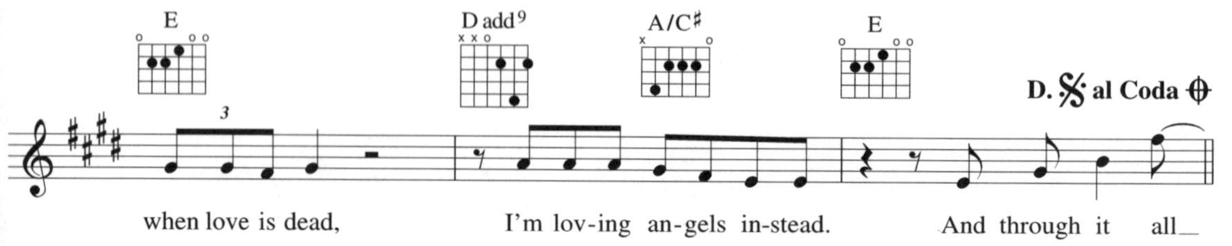
E
D add9
A/C♯
E
D.𝄋 al Coda
3
when love is dead, I'm lov-ing an-gels in-stead. And through it all

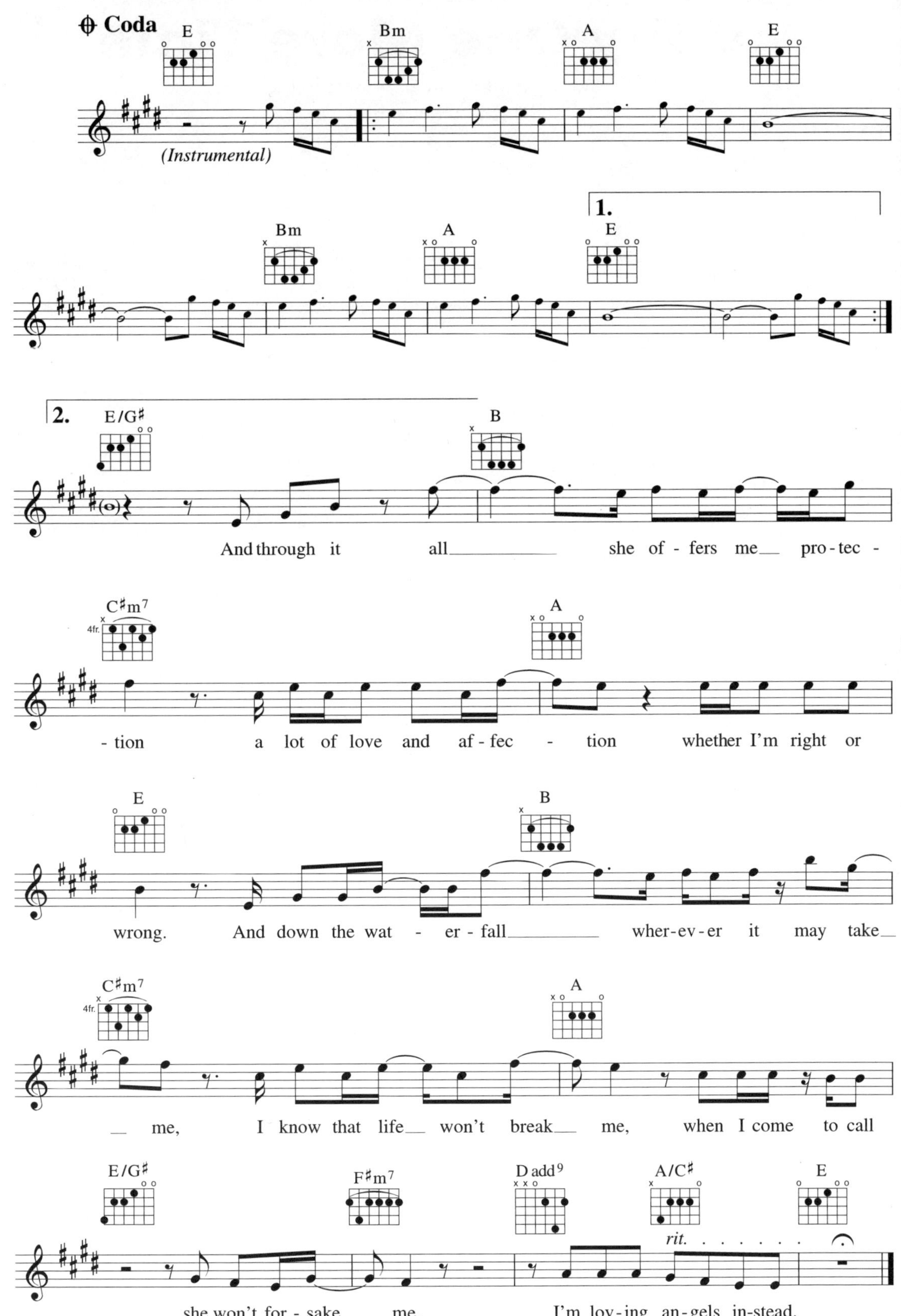
Coda
E
Bm
A
E
(Instrumental)
Bm
A
1.
E
2.
E/G♯
B
And through it all she of - fers me pro - tec - tion
C♯m7
4fr.
A
a lot of love and af - fec - tion whether I'm right or wrong.
E
B
And down the wat - er - fall wher - ev - er it may take me,
C♯m7
4fr.
A
I know that life won't break me, when I come to call
E/G♯
F♯m7
D add9
A/C♯
E
rit.
she won't for - sake me. I'm lov - ing an - gels in - stead.

...Baby One More Time

Words & Music by Max Martin

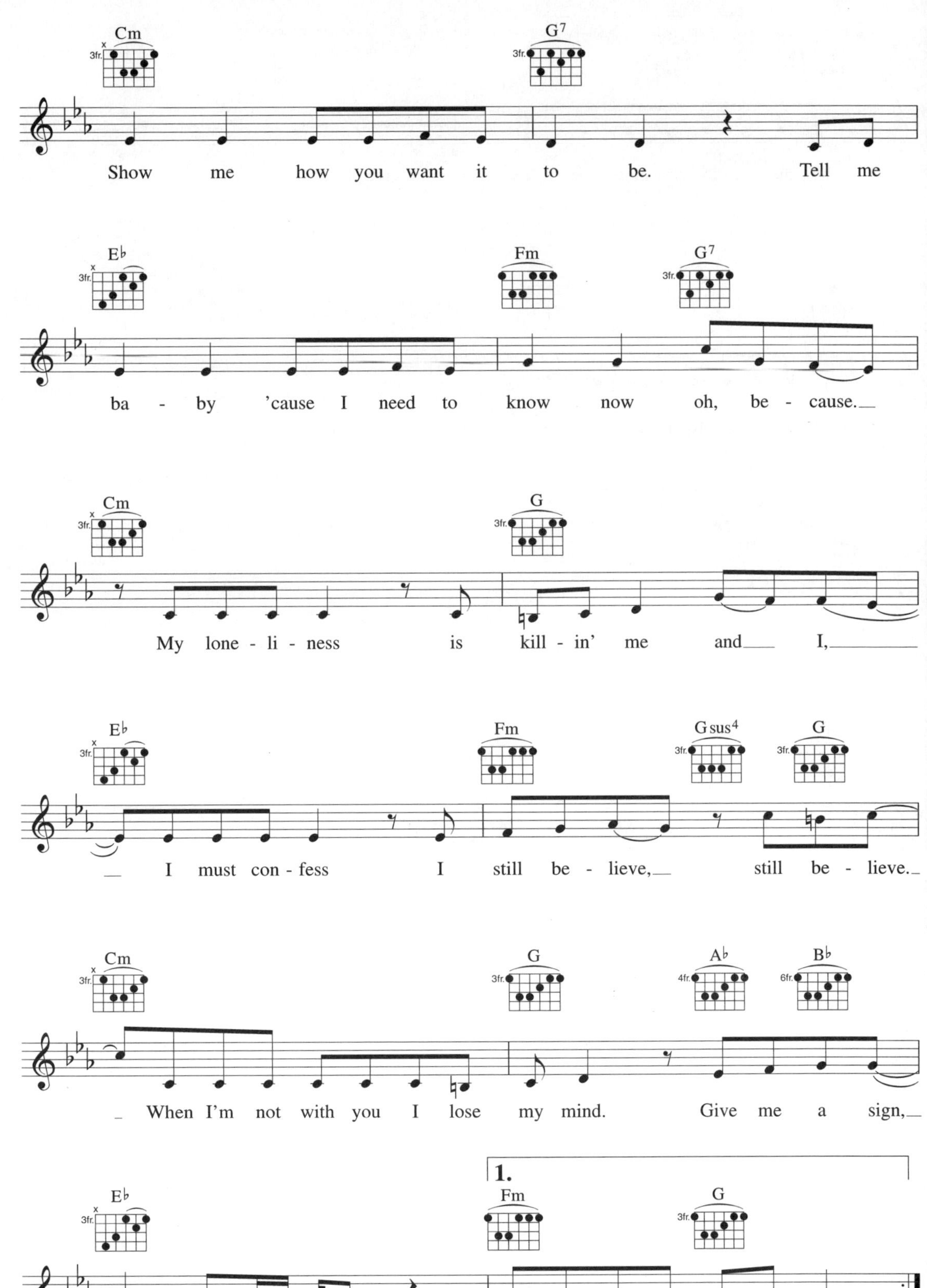
Cm G7
Show me how you want it to be. Tell me
E♭ Fm G7
ba - by 'cause I need to know now oh, be - cause.
Cm G
My lone - li - ness is kill - in' me and I,
E♭ Fm Gsus4 G
I must con - fess I still be - lieve, still be - lieve.
Cm G A♭ B♭
When I'm not with you I lose my mind. Give me a sign,
1.
E♭ Fm G
hit me ba - by one more time.

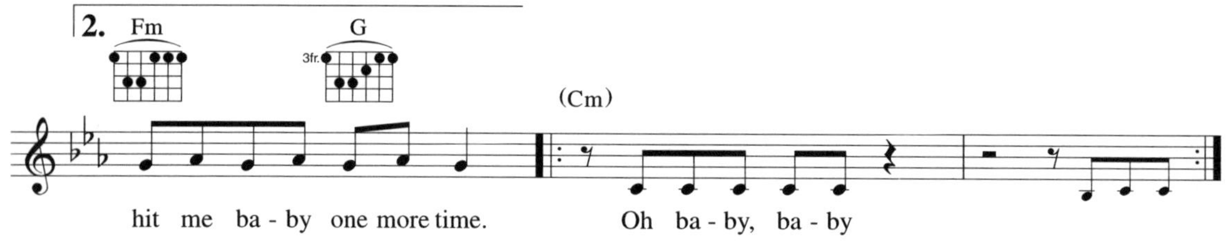
2.
Fm
G
(Cm)
hit me ba - by one more time.
Oh ba - by, ba - by

Cm
G7
E♭
Oh ba-by, ba-by how was I sup - posed to know?

Fm
Gsus4
G
A♭
B♭
Oh pret-ty ba-by I should-n't have let you go.
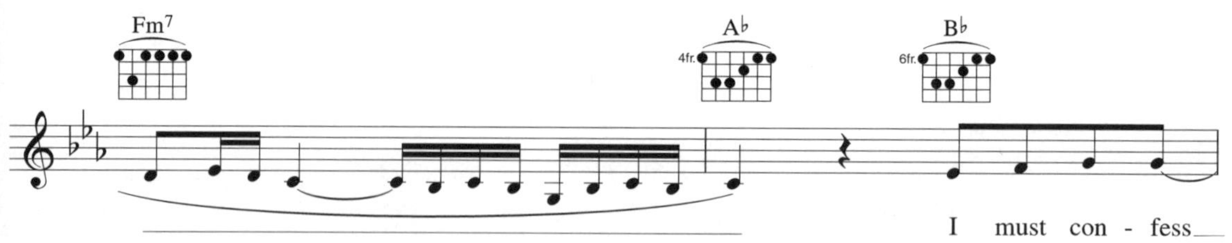
Fm7
A♭
B♭
I must con - fess

Cm
G
that my lone - li - ness is kill - in' me now,

E♭
Fm
Gsus4
G
don't you know I still be - lieve

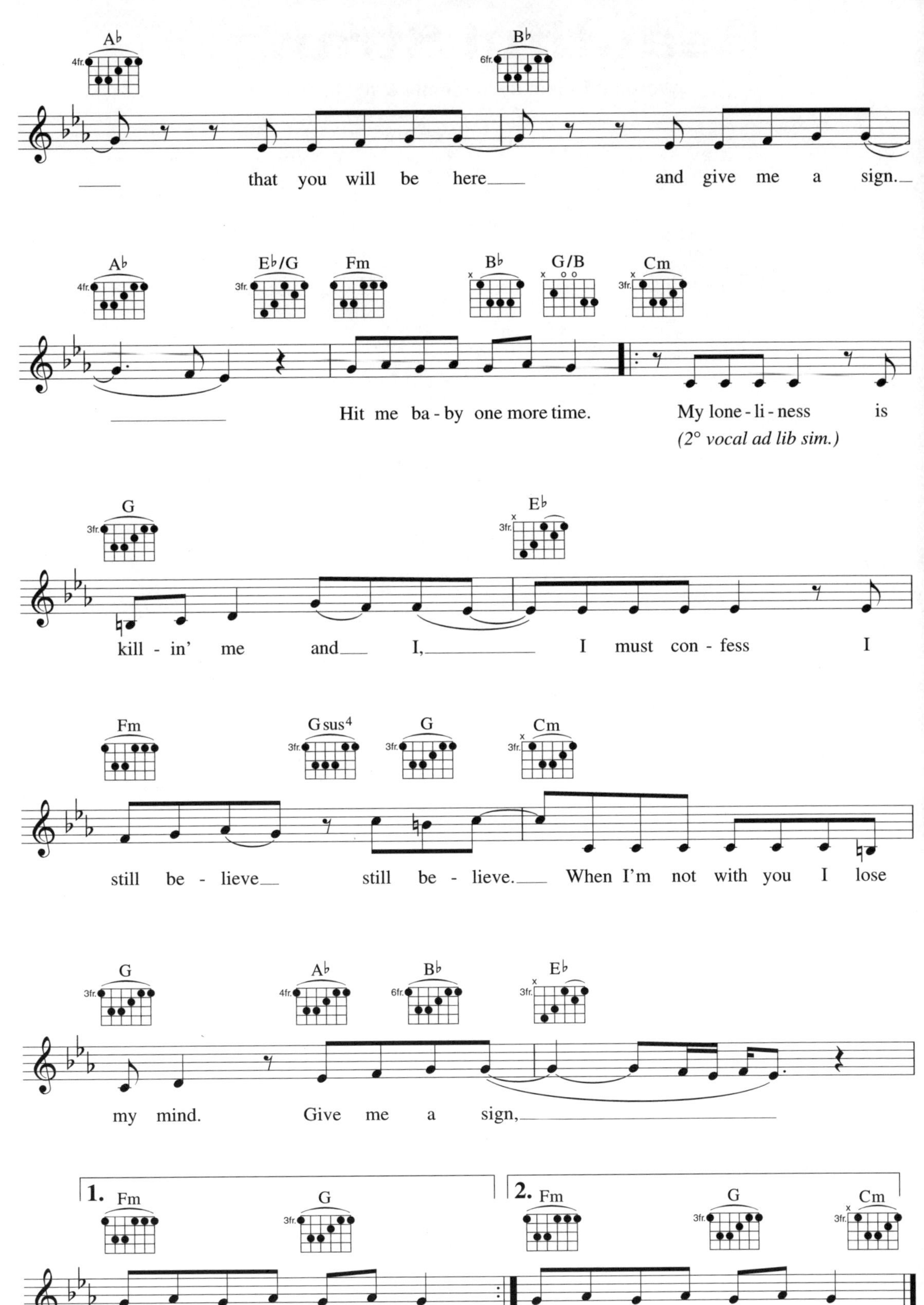

A♭ B♭
4fr. 6fr.
that you will be here and give me a sign.
A♭ E♭/G Fm B♭ G/B Cm
Hit me ba - by one more time. My lone - li - ness is
(2° vocal ad lib sim.)
G E♭
kill - in' me and I, I must con - fess I
Fm Gsus4 G Cm
still be - lieve still be - lieve. When I'm not with you I lose
G A♭ B♭ E♭
my mind. Give me a sign,
1. Fm G
hit me ba - by one more time.
2. Fm G Cm
hit me ba - by one more time.

Beautiful Stranger

Words & Music by Madonna & William Orbit

C♯7sus4
C♯7
C♯7sus4
If I'm smart_ then I'll run a - way,_ but I'm not_ so I
on (𝄋) If I'm smart_ then I'll run a - way,_ but I'm not_ so I
C♯7
C♯7sus4
C♯7
guess I'll__ stay. Heav-en for - bid,___ I'll take my chance_ on a
guess I'll__ stay. Have-n't you heard,_ I fell in love__ with a
C♯7sus4
C♯7
beau - ti - ful stran - - ger.
beau - ti - ful stran - - ger.
B
A
I looked in - to your___ eyes and my world_
I looked in - to your___ face my heart was__
C♯7sus4
C♯7
B
_ came tum - bl - ing down.__ You're the Dev - il in
dancing all ov - er the place.__ I'd like to change my point
A
C♯7sus4
C♯7
dis - guise, that's why I'm sing - ing this song.
of view, if I could just for - get a - bout___ you.___
F♯
F♯sus4
E
To know___ you___ is to love__

B
To Coda 1
C♯7
C♯7sus4
you. You're ev - 'ry - where I go,
C♯7
C♯7sus4
To Coda 2
F♯
and ev - 'ry - bo - dy knows to love you
E
B
C♯7
is to be part of you. I paid for you with
C♯7sus4
C♯7
C♯7sus4
tears, and swal-lowed all my pride.
E
B
F♯
A
C♯7
Duh duh duh duh da dum da dum da da da da dum, beau - ti - ful
E
B
F♯
A
stran - ger. Duh duh duh duh da dum da dum da da da da dum,
C♯7
C♯7sus4
C♯7
D.S. al Coda 1
beau - ti - ful stran - ger.

Coda 1
C♯7sus4
C♯7
You're ev - 'ry - where I go,
C♯7sus4
C♯7
D.%% al Coda 2
and ev - 'ry - bo - dy knows.
Coda 2
C♯7sus4
C♯7
C♯7sus4
I paid for you with tears, and swal-lowed all my
C♯7
E
B
F♯
A
pride. Duh duh duh duh da dum da dum da da da da dum,
C♯7
E
B
beau - ti - ful stran - ger. Duh duh duh duh da dum da dum
F♯
A
C♯7
da da da da dum, beau - ti - ful stran - ger.
C♯7
C♯7sus4
C♯7
C♯7sus4
C♯7
C♯7sus4
C♯7
C♯7sus4
Repeat to fade
(Instrumental)

Common People

Words by Jarvis Cocker
Music by Pulp

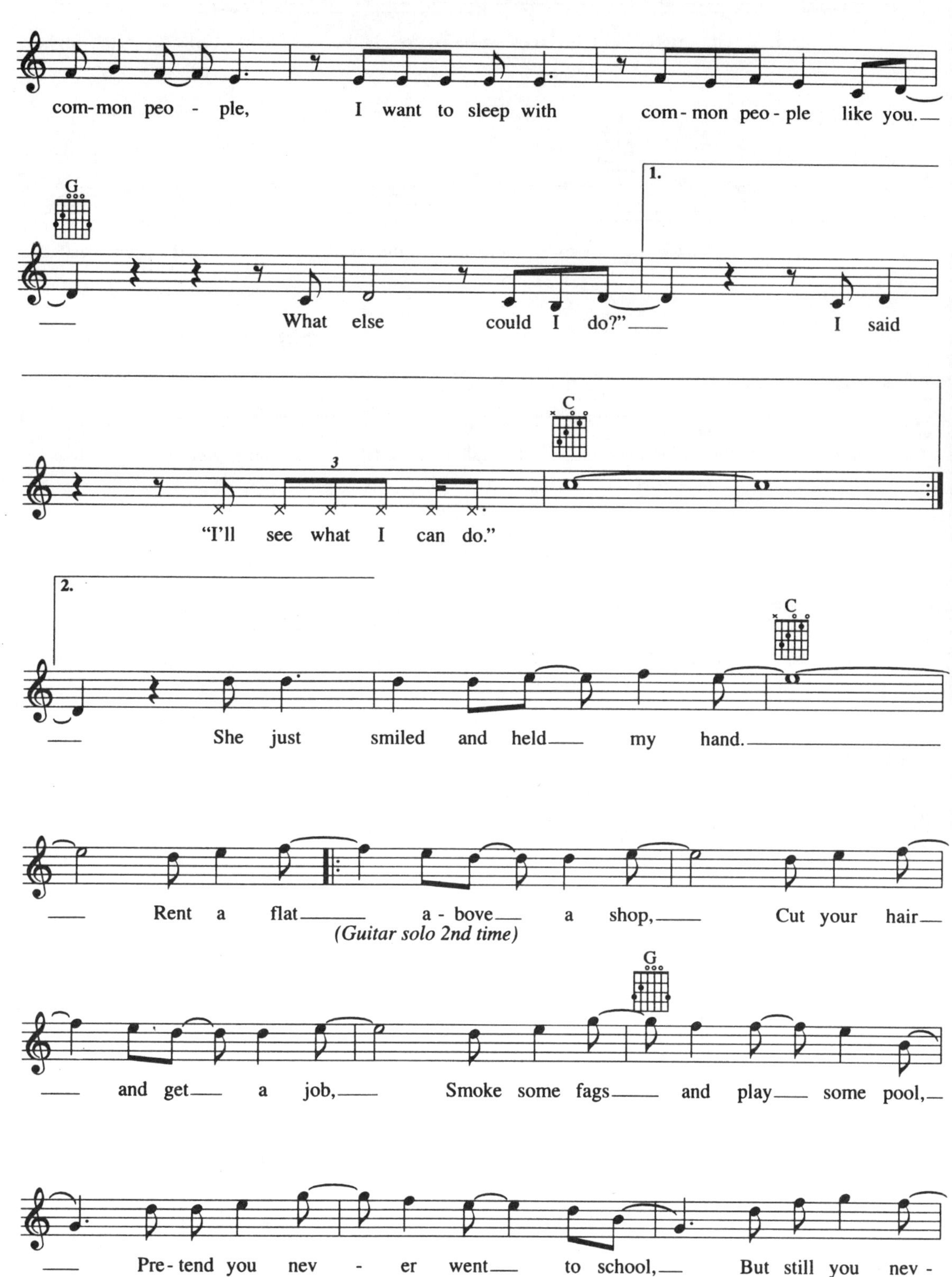
com-mon peo - ple, I want to sleep with com-mon peo-ple like you.
G
What else could I do?"
1.
I said
"I'll see what I can do."
C
2.
She just smiled and held my hand.
C
Rent a flat a - bove a shop, Cut your hair
(Guitar solo 2nd time)
and get a job, Smoke some fags and play some pool,
G
Pre-tend you nev - er went to school, But still you nev -

C
- er get it right 'cos when you're laid in bed at night
G
watch - ing roach - es climb the wall, If you called
F
your dad he could stop it all, yeah! You'll nev - er live like
com - mon peo - ple, You'll nev - er do what - ev - er com - mon peo - ple do,
C
Nev - er fail like com - mon peo - ple, You'll nev - er watch your life
G
slide out of view, And dance and drink and screw,
C
Be - cause there's no - thing else to do.

2. I took her to a supermarket,
I don't know why but I had to start it somewhere,
So it started there.
I said "Pretend you've got no money,"
But she just laughed and said
"Oh you're so funny!"
I said "Yeah?"
(Spoken): "Well,
"I can't see anyone else smiling in here,"
"Are you sure?"

CHORUS 1:
You want to live like common people,
You want to see whatever common people see,
Want to sleep with common people,
You want to sleep with common people like me.
But she didn't understand,
She just held my hand.

3. *Guitar solo*

CHORUS 2:
Sing along with the common people,
Sing along and it might just get you through,
Laugh along with the common people,
Laugh along even though they're laughing at you,
And the stupid things that you do,
Because you think that poor is cool.

The Day We Caught The Train

Words & Music by Steve Cradock, Simon Fowler, Oscar Harrison & Damon Minchella

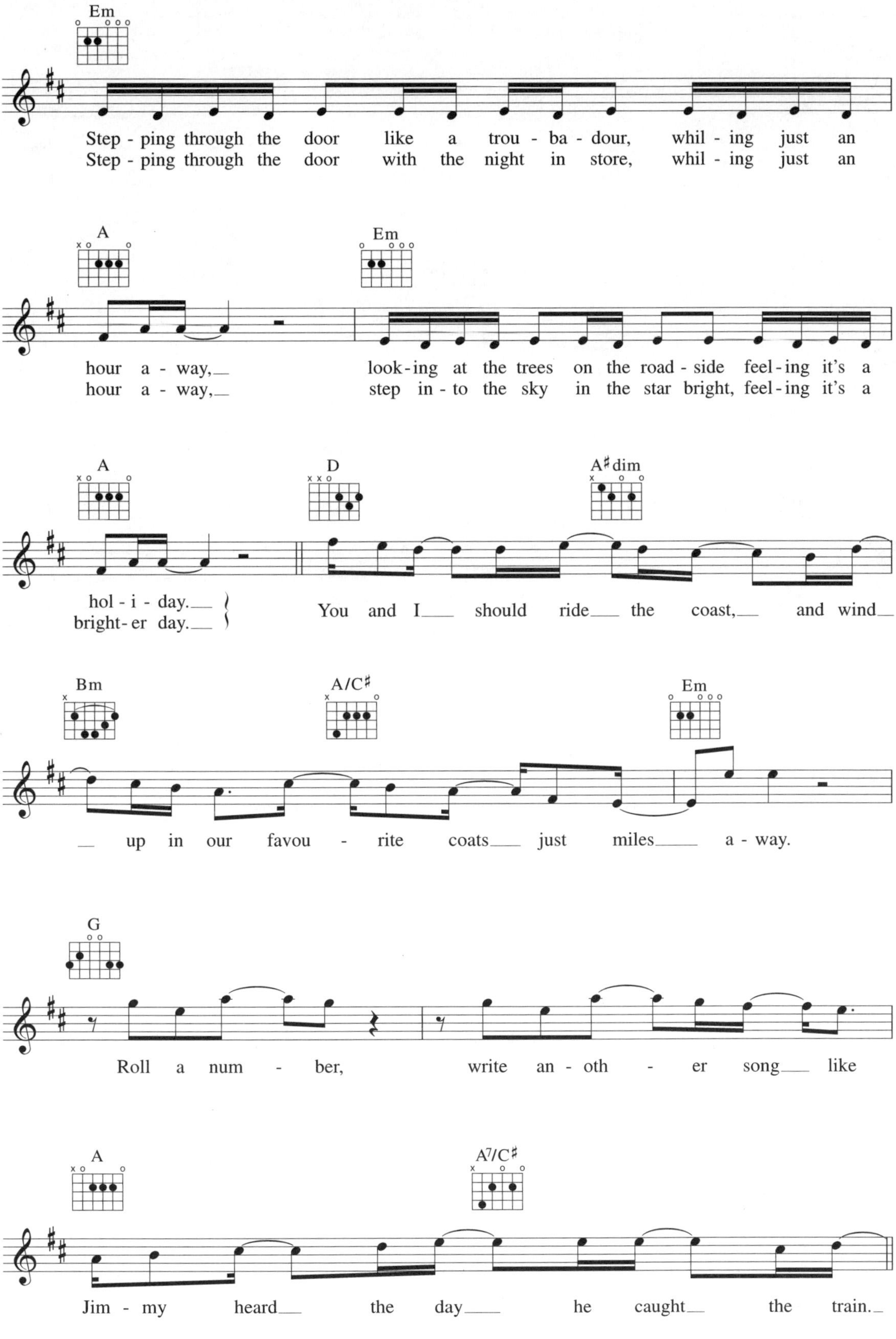

Em

Step - ping through the door like a trou - ba - dour, whil - ing just an
Step - ping through the door with the night in store, whil - ing just an

A Em

hour a - way, looking at the trees on the road - side feel - ing it's a
hour a - way, step in - to the sky in the star bright, feel - ing it's a

A D A♯dim

hol - i - day. You and I should ride the coast, and wind
bright - er day.

Bm A/C♯ Em

up in our favou - rite coats just miles a - way.

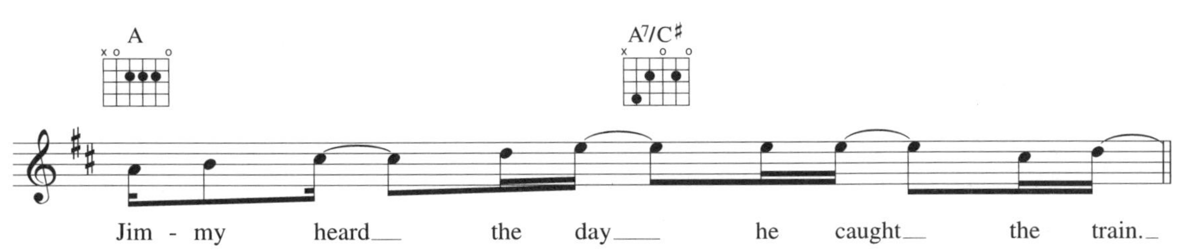

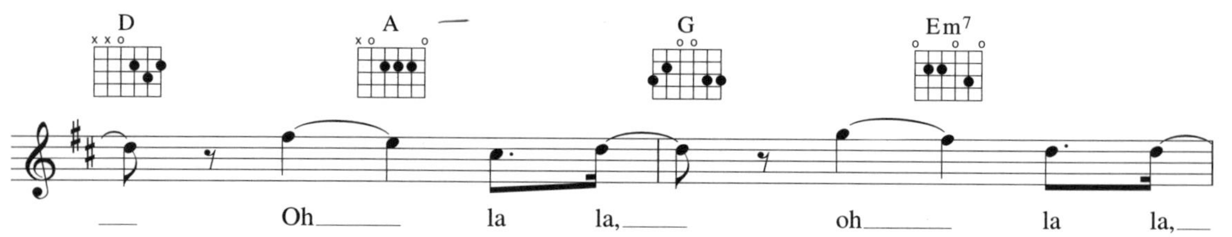
D
A
G
Em7
Oh la la, oh la la,

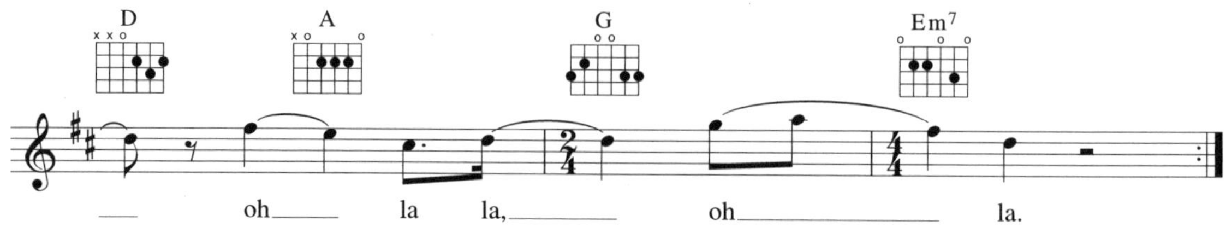
D
A
G
Em7
oh la la, oh la.

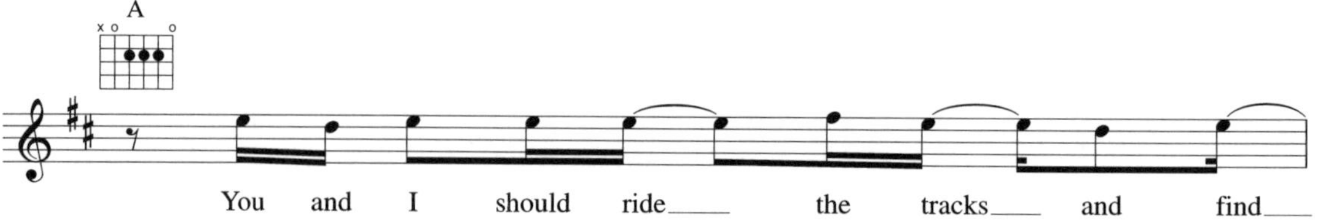
A
You and I should ride the tracks and find

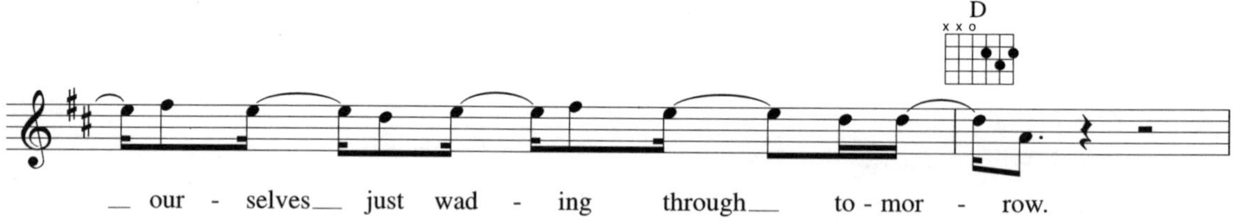
D
our - selves just wad - ing through to - mor - row.

A
And you and I when we're com - ing down, we're on - ly

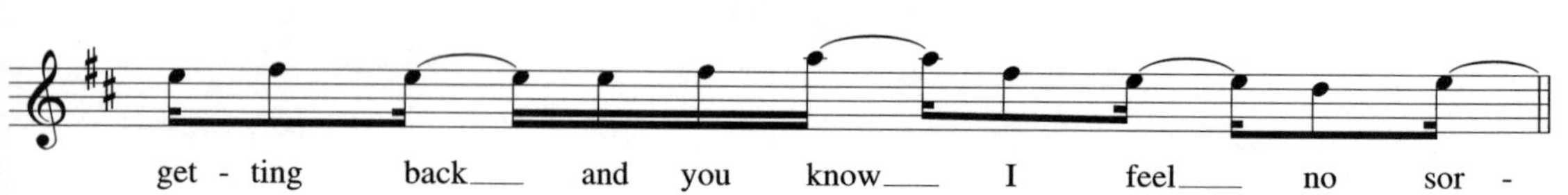
get - ting back and you know I feel no sor -

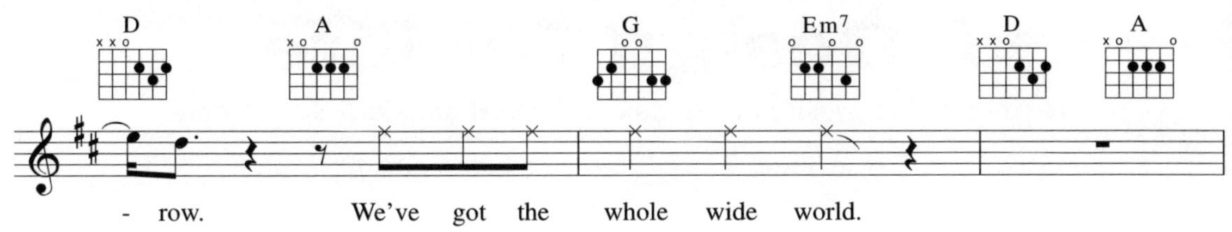
D
A
G
Em7
D
A
- row. We've got the whole wide world.

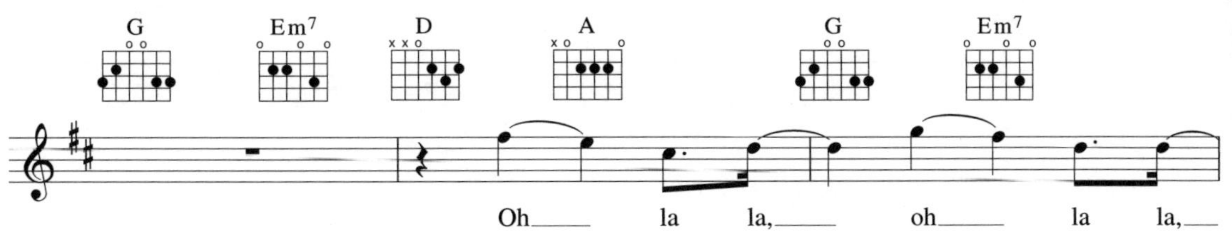
G
Em7
D
A
G
Em7
Oh la la, oh la la,

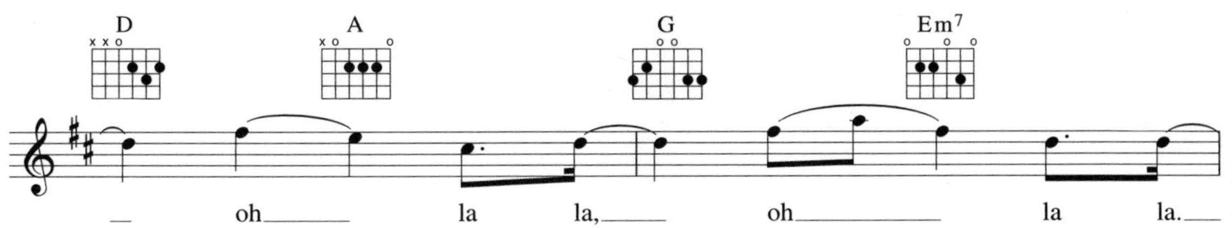
D
A
G
Em7
oh la la, oh la la.

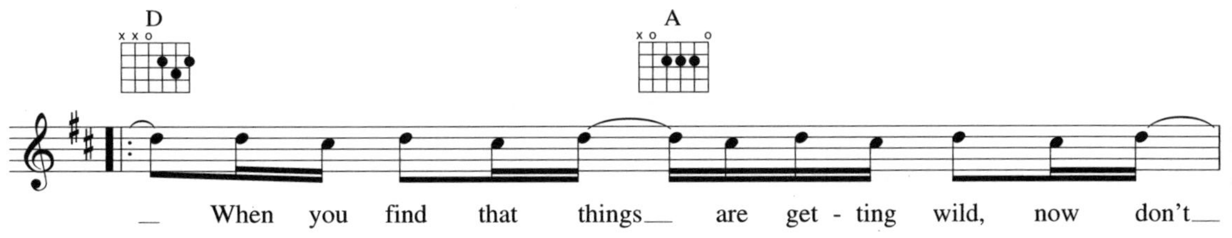
D
A
When you find that things are get - ting wild, now don't

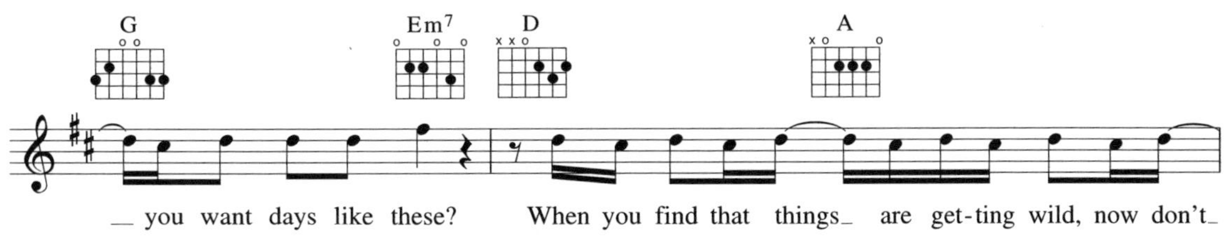
G
Em7
D
A
you want days like these? When you find that things are get-ting wild, now don't

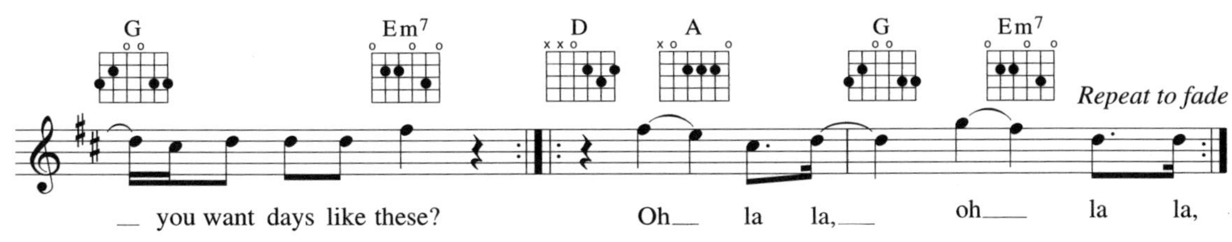
G
Em7
D
A
G
Em7
Repeat to fade
you want days like these? Oh la la, oh la la,

A Design For Life

Words & Music by Nicky Wire, James Dean Bradfield & Sean Moore

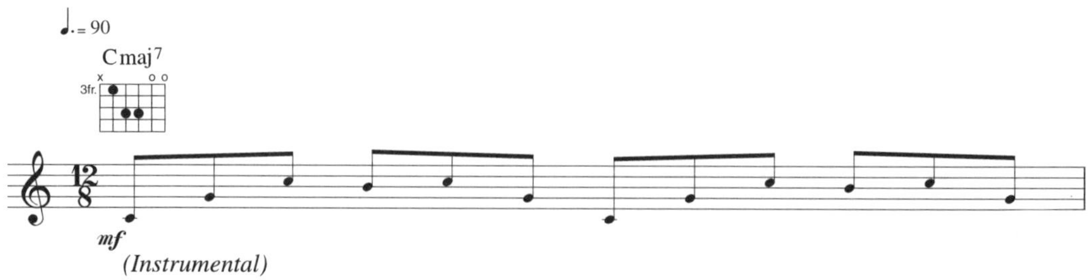

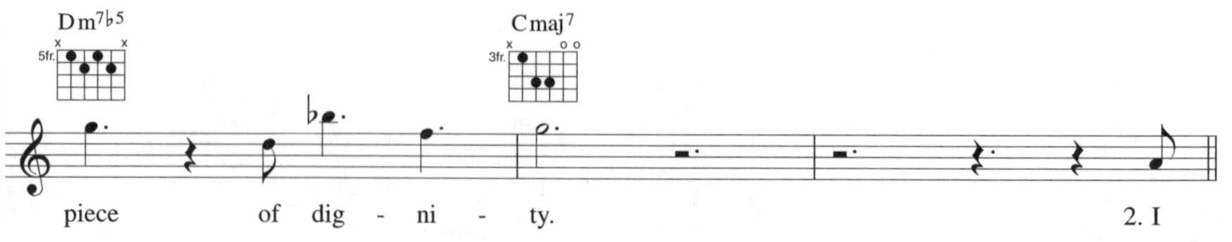

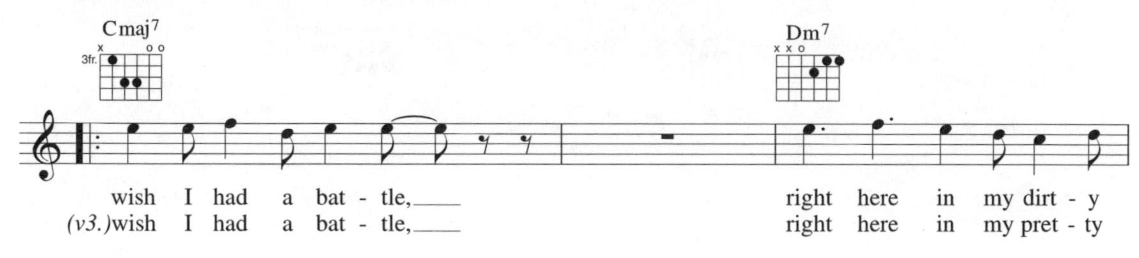
Cmaj7
3fr.
Dm7
wish I had a bat - tle,
(v3.)wish I had a bat - tle,
right here in my dirt - y
right here in my pret - ty

G
face.
face.
to wear the scars
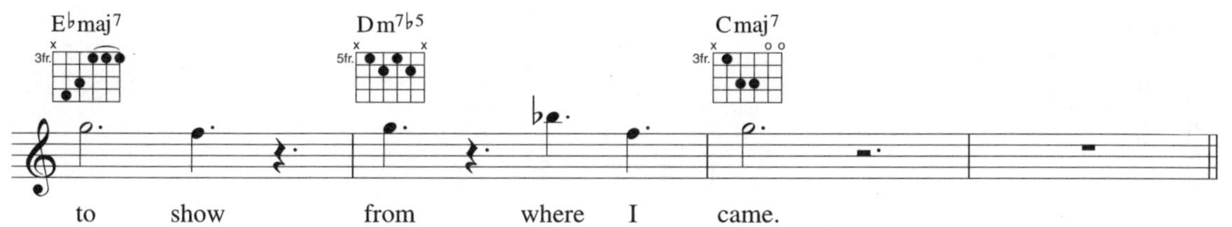
E♭maj7
3fr.
Dm7♭5
5fr.
Cmaj7
3fr.
to show from where I came.
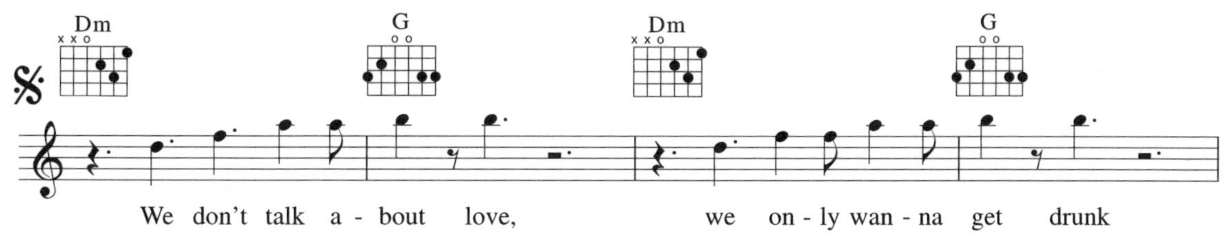
Dm
G
Dm
G
We don't talk a - bout love,
we on - ly wan - na get drunk
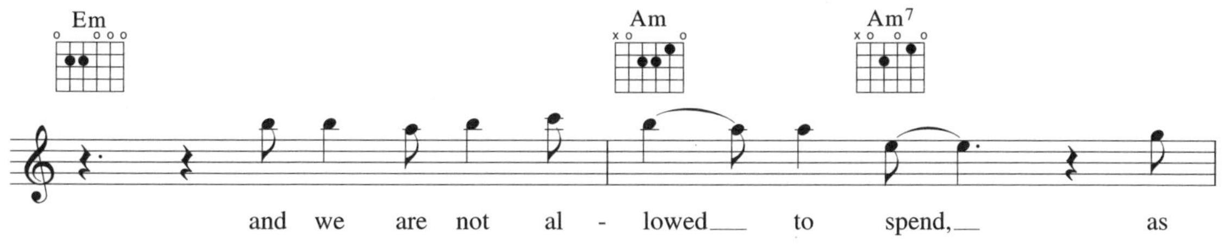
Em
Am
Am7
and we are not al - lowed to spend, as

F
Am
we are told that this is the end.
A de - sign

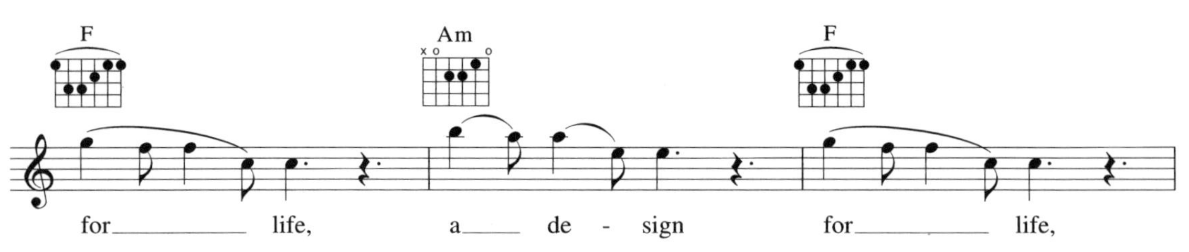
F
Am
F
for life, a de - sign for life,

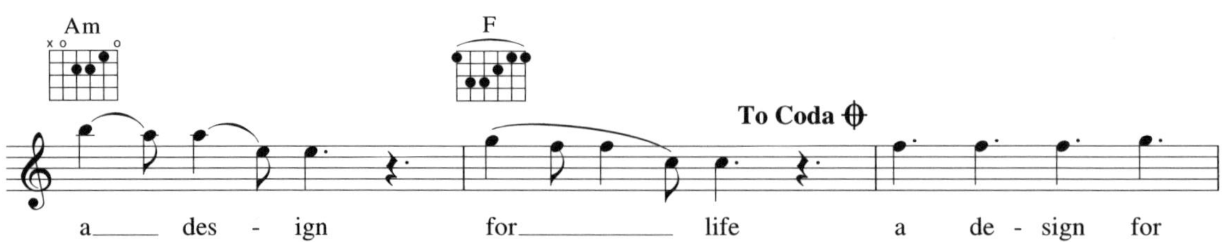
Am
F
To Coda
a des - ign for life a de - sign for

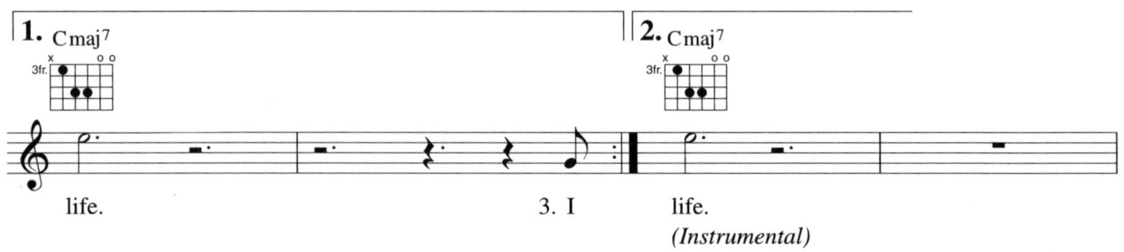
1. Cmaj7
2. Cmaj7
life. 3. I life.
(Instrumental)

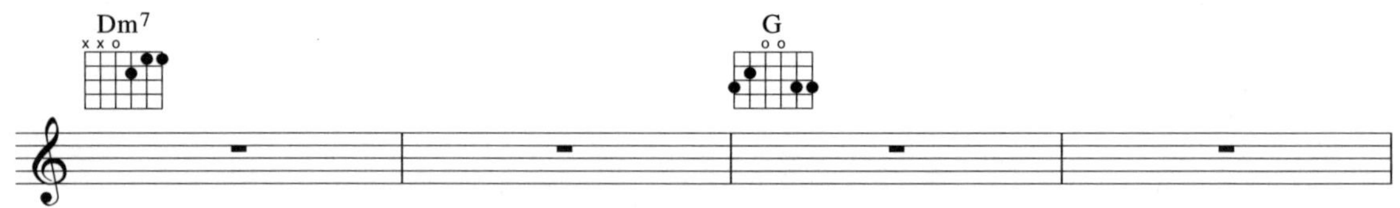
Dm7
G

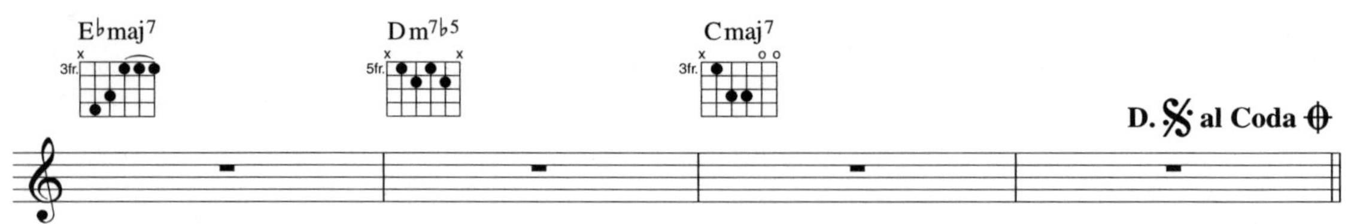
E♭maj7
Dm7♭5
Cmaj7
D.𝄋 al Coda

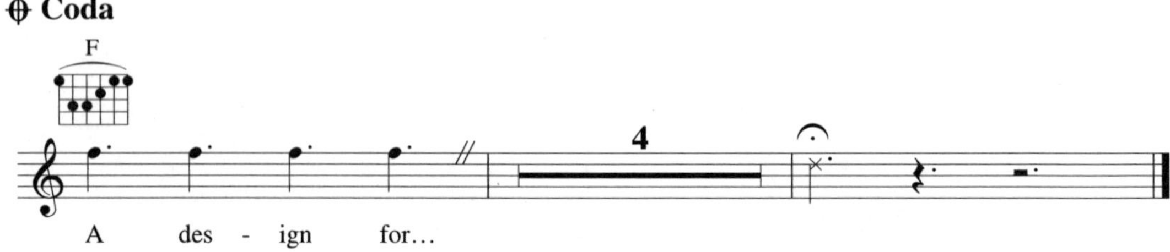
Coda
F
4
A des - ign for…

Don't Look Back In Anger

Words & Music by Noel Gallagher

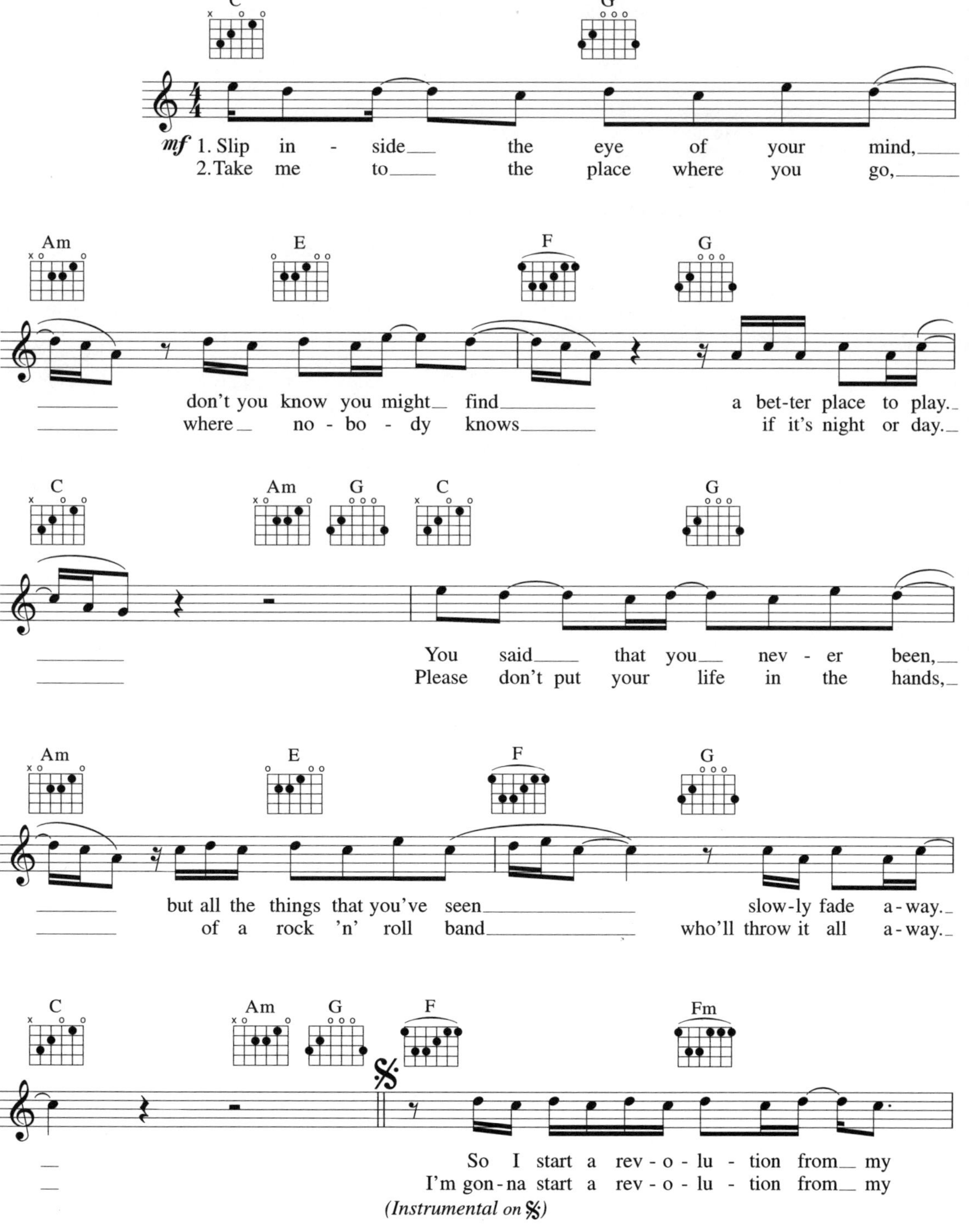

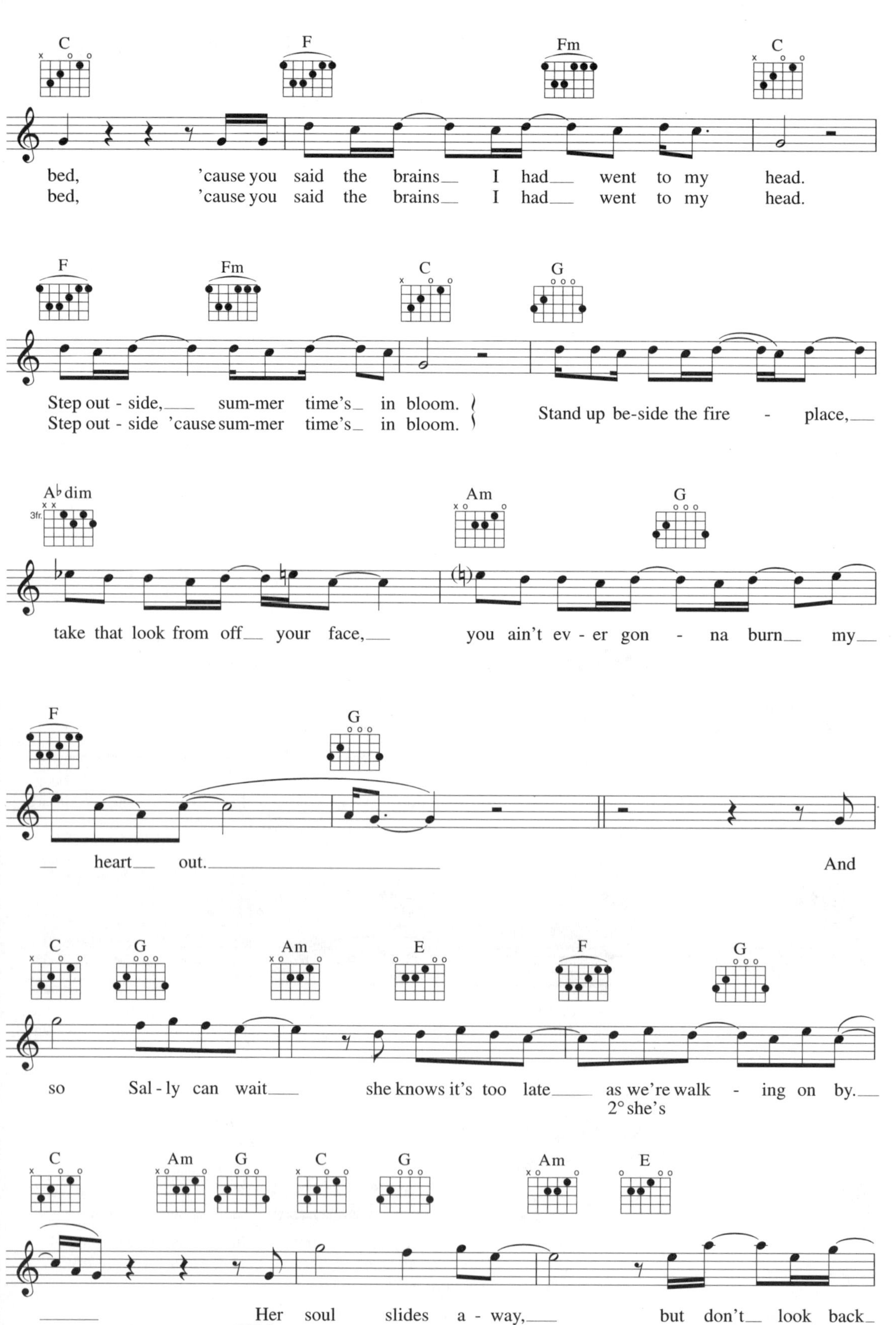
C F Fm C
bed, 'cause you said the brains I had went to my head.
bed, 'cause you said the brains I had went to my head.
F Fm C G
Step out - side, sum-mer time's in bloom.
Step out - side 'cause sum-mer time's in bloom.
Stand up be-side the fire - place,
A♭dim Am G
3fr.
take that look from off your face, you ain't ev - er gon - na burn my
F G
heart out.
And
C G Am E F G
so Sal - ly can wait she knows it's too late as we're walk - ing on by.
2° she's
C Am G C G Am E
Her soul slides a - way, but don't look back
2° My

1.
F G C G Am E
To Coda
in an - ger, I heard you say.
1. cont.
F G C Am G
2.
C Am G
D.S. al Coda
Coda
C Am G C G Am E
So Sal - ly can wait she knows it's too late
F G C Am G C G
as she's walk - ing on by.
My soul slides a - way,
Am F
but don't look back in an - ger, don't look
Fm C G
back in an - ger, I heard you say,
Am E F Fm C
at least not to - day.

Don't Speak

Words & Music by Eric Stefani & Gwen Stefani

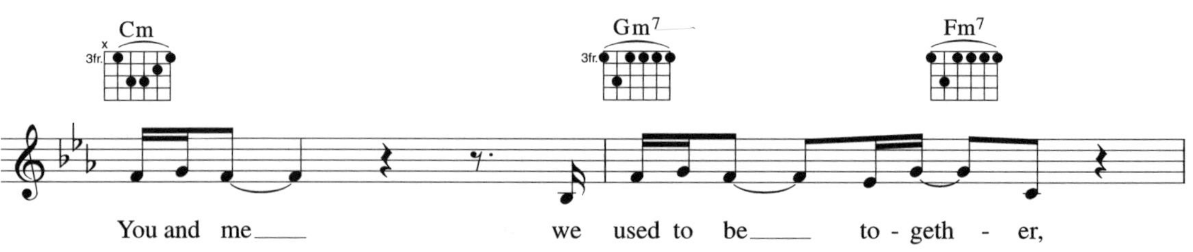

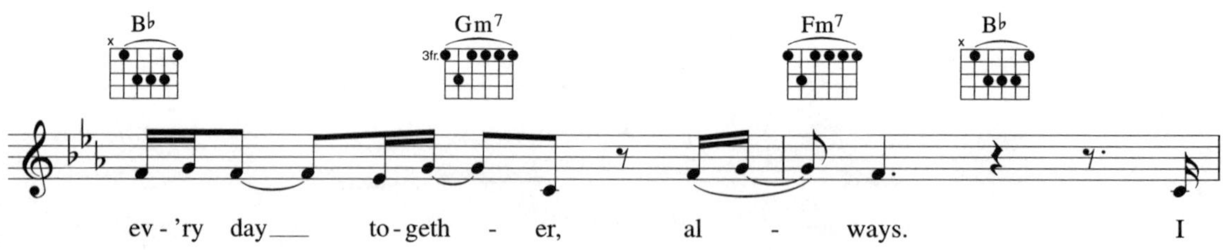

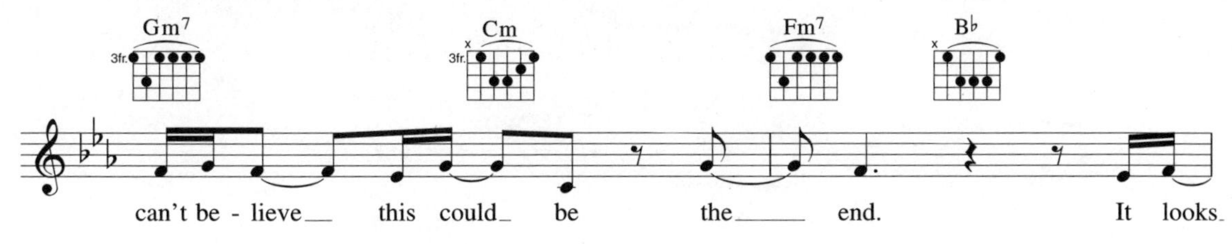
Gm7
3fr.
Cm
3fr.
Fm7
B♭
can't be - lieve this could be the end. It looks

Cm
3fr.
Gm7
3fr.
Fm7
B♭
as though you're let - ting go, and
we die both you and I

E♭
6fr.
B♭
C
if it's real then I don't want to know.
with my head in my hands I'll soon be cry - ing.

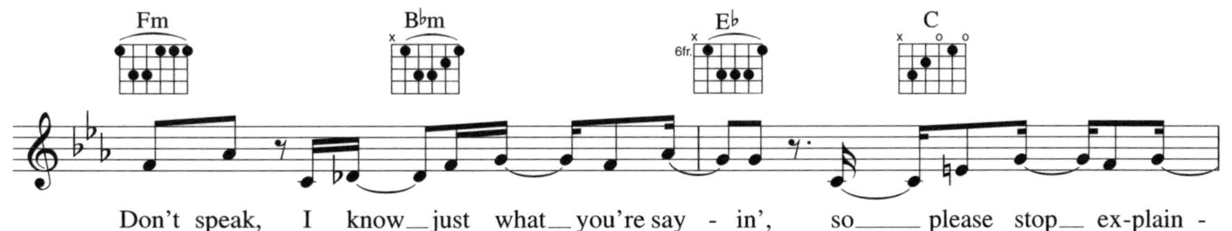
Fm
B♭m
E♭
6fr.
C
Don't speak, I know just what you're say - in', so please stop ex-plain -

B♭m
C
Fm
B♭m
C
- ing, don't tell me 'cause it hurts.

Fm
B♭m
E♭
6fr.
C
Don't speak, I know what you're think - in' I don't need your rea -

B♭m
C
1. Fm
B♭m
E♭
6fr.
sons, don't tell me cause it hurts. Old

1. cont.
Cm
3fr.
Gm7
3fr.
Fm7
mem-o - ries, they can be in - vit - ing but some are

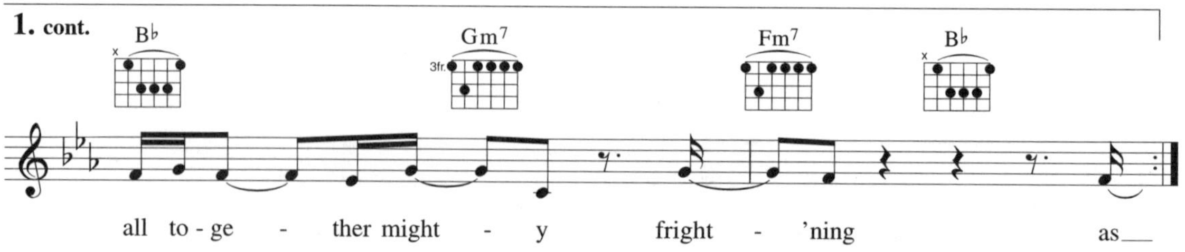
1. cont.
B♭
Gm7
3fr.
Fm7
B♭
all to - ge - ther might - y fright - 'ning as

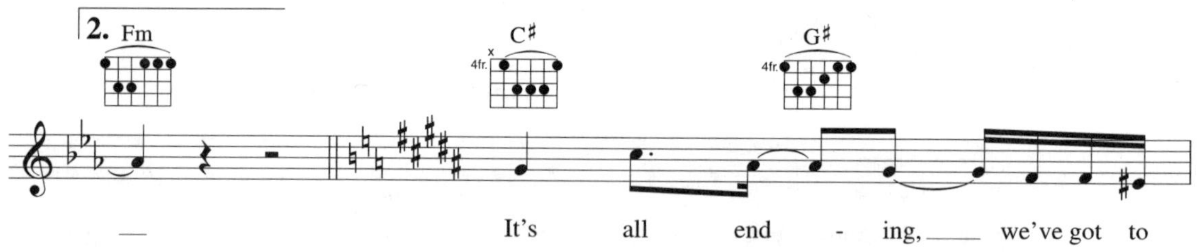
2. Fm
C♯
4fr.
G♯
4fr.
It's all end - ing, we've got to

B
F♯
A
5fr.
D♯7
6fr.
G♯sus4
4fr.
G♯
4fr.
stop pre - tend - ing who we are.

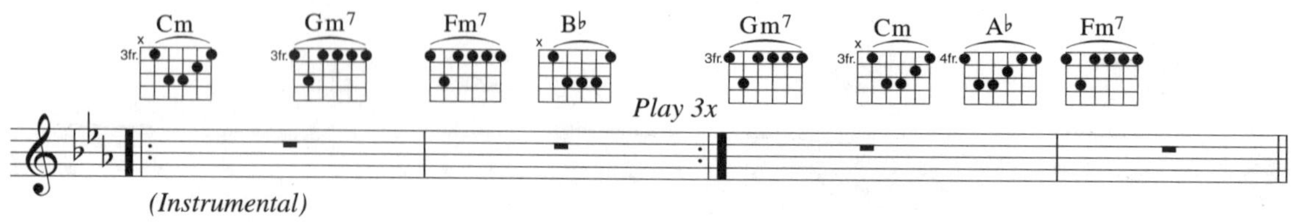
Cm
3fr.
Gm7
3fr.
Fm7
B♭
Play 3x
Gm7
3fr.
Cm
3fr.
A♭
4fr.
Fm7
(Instrumental)

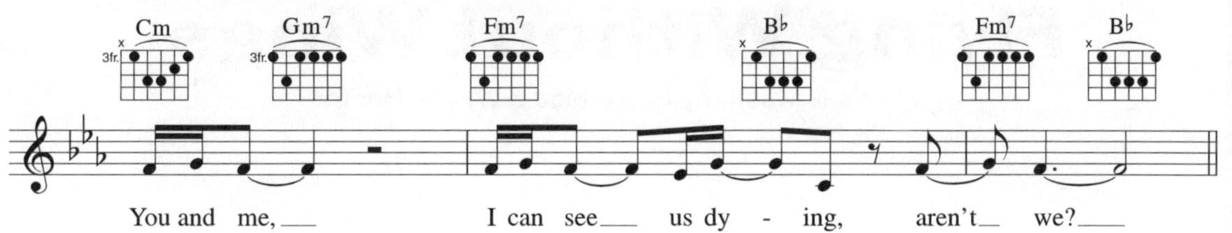
Cm
Gm7
Fm7
B♭
Fm7
B♭
You and me,
I can see us dy - ing,
aren't we?

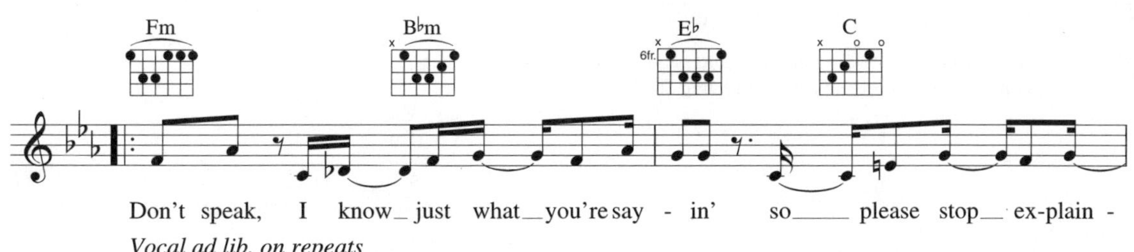
Fm
B♭m
E♭
C
Don't speak, I know just what you're say - in' so please stop ex-plain -
Vocal ad lib. on repeats

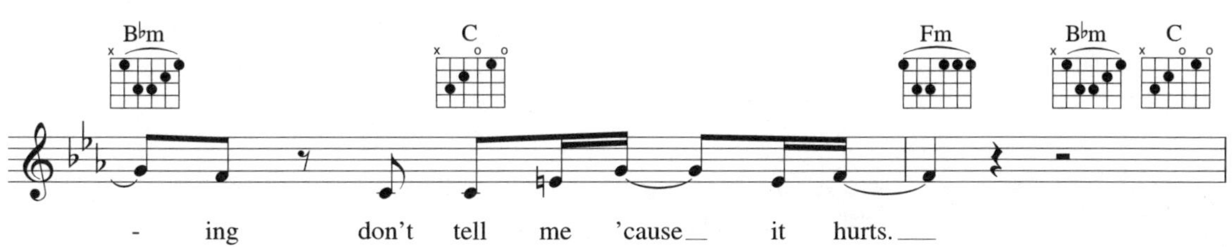
B♭m
C
Fm
B♭m
C
- ing don't tell me 'cause it hurts.

Fm
B♭m
E♭
C
Don't speak, I know what you're think - in' I don't need your rea -

B♭m
C
Fm
B♭m
Repeat to fade
- sons, don't tell me 'cause it hurts. Don't tell me 'cause it

Flying Without Wings

Words & Music by Steve Mac & Wayne Hector

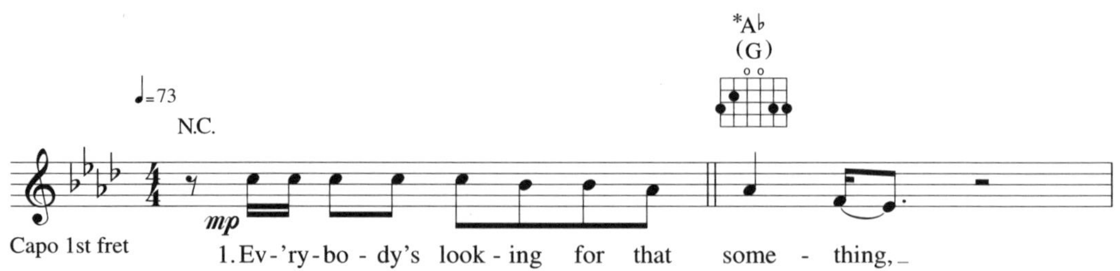

* Symbols in parentheses represent chord names with respect to capoed gtr.
Symbols above represent actual sounding chords.

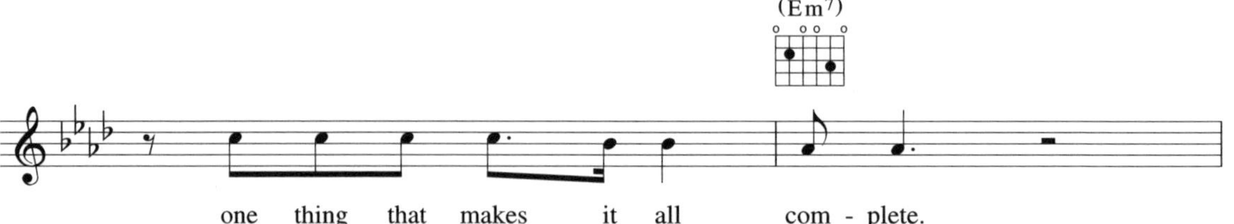

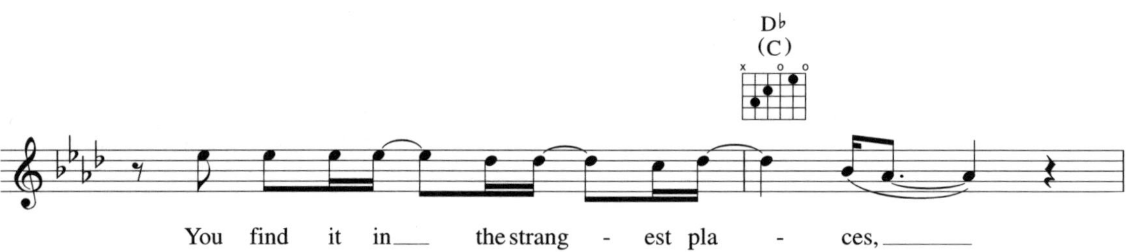

Fm7
(Em7)
some find it in their lov - er's eyes.
D♭
(C)
Who can de - ny the joy it brings when you've found that spe - cial
E♭
(D)
A♭
(G)
thing? You're fly - ing with-out wings.
2. Some find it shar - ing ev - 'ry
A♭
(G)
E♭/G
(D/F♯)
morn - ing.
(Verse 3(𝄋) see block lyric)
Some in their so - li - ta -
Fm7
(Em7)
- ry lives.
You find it in the words of
D♭
(C)
oth - ers,
a sim - ple line can make you

E♭ (D)
E♭11 (D11)
E♭ (D)
laugh or cry. You find it in the deep - est
A♭ (G)
E♭/G (D/F♯)
friend - ships, the kind you cher - ish all
Fm7 (Em7)
your life, and when you know how much that
D♭ (C)
E♭ (D)
To Coda
means, you've found that spe - cial thing, you're fly - ing with - out wings.
A♭ (G)
E♭/G (D/F♯)
So, im - poss - i -
D♭ (C)
E♭ (D)
- ble as they may seem you've got to
Fm7 (Em7)
E♭/G (D/F♯)
A♭ (G)
fight for ev - er - y dream. 'Cause who's to

Verse 3:
Well, for me it's waking up beside you
To watch the sun rise on your face
To know that I can say I love you
In any given time or place
It's little things that only I know
Those are the things that make you mine
And it's like flying without wings
'Cause you're my special thing
I'm flying without wings.

Female Of The Species

Words & Music by Tommy Scott, James Edwards, Francis Griffiths & Andrew Parle

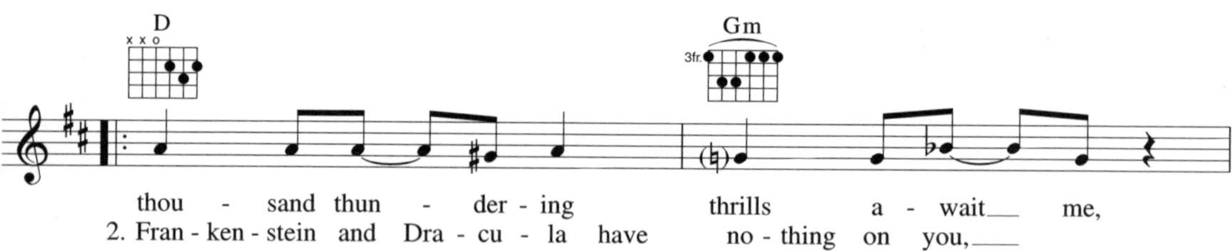

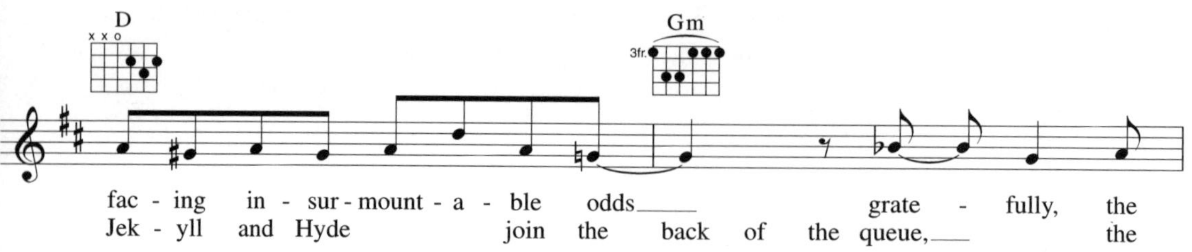

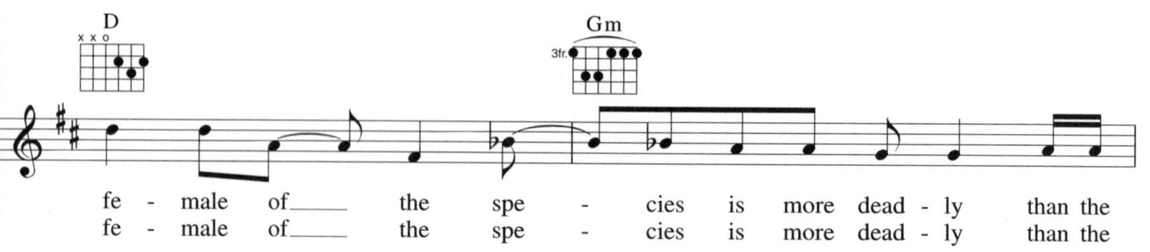

D
male. Shock, shock, hor - ror hor - ror,
male. Oh she wants to con - quer the world
Gm
D
shock, shock hor - ror. I'll shout my - self hoarse for your
com - plete - ly but first she'll con - quer
Gm
D
sup - er - nat - ur - al force the fe - male of the spe -
me dis - creet - ly the fe - male of the spe -
Gm
D
- cies is more dead - ly than the male.
- cies is more dead - ly than the male.
Oh
E♭maj7
C7
E♭maj7
she deals in witch - craft and one kiss and
C7
B♭
Dm7
I'm zapped. Oh how can hea - ven hold a place for me, when a

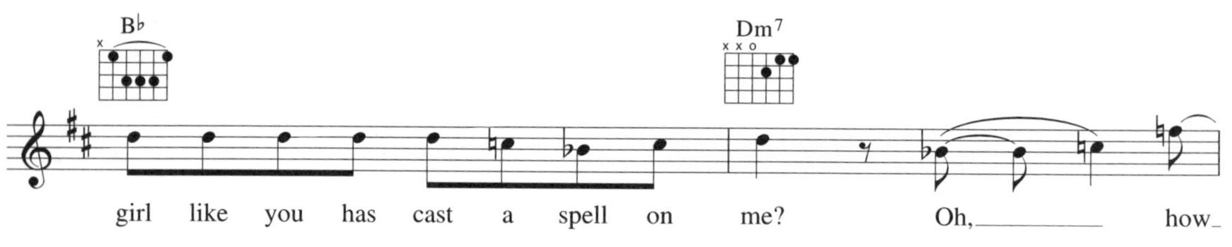
B♭
Dm7
girl like you has cast a spell on me? Oh, how

B♭
Dm7
can hea - ven hold a place for me, when a

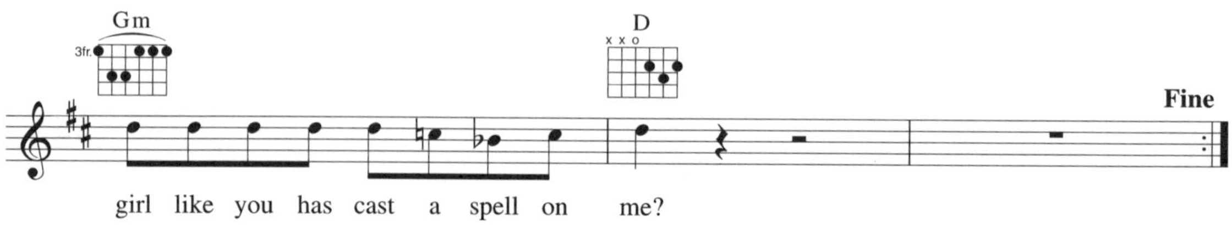
Gm
D
Fine
girl like you has cast a spell on me?

D
Gm
D
(Instrumental)

Gm
D

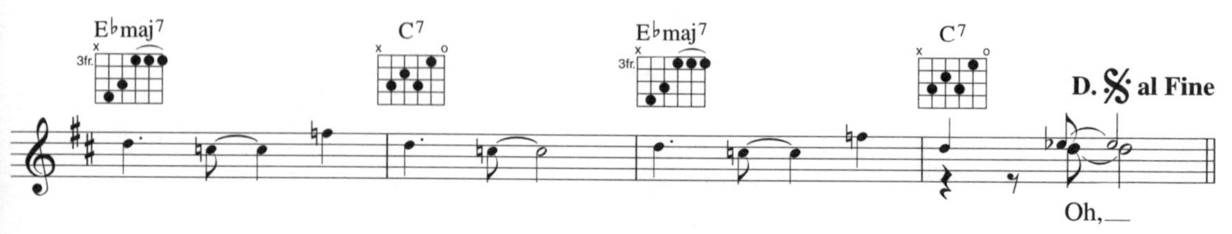
E♭maj7
C7
E♭maj7
C7
D.𝄋 al Fine
Oh,

Girl From Mars

Words & Music by Tim Wheeler

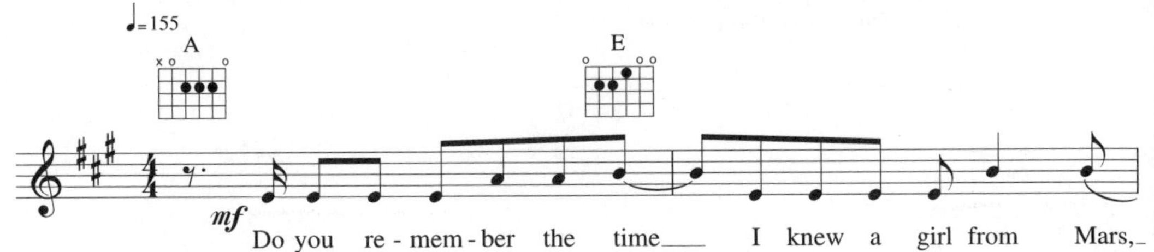

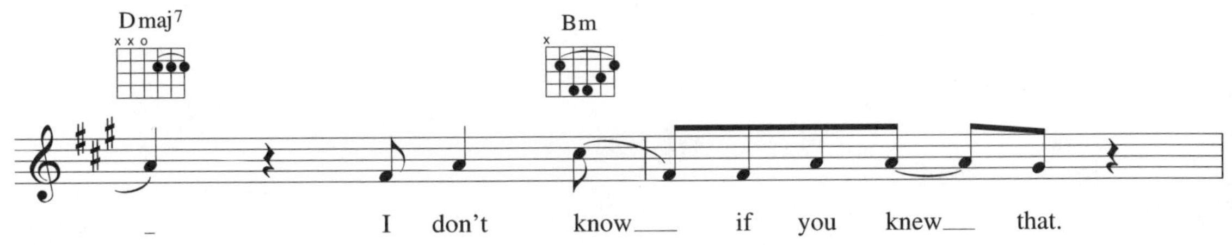

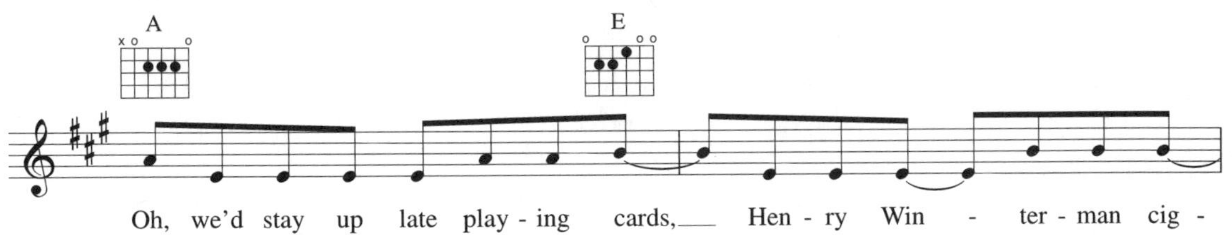

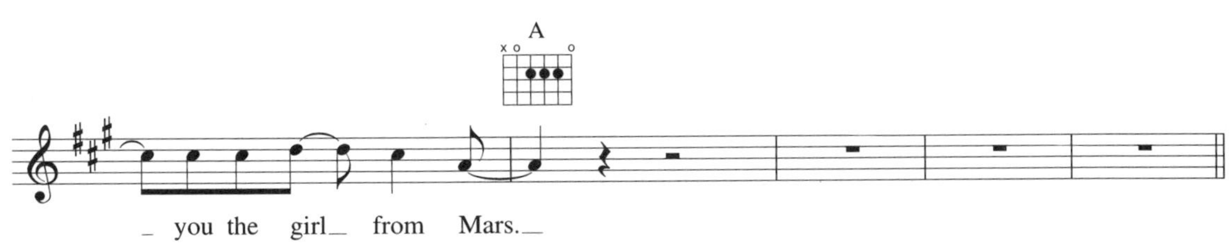

A E D
1. Sit - ting in a dream - y daze by the wa -
2. Surg - ing through the dark - ness ov - er the moon -
Bm D E
- ter's edge, on a cool sum - mer night.
- lit strand, elec - tri - ci - ty in the air.
A E D
Fire - flies and stars in the sky, gen - tle glow -
Twist - ing all through the night on the ter -
Bm D E A E
- ing light, from your cig - ar - ette. The breeze blow -
race, now that sum - mer is here. I know that you
D Bm D
- ing soft - ly on my face re - minds
are al - most in love with me, I can see
E A E
me of some - thing else. Some - thing that in
it in your eyes. Strange lights shim -

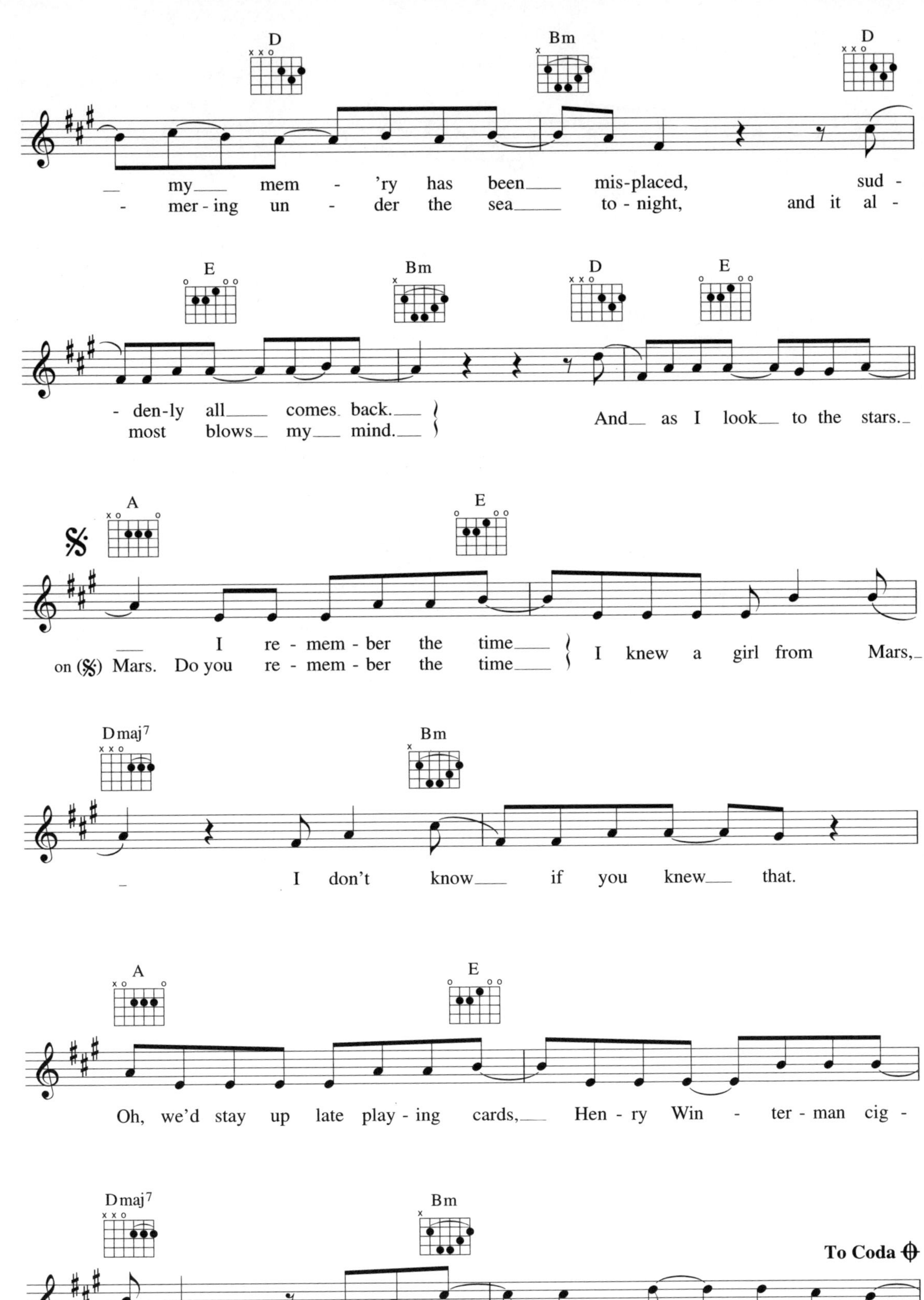
D
Bm
D
my mem - 'ry has been mis-placed, sud -
- mer - ing un - der the sea to - night, and it al -
E
Bm
D
E
- den-ly all comes back.
most blows my mind.
And as I look to the stars.
A
E
I re - mem - ber the time
on (%) Mars. Do you re - mem - ber the time
I knew a girl from Mars,
Dmaj7
Bm
I don't know if you knew that.
A
E
Oh, we'd stay up late play - ing cards, Hen - ry Win - ter - man cig -
Dmaj7
Bm
To Coda
- ars, and she nev - er told me her name,

D
E
A
I still love you the girl from Mars.

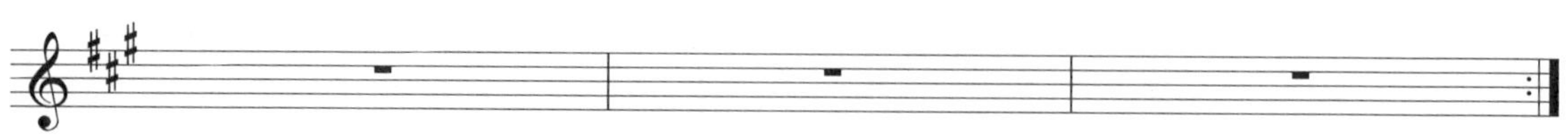

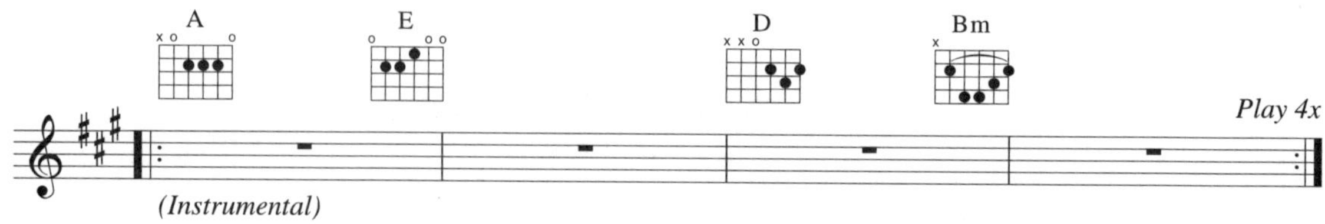
A
E
D
Bm
Play 4x
(Instrumental)

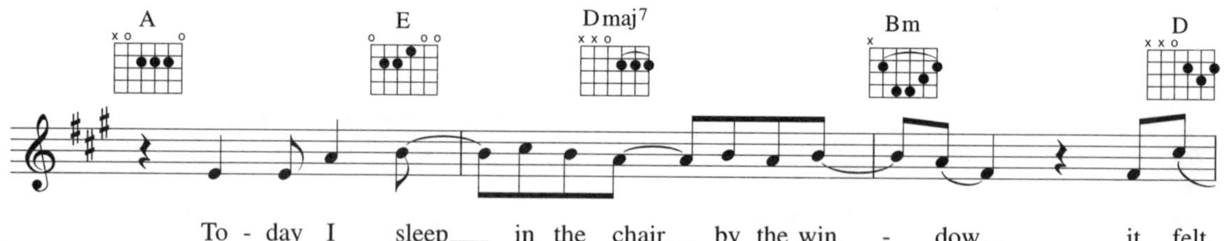
A
E
Dmaj7
Bm
D
To - day I sleep in the chair by the win - dow, it felt

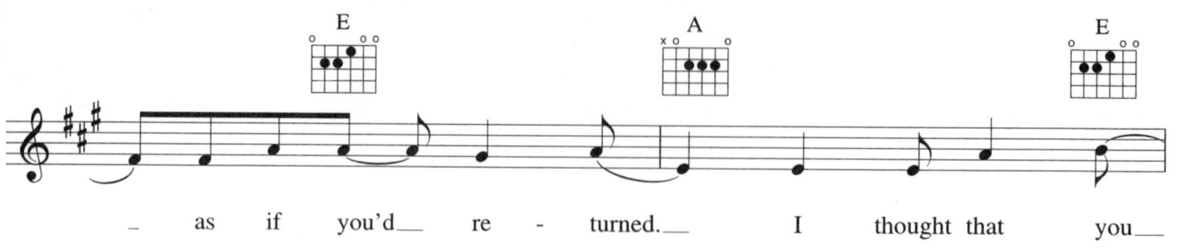
E
A
E
as if you'd re - turned. I thought that you

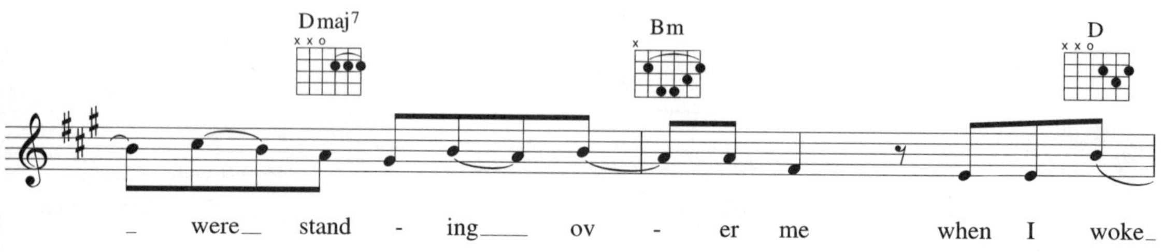
Dmaj7
Bm
D
were stand - ing ov - er me when I woke

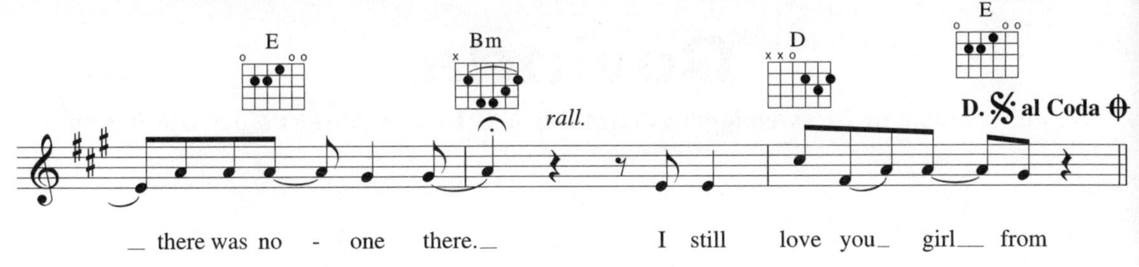
E
Bm
D
E
rall.
D.𝄋 al Coda
there was no - one there.
I still love you girl from

Coda
A
E
do you re - mem - ber the time I knew a girl from Mars,

D
Bm
I don't know if you knew that.

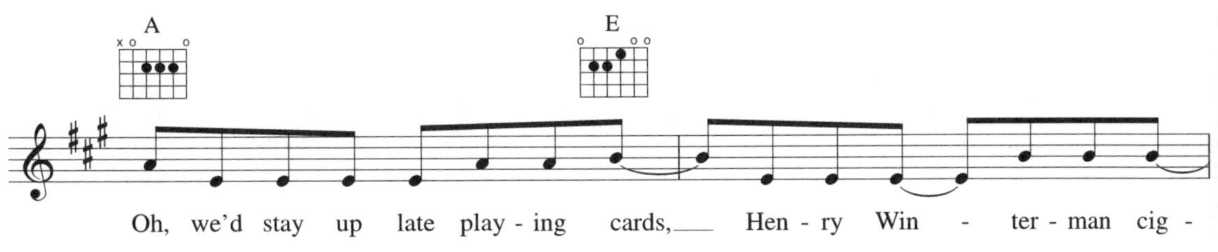
A
E
Oh, we'd stay up late play - ing cards, Hen - ry Win - ter - man cig -

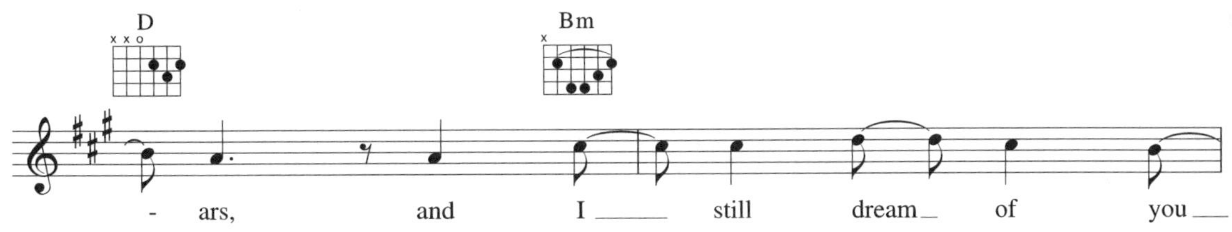
D
Bm
- ars, and I still dream of you

D
E
A
I still love you the girl from Mars.

Govinda

Words & Music by Crispian Mills, Alonza Bevan, Paul Winter-Hart & Jay Darlington

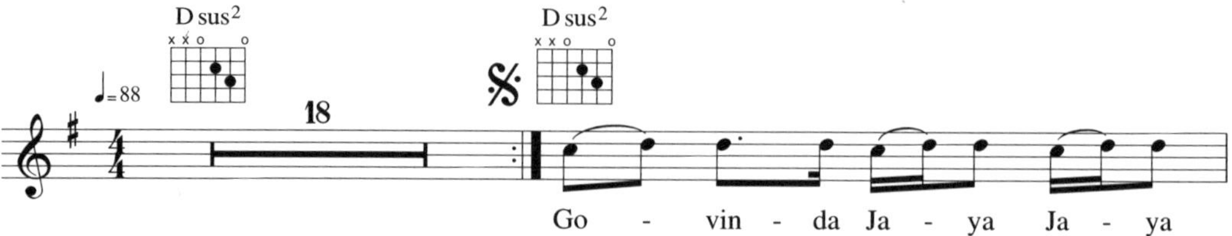

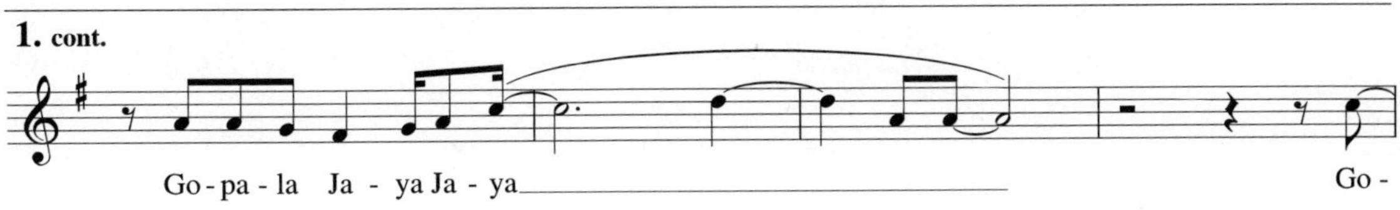
1. cont.
Go-pa-la Ja - ya Ja - ya
Go -

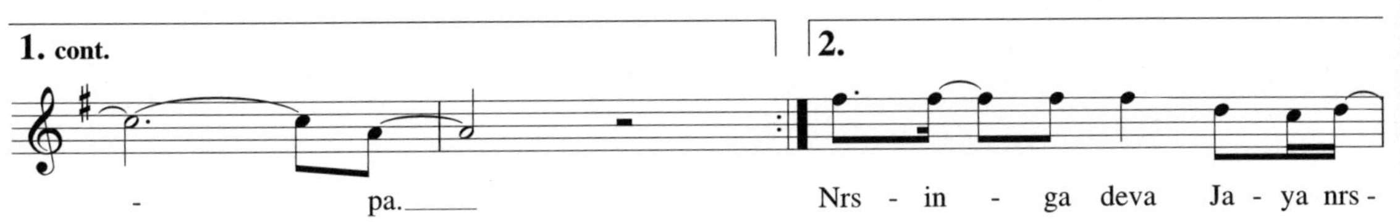
1. cont.
2.
- pa.
Nrs - in - ga deva Ja - ya nrs -

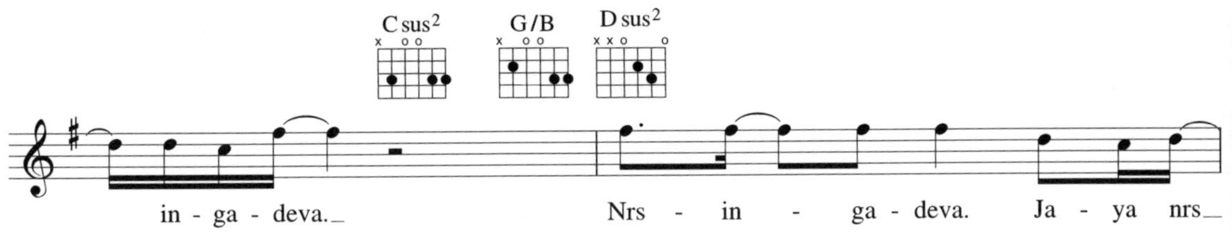
C sus2
G/B
D sus2
in - ga - deva.
Nrs - in - ga - deva. Ja - ya nrs

C sus2
G/B
D sus2
C sus2
G/B
in-ga-de-va.
Nrs - in - ga-deva Ja - ya nrs
in-ga - deva.

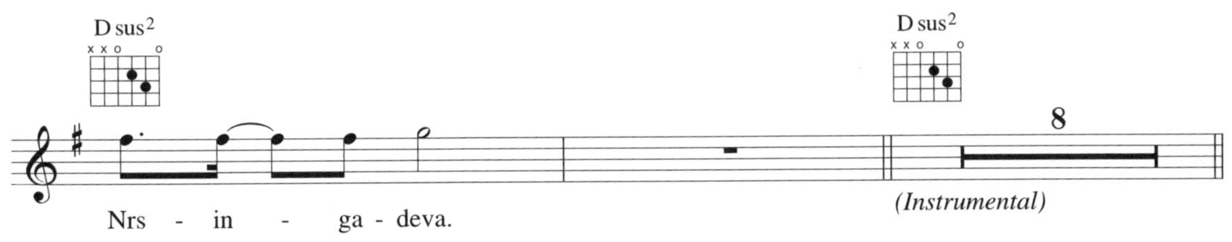
D sus2
D sus2
8
Nrs - in - ga - deva.
(Instrumental)

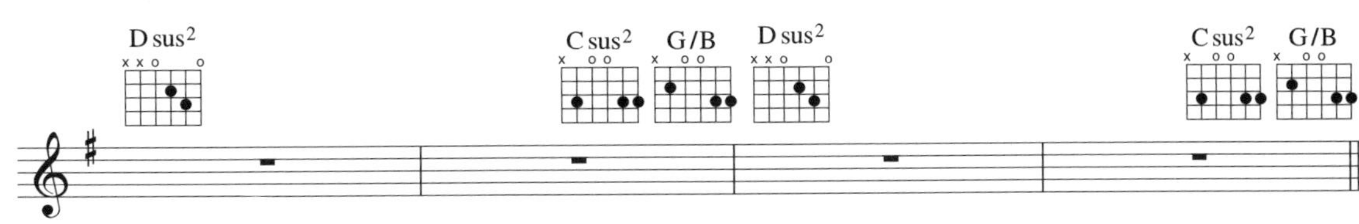
D sus2
C sus2
G/B
D sus2
C sus2
G/B

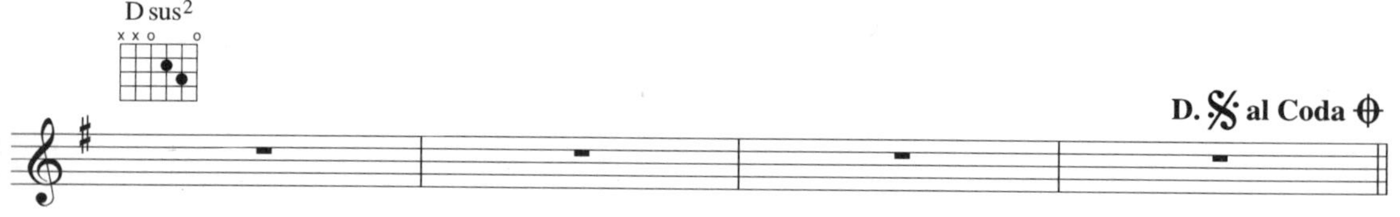
D sus2
D. 𝄋 al Coda 𝄌

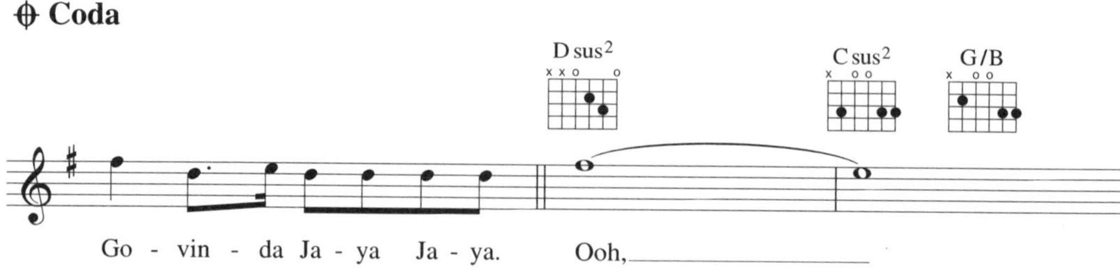
𝄌 Coda
D sus2
C sus2
G/B
Go - vin - da Ja - ya Ja - ya. Ooh,

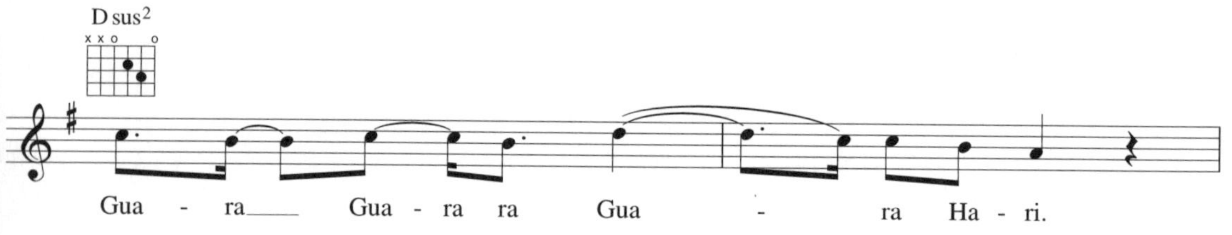
D sus2
Gua - ra Gua - ra ra Gua - ra Ha - ri.

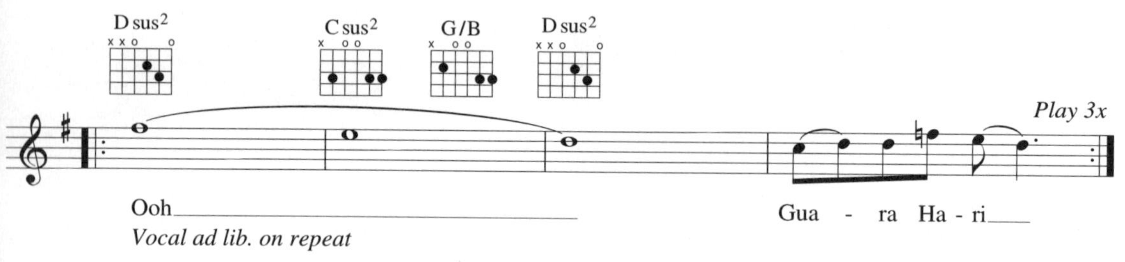
D sus2
C sus2
G/B
D sus2
Play 3x
Ooh
Vocal ad lib. on repeat
Gua - ra Ha - ri

D sus2
Go - vin - da.

Half The World Away

Words & Music by Noel Gallagher

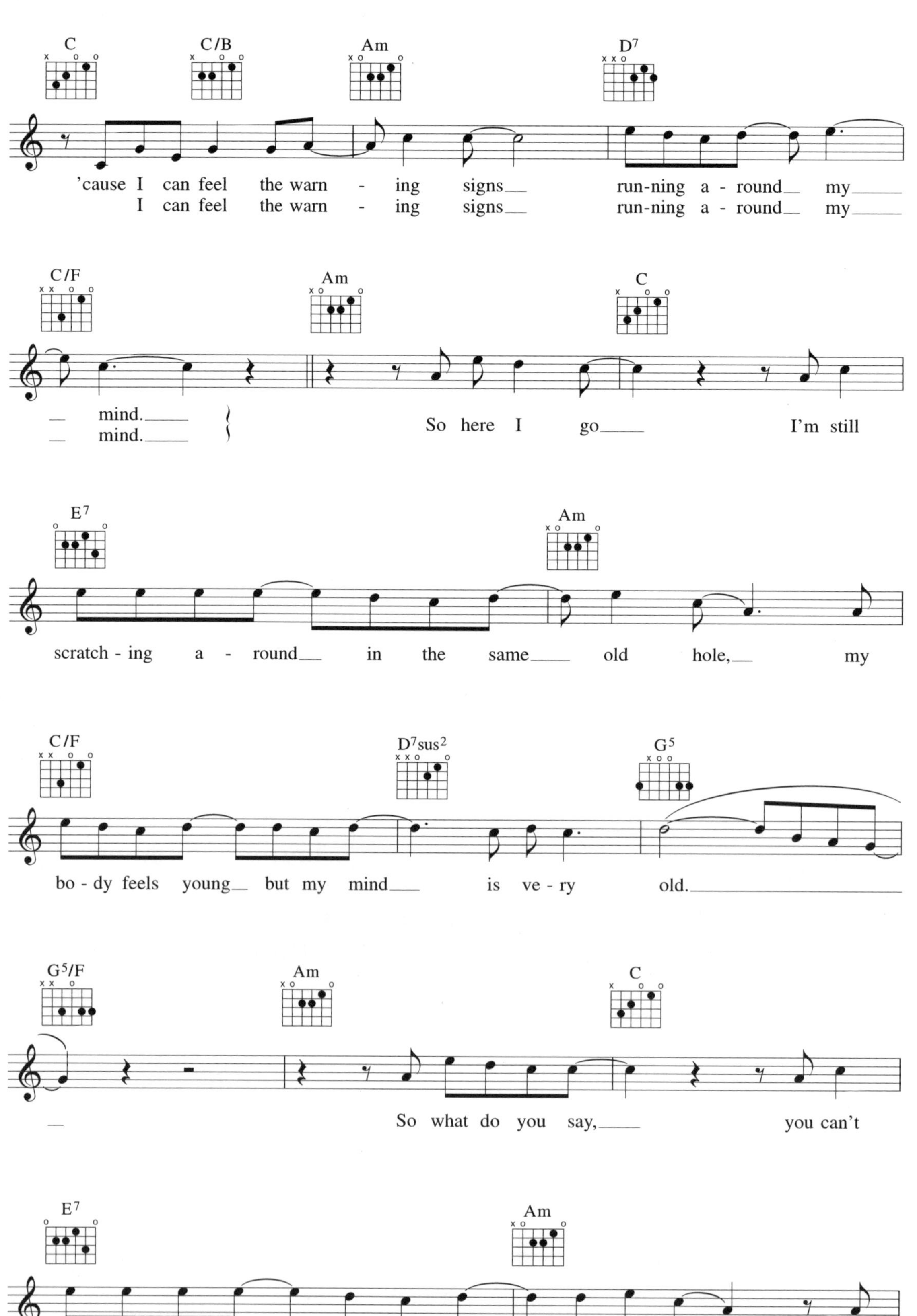
C C/B Am D7
'cause I can feel the warn - ing signs running a - round my
I can feel the warn - ing signs running a - round my
C/F Am C
mind. So here I go I'm still
mind.
E7 Am
scratch - ing a - round in the same old hole, my
C/F D7sus2 G5
bo - dy feels young but my mind is ve - ry old.
G5/F Am C
So what do you say, you can't
E7 Am
give me the dreams that are mine an - y - way, you're

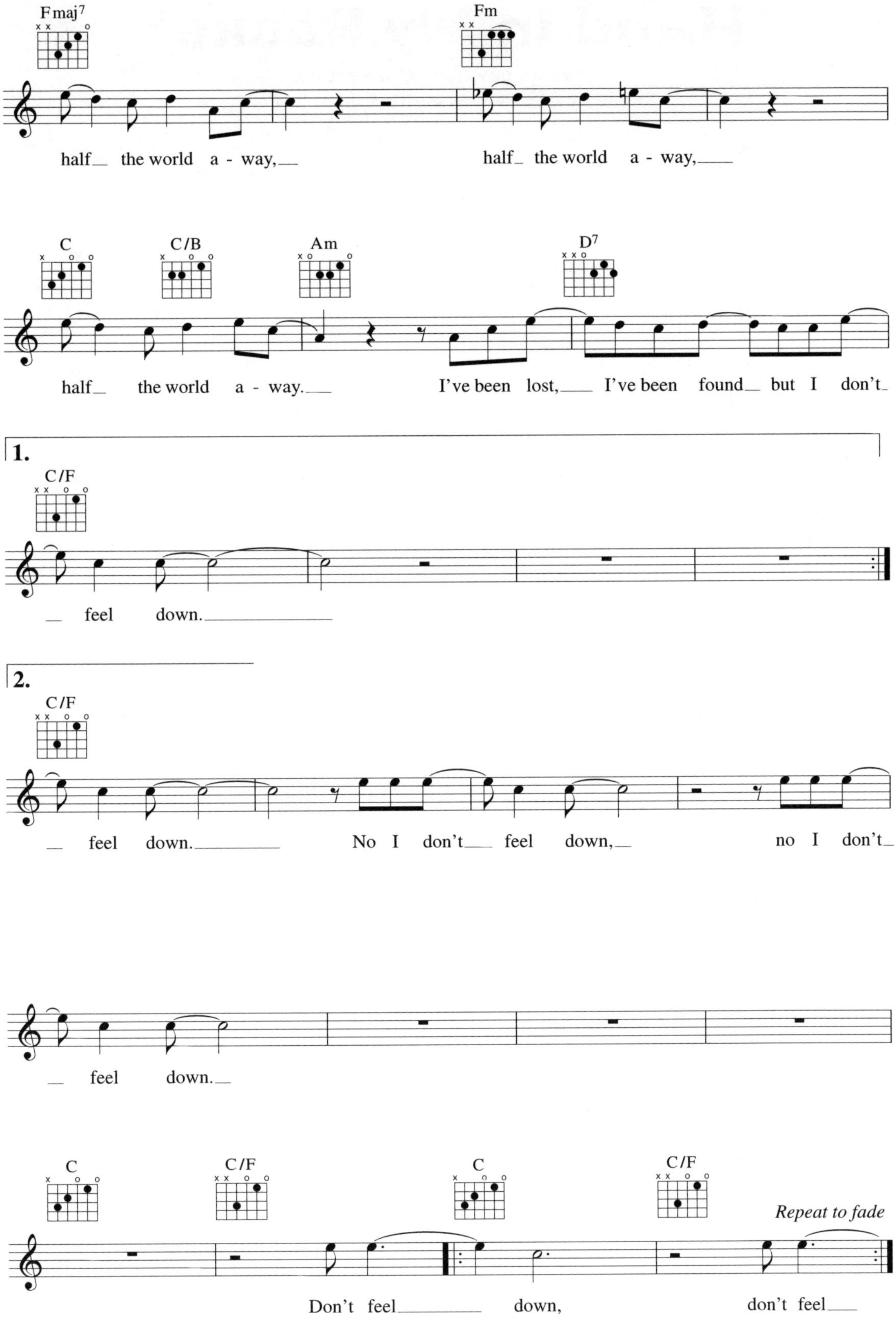

Fmaj7 Fm

half the world a - way, half the world a - way,

C C/B Am D7

half the world a - way. I've been lost, I've been found but I don't

1\.

C/F

feel down.

2\.

C/F

feel down. No I don't feel down, no I don't

Hand In My Pocket

Words by Alanis Morissette
Music by Alanis Morissette & Glen Ballard

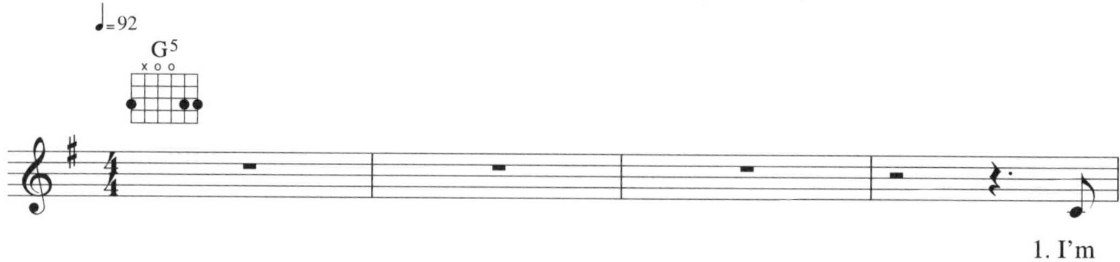

lost but I'm hope - ful, ba - by. And what it all comes down
wrong and I'm sor - ry, ba - by. And what it all comes down
G5/F
Csus2
to is that ev - 'ry-thing's gon - na be
to is that ev - 'ry-thing's gon - na be
G5
fine, fine, fine, 'cause I've got
quite al - right, 'cause I've got
G5/F
Csus2
G5/D
To Coda
one hand in my pock - et and the oth - er one is giv-in' a high five.
one hand in my pock - et and the oth - er one flick - in' a cig - ar - ette.
G5
1.2.
3.
D.S. al Coda
2. I feel
4. I'm
Coda
G5
And what it all comes down

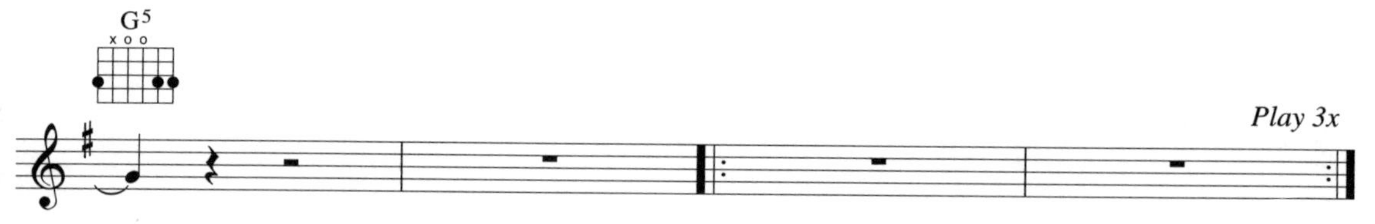

Verse 3:
Harmonica solo:
And what it all comes down to
Is that I haven't got it all figured out just yet
'Cause I've got one hand in my pocket
And the other one is givin' a peace sign.

Verse 4:
I'm free but I'm focussed
I'm green but I'm wise
I'm hard but I'm friendly baby
I'm sad but I'm laughing
I'm brave but I'm chicken-shit
I'm sick but I'm pretty, baby

And what it all boils down to
Is that no one's really got it all figured out just yet
But I've got one hand in my pocket
And the other one is playin' a piano.

I Believe I Can Fly

Words & Music by R. Kelly

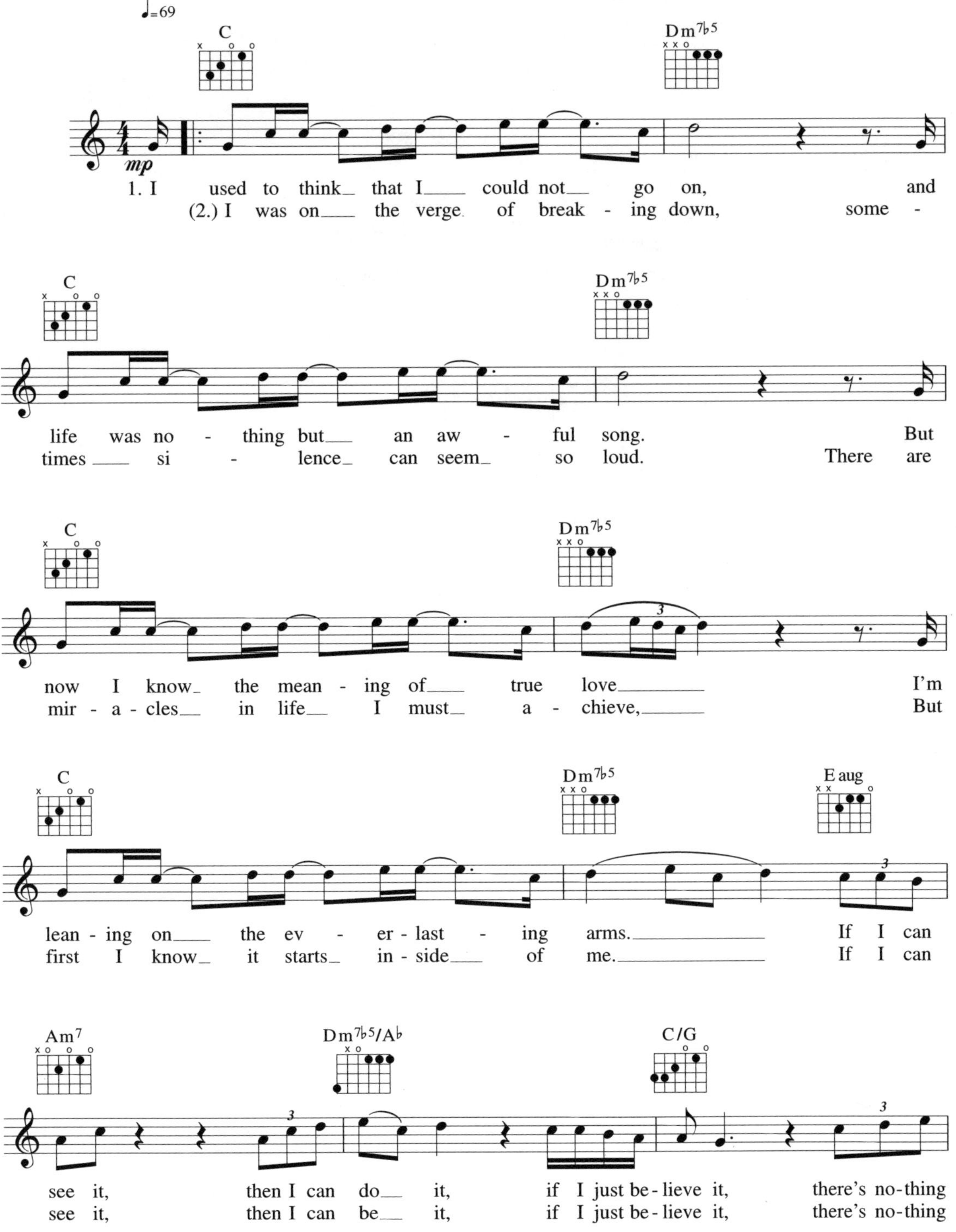

F/G
G
C
to it. I be-lieve I can fly. I be-lieve I can
to it.
Am7
Dm7
touch the sky, I think a-bout it ev-'ry night and day, spread my wings and
F/G
E7
Am7
fly a-way, I be-lieve I can soar, see me run-ning through that
Dm7♭5/A♭
C/G
op - en door, I be-lieve I can fly, I be-lieve I can
1.
Dm7♭5
Am7
Fmaj7/G
3
fly, I be-lieve I can fly. 2. See
2.
Am7
Dm9
C/G
fly, 'cause I be - lieve in you, oh

F/G
B♭m7
If I can see it then I can
G♭m7/A
D♭/A♭
do it, if I just be - lieve it, there's no-thing
G♭/A♭
A♭
D♭
to it. I be-lieve I can fly, I be-lieve I can
B♭m7
E♭m7
touch the sky. I think a-bout it ev-'ry night and day, spread my wings and
G♭/A♭
F/A
B♭m7
fly a - way. I be-lieve I can soar. See me run-ning through that
G♭m7/A
D♭/A♭
op - en door. I be-lieve I can fly. I be-lieve I can
G♭m7/A
D♭/A♭
G♭m7/A
D♭
Repeat ad lib
rall.
fly. I be - lieve I can fly.

I'll Be There For You

Words & Music by Michael Skloff, Allee Willis, Philip Solem, David Crane, Marta Kauffman & Danny Wilde

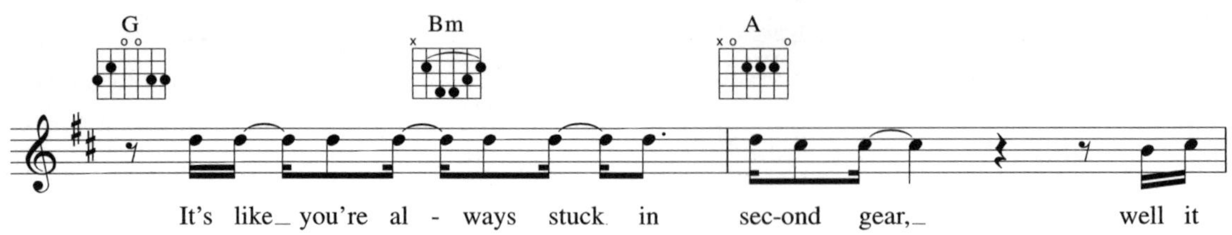

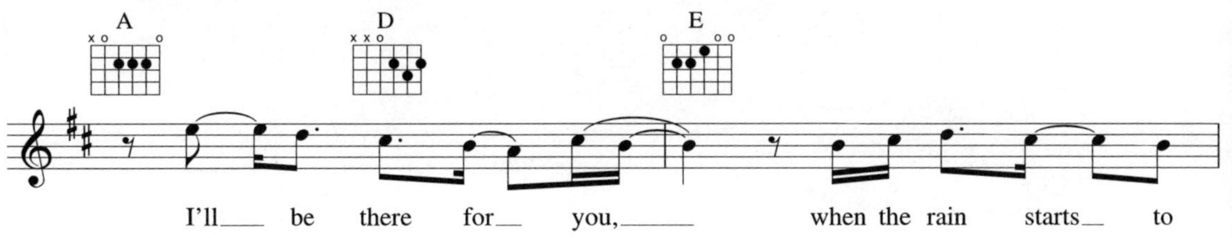
A
D
E
I'll__ be there for__ you,____ when the rain starts__ to

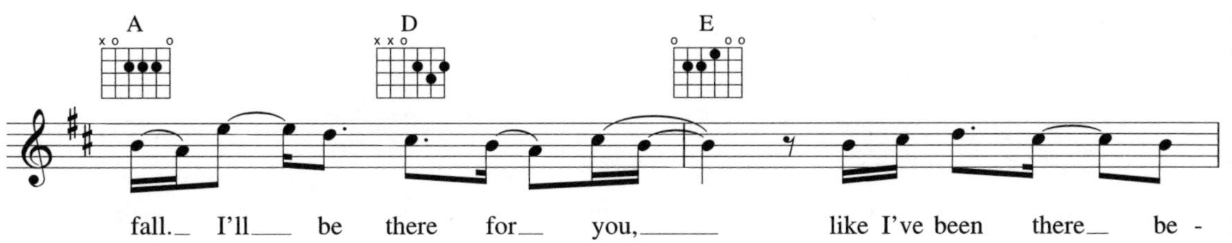
A
D
E
fall._ I'll__ be there for__ you,____ like I've been there__ be -

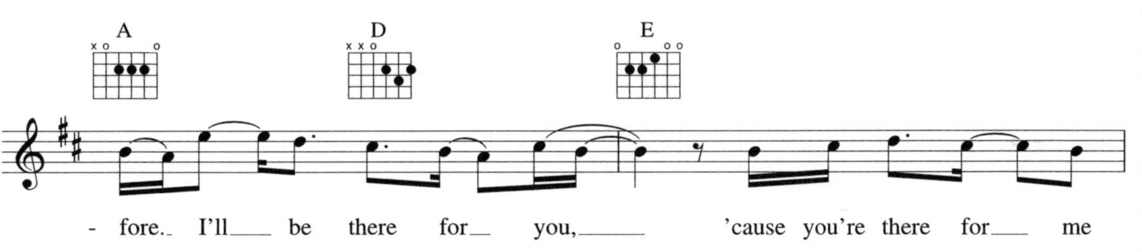
A
D
E
- fore._ I'll__ be there for__ you,____ 'cause you're there for__ me

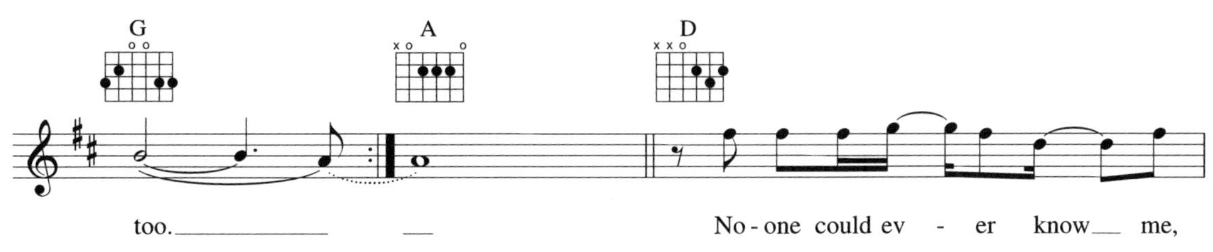
G
A
D
too.__________ __ No - one could ev - er know__ me,

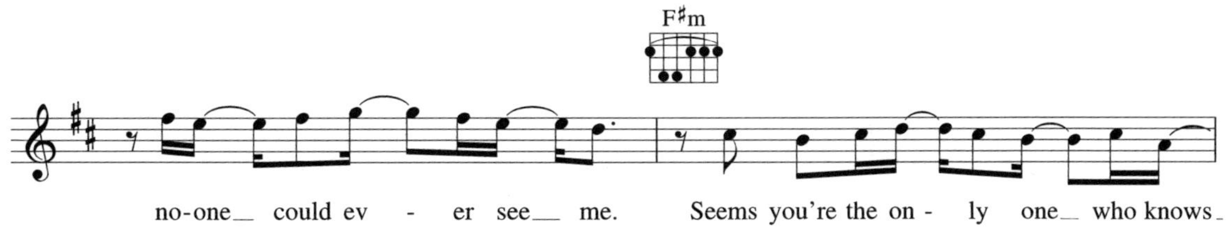
F♯m
no-one__ could ev - er see__ me. Seems you're the on - ly one_ who knows_

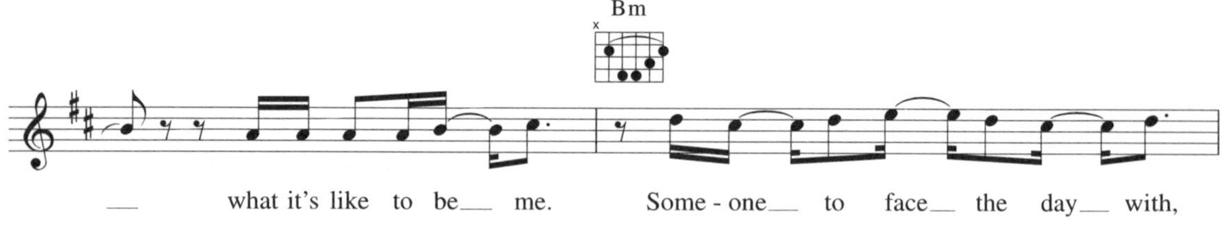
Bm
what it's like to be me. Some-one to face the day with,

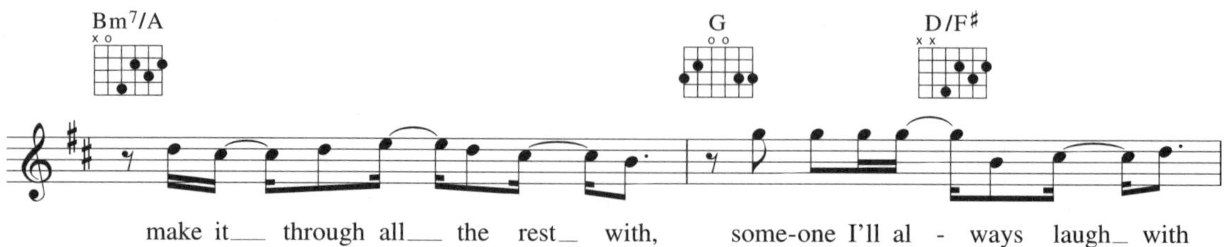
Bm7/A
G
D/F♯
make it through all the rest with, some-one I'll al - ways laugh with

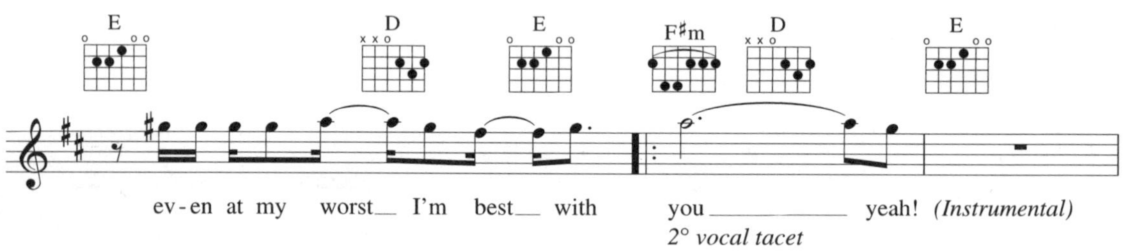
E
D
E
F♯m
D
E
ev-en at my worst I'm best with you yeah! (Instrumental)
2° vocal tacet

A
D
E
G
Bm
It's like you're al - ways stuck in

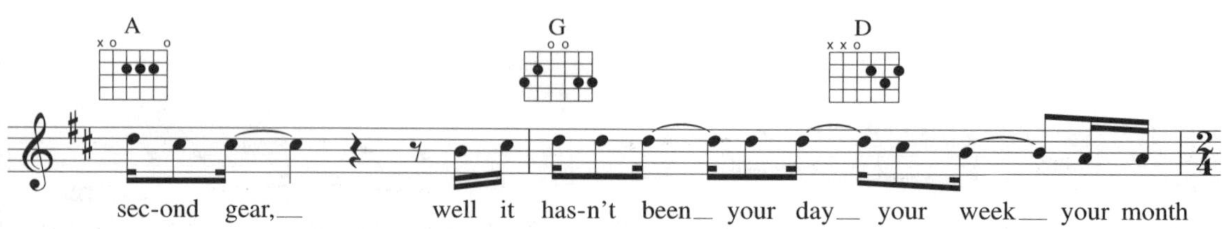
A
G
D
sec-ond gear, well it has-n't been your day your week your month

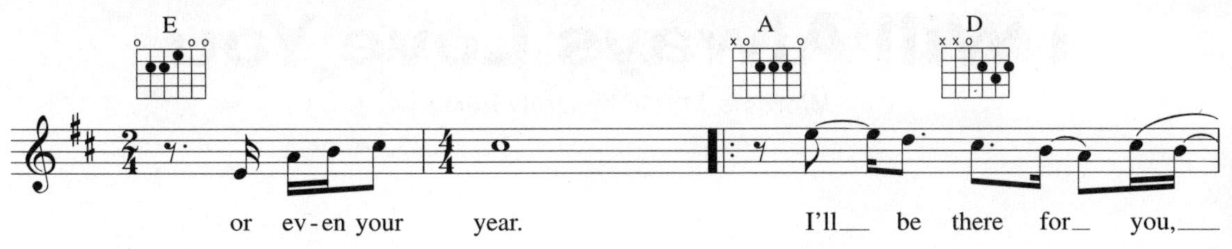

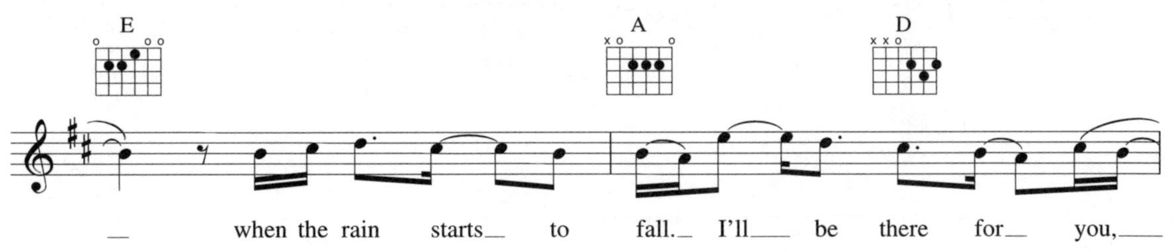

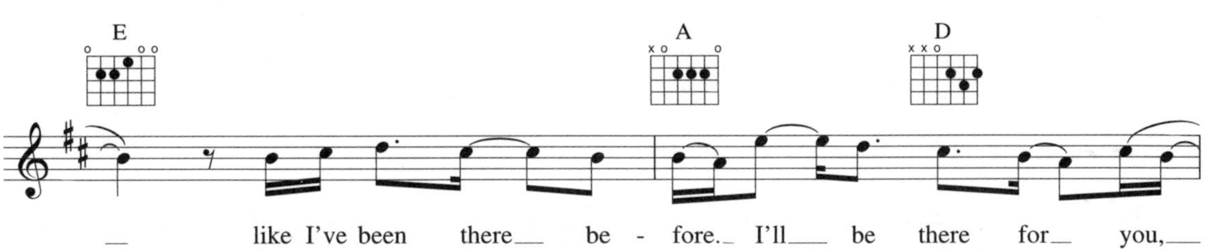

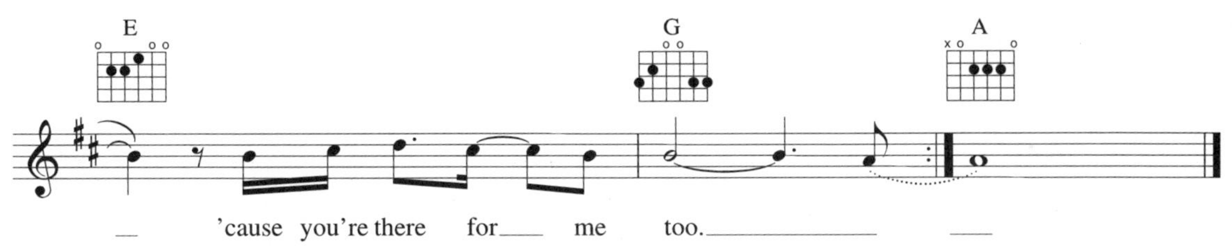

Verse 3:
You're still in bed at ten and work began at eight
You've burned your breakfast so far, things are going great
Your mother warned you there'd be days like these
But she didn't tell you when the world has brought?
You down to your knees.

I Will Always Love You

Words & Music by Dolly Parton

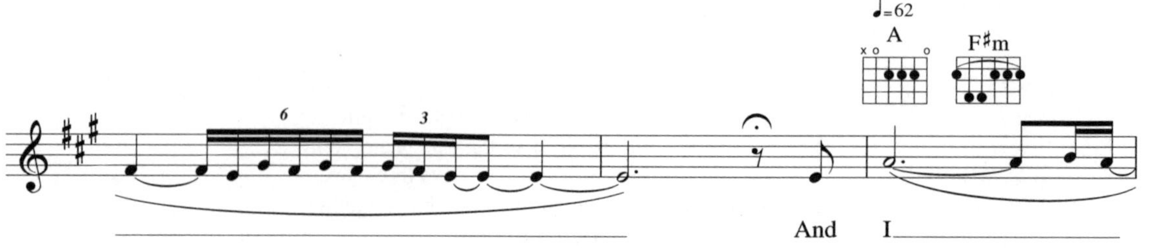

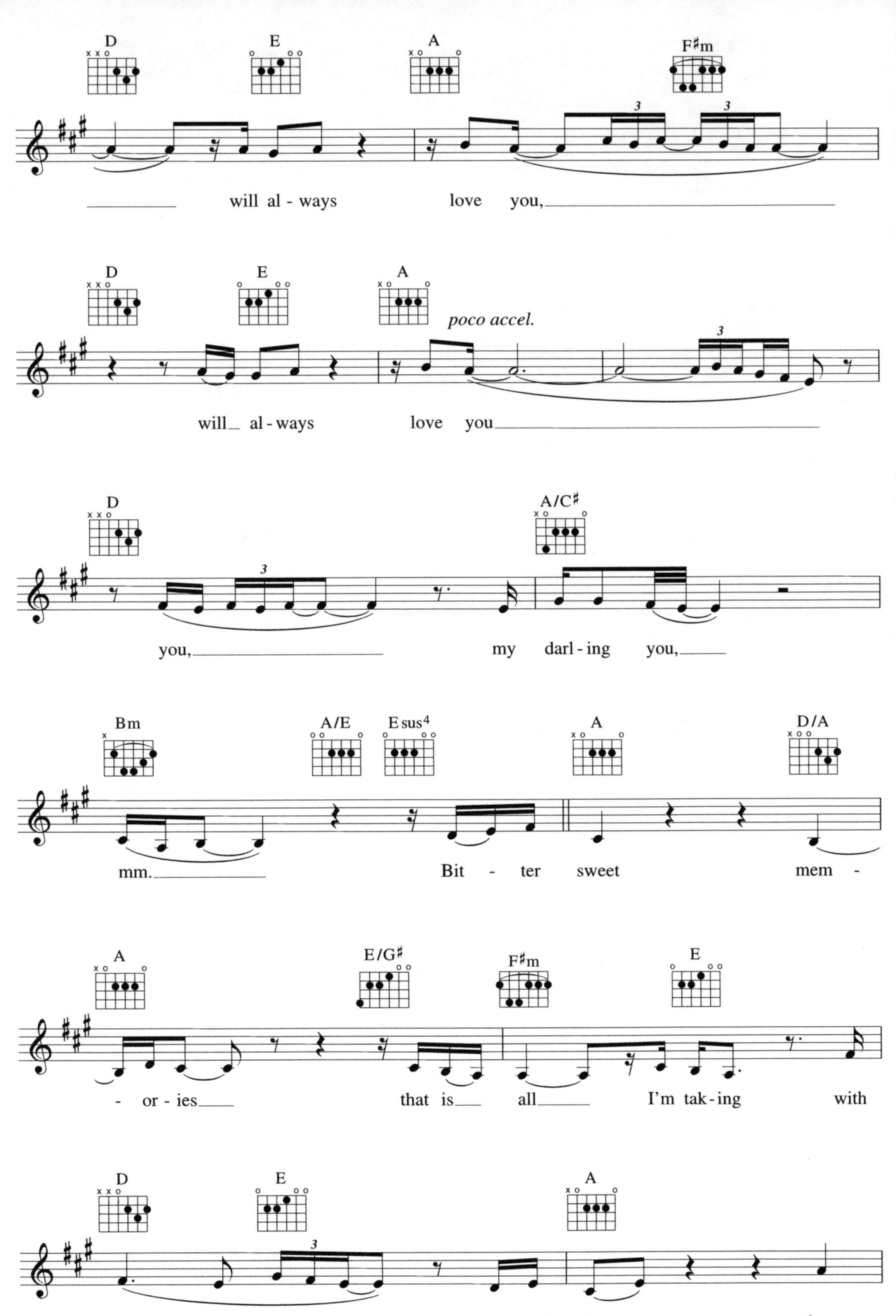
D
E
A
F♯m
will al - ways
love you,
D
E
A
poco accel.
will al - ways
love you
D
A/C♯
you,
my darl - ing you,
Bm
A/E
Esus4
A
D/A
mm.
Bit - ter sweet mem -
A
E/G♯
F♯m
E
- or - ies
that is all
I'm tak - ing with
D
E
A
me.
So good - bye,
please

E/G♯ F♯m E
3 3 3
don't cry, we both know I'm not what you, you
D E A F♯m
3
need. And I
D E A F♯m
6
will al - ways love you, I
D E A D/A A E
6
will al - ways love you.
A D/A A E/G♯
3
1° vocal tacet/instrumental
(2.) hope life treats you kind, and I
F♯m E D E
3 3 3
hope you have all you dreamed of. And I wish

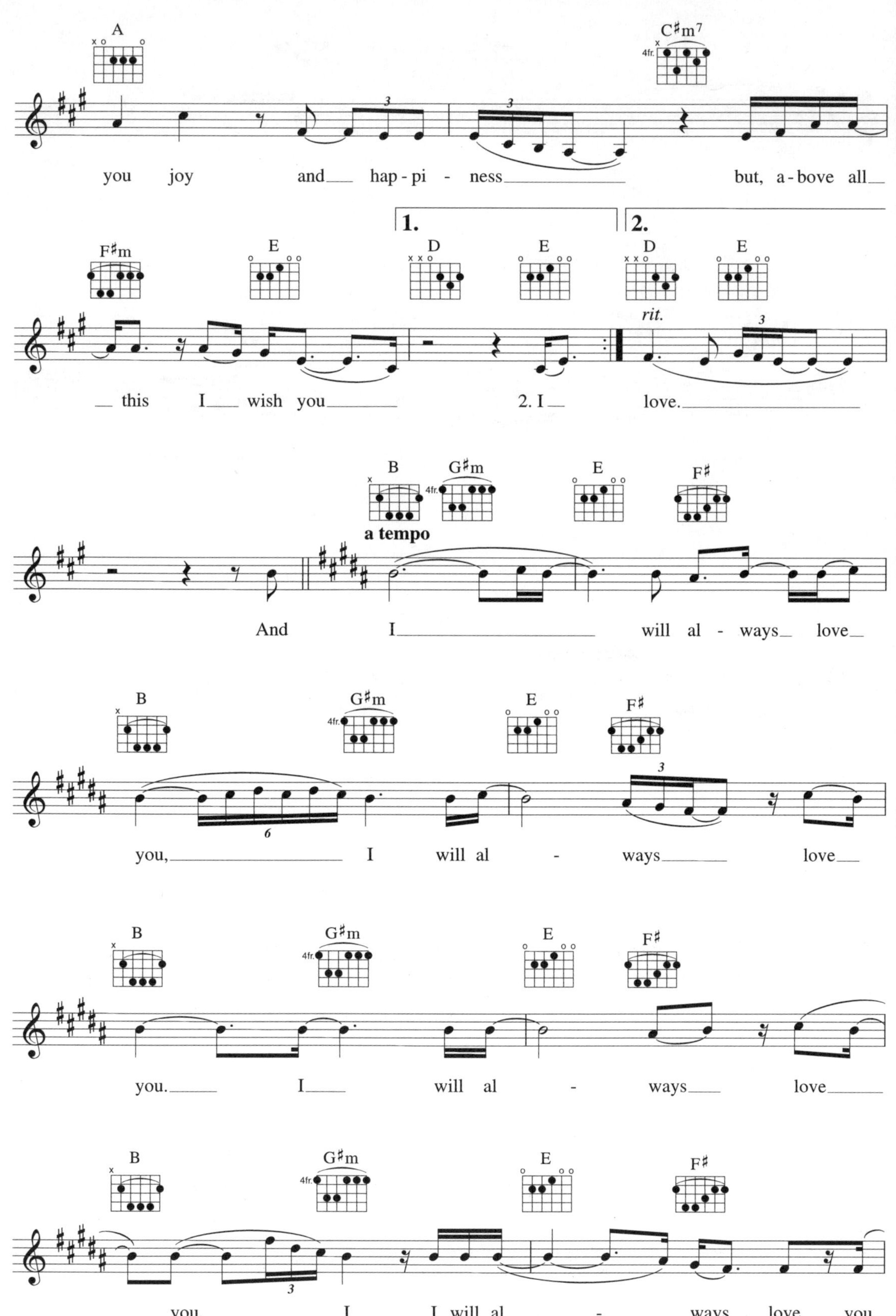
A
C♯m7
4fr.
you joy and happiness but, above all
1.
2.
F♯m
E
D
E
D
E
rit.
this I wish you 2. I love.
B
G♯m
E
F♯
a tempo
And I will always love
you, I will always love
you. I will always love
you, I I will always love you.

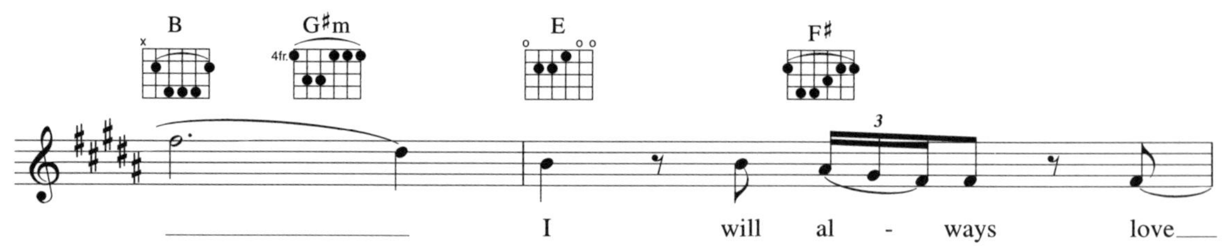
B
G♯m
4fr.
E
F♯
I will al - ways love

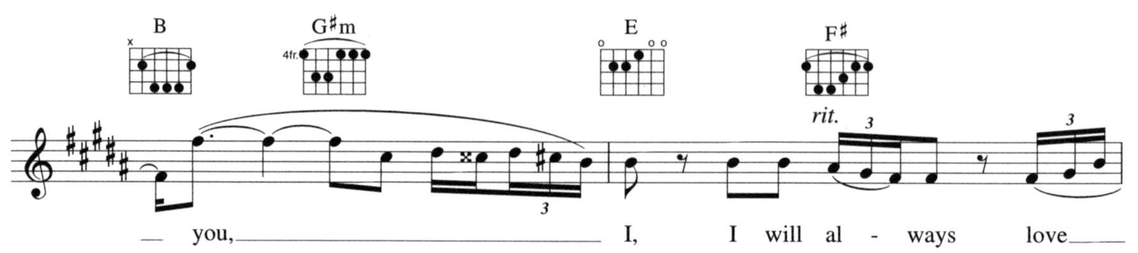
B
G♯m
4fr.
E
F♯
rit.
you, I, I will al - ways love

N.C.
you,

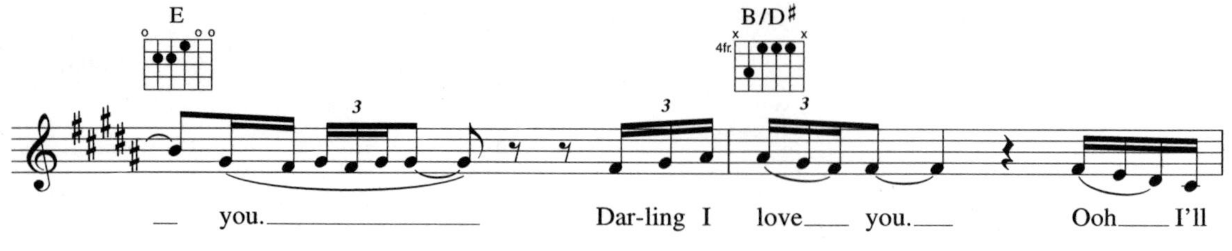
E
B/D♯
4fr.
you. Dar-ling I love you. Ooh I'll

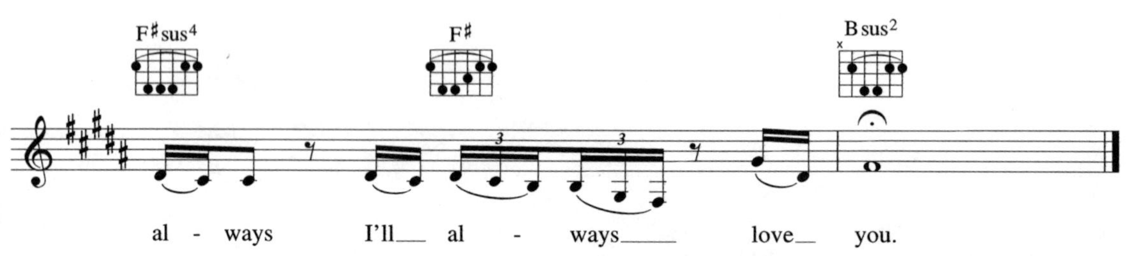
F♯sus4
F♯
B sus2
al - ways I'll al - ways love you.

Ironic

Words by Alanis Morissette
Music by Alanis Morissette & Glen Ballard

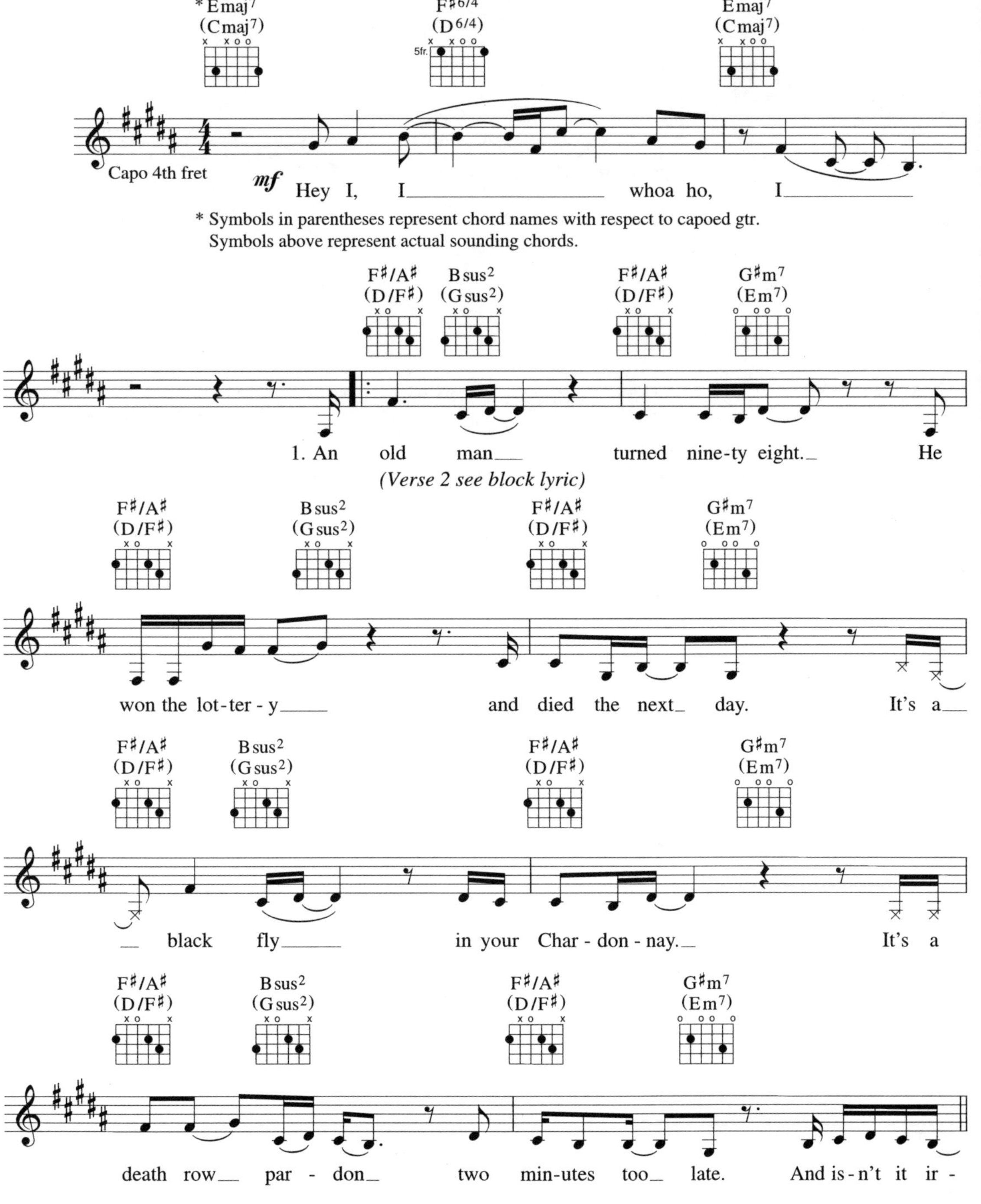

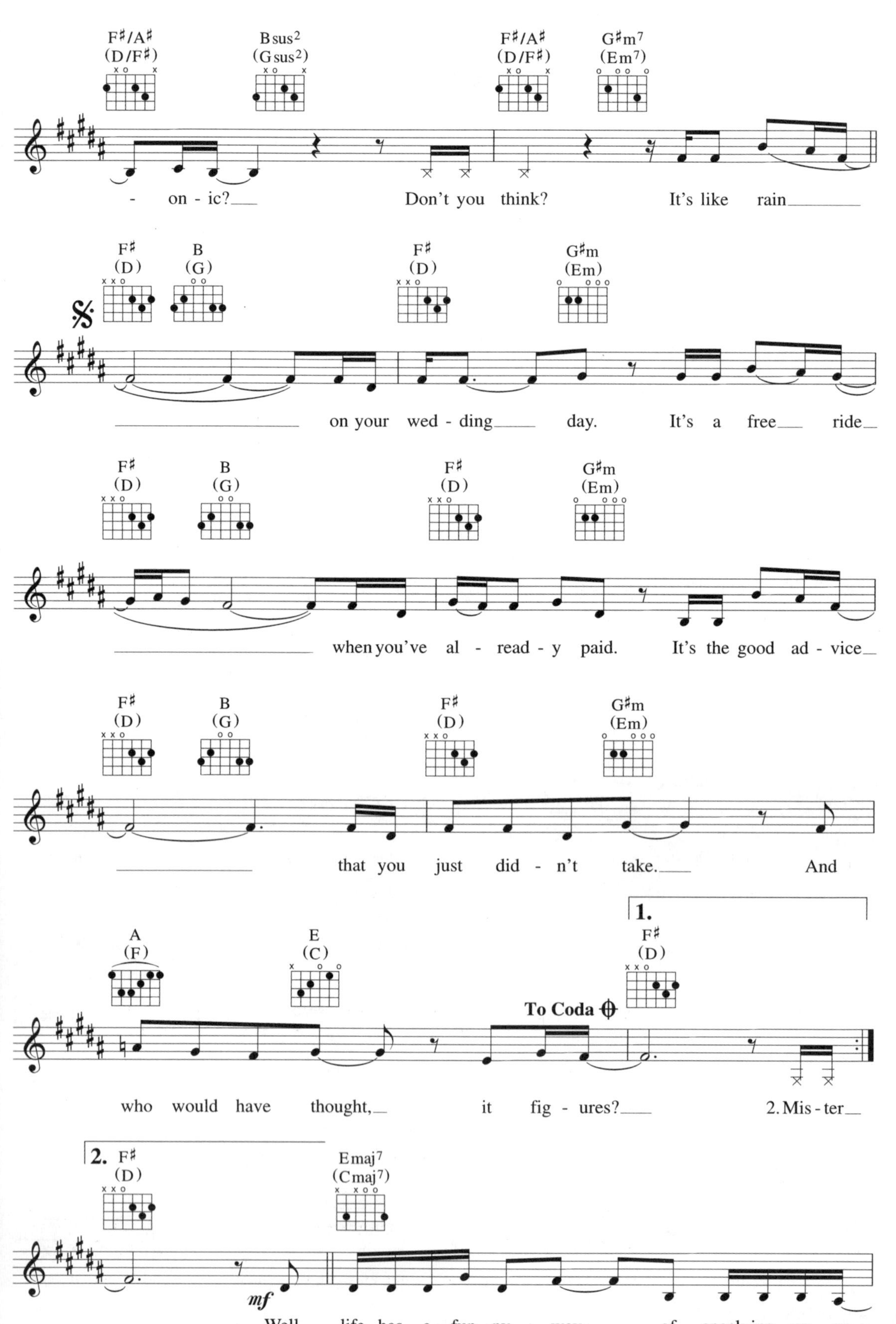
F♯/A♯ (D/F♯) Bsus2 (Gsus2) F♯/A♯ (D/F♯) G♯m7 (Em7)
- on - ic? Don't you think? It's like rain
F♯ (D) B (G) F♯ (D) G♯m (Em)
on your wed - ding day. It's a free ride
when you've al - read - y paid. It's the good ad - vice
that you just did - n't take. And
A (F) E (C) 1. F♯ (D)
To Coda
who would have thought, it fig - ures? 2. Mis - ter
2. F♯ (D) Emaj7 (Cmaj7)
mf
Well, life has a fun - ny way of sneak-ing up on

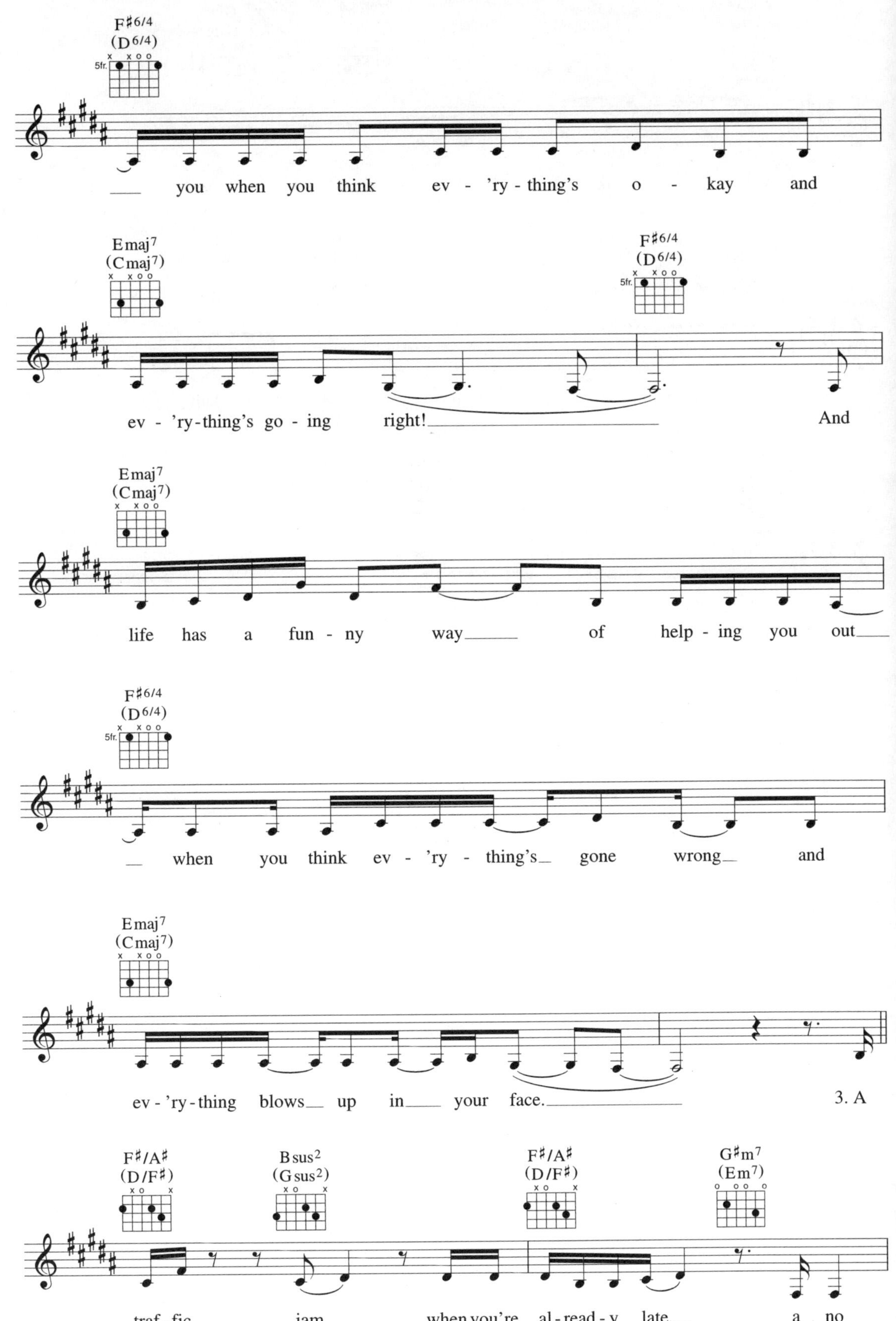
F♯6/4
(D6/4)
5fr.
you when you think ev - 'ry - thing's o - kay and
Emaj7
(Cmaj7)
F♯6/4
(D6/4)
5fr.
ev - 'ry - thing's go - ing right!
And
Emaj7
(Cmaj7)
life has a fun - ny way of help - ing you out
F♯6/4
(D6/4)
5fr.
when you think ev - 'ry - thing's gone wrong and
Emaj7
(Cmaj7)
ev - 'ry - thing blows up in your face.
3. A
F♯/A♯
(D/F♯)
Bsus2
(Gsus2)
F♯/A♯
(D/F♯)
G♯m7
(Em7)
traf - fic jam when you're al - read - y late, a no

F♯/A♯ (D/F♯)
Bsus2 (Gsus2)
G♯m7 (Em7)
smok - ing sign on your cig-ar-ette break. It's like
ten thou-sand spoons when all you need is a knife. It's
meet-ing the man of my dreams, and then meet-
-ing his beau-ti-ful wife. And is-n't it ir-
-on-ic. Don't you think? A lit-tle too
ir-on-ic, and yeah, I real-ly do think. It's like rain
D.S. al Coda

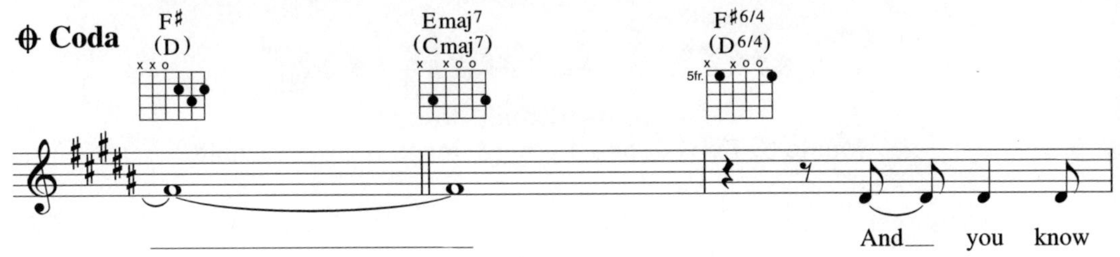

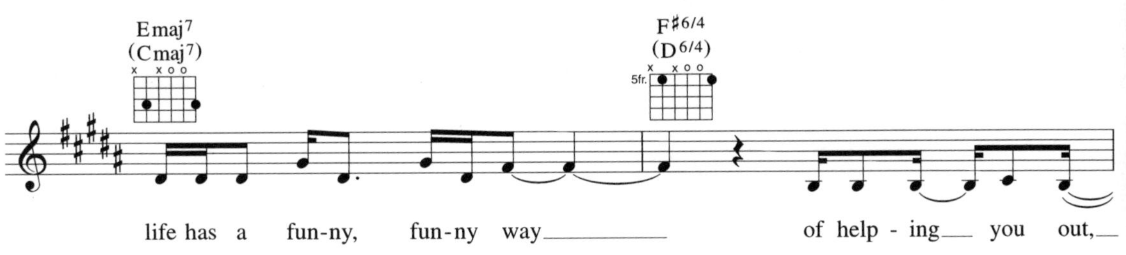

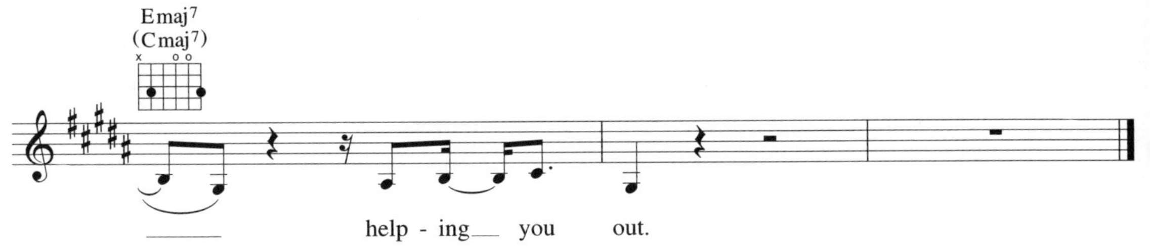

Verse 2:
Mister Play It Safe was afraid to fly
He packed his suitcase and kissed his kids goodbye
He waited his whole damn life to take that flight
And as the plane crashed down he thought, "Well isn't this nice?"

And isn't it ironic, don't you think?

It's like rain on your wedding day
It's a free ride when you've already paid
It's the good advice that you just didn't take
And who would have thought, it figures.

Just Looking

Words by Kelly Jones
Music by Kelly Jones, Richard Jones & Stuart Cable

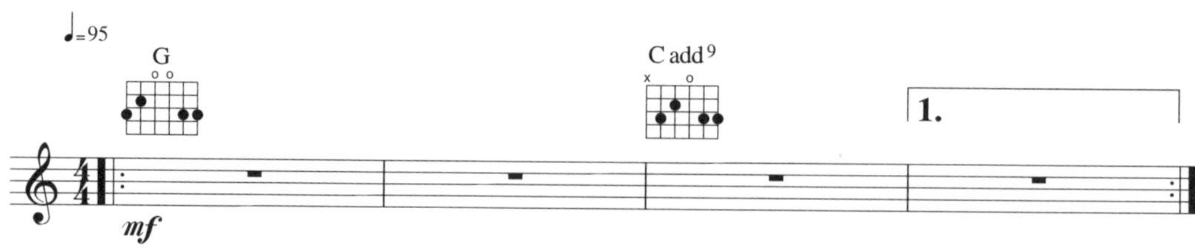

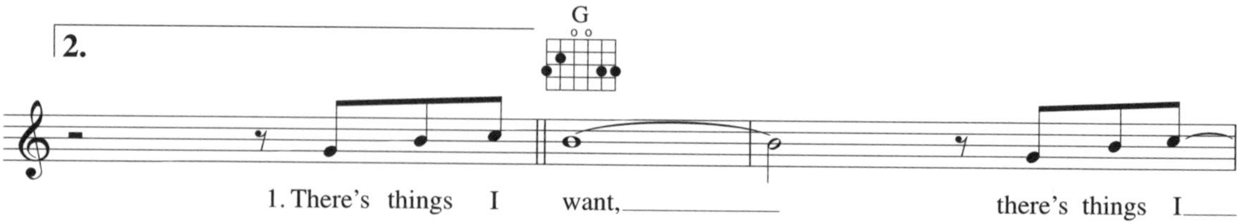

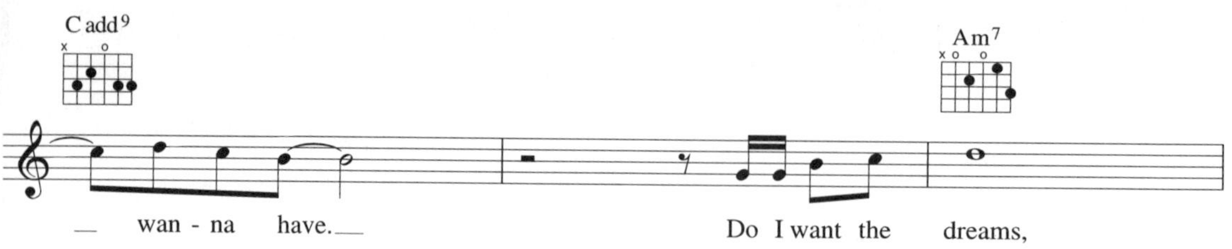

G
C add9
wife
the word per - fect ain't quite right,
seen,
an - oth - er could a' been,
(Verse 4(𝄋) see block lyric)
G
shop-pin' ev - 'ry day,
take it back the
you drenched my head
and said what
C add9
Am7
next break.
They say the more you fly the
I said.
Said that life is what you
F sus2
more you risk your li - - - - fe.
make of it yet most of us just fake.
And I'm just
G
C add9
look - in',
I'm not buy - ing.
I'm just look - in'
it keeps me

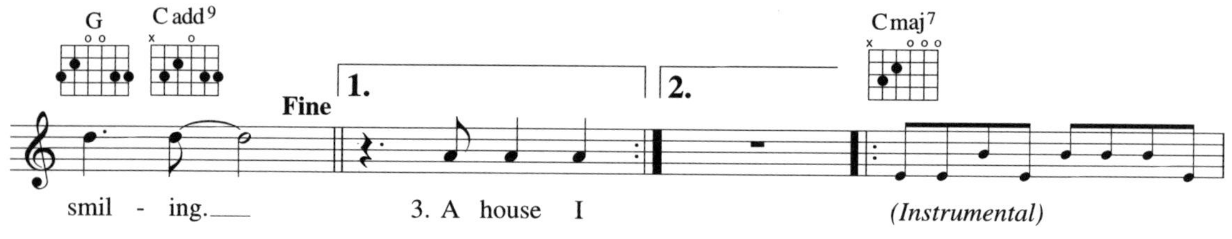

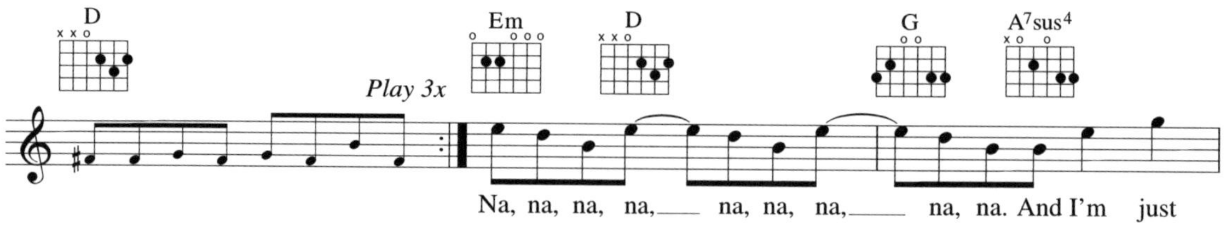

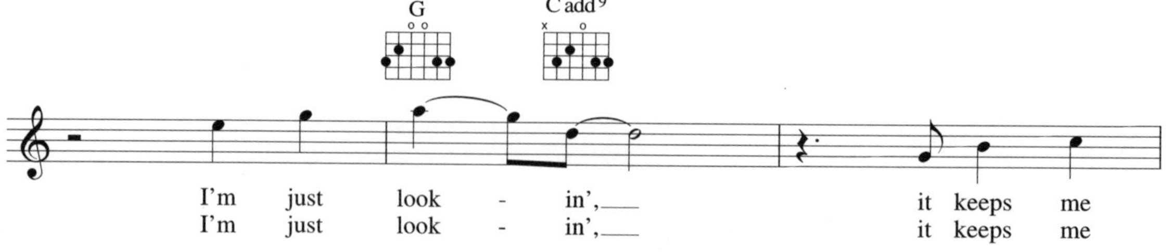

Verse 4:
There's things I want
There's things I think I want
There's things I've had
There's things I wanna have
They say the more you fly
The more you risk your life.

The Life Of Riley

Words & Music by Ian Broudie

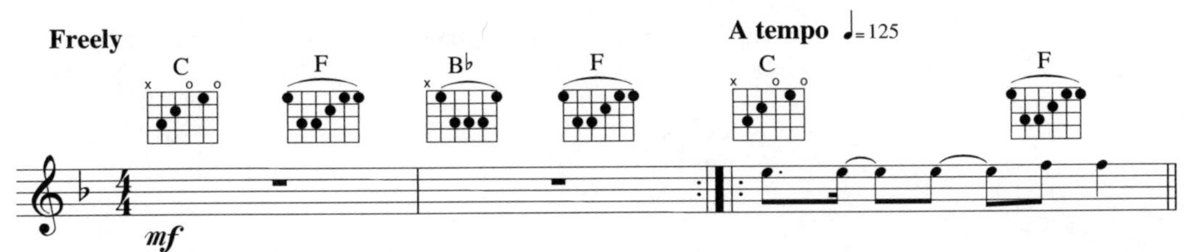

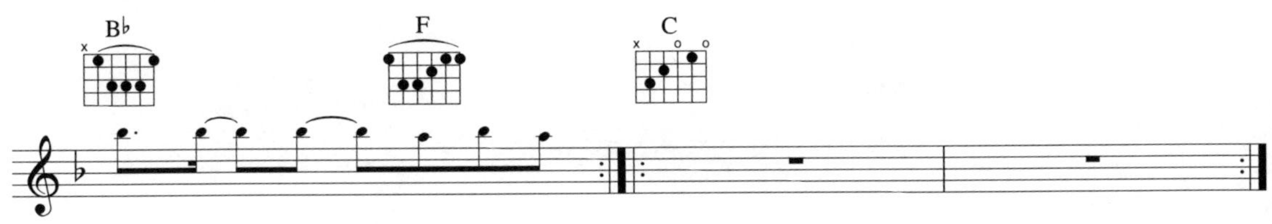

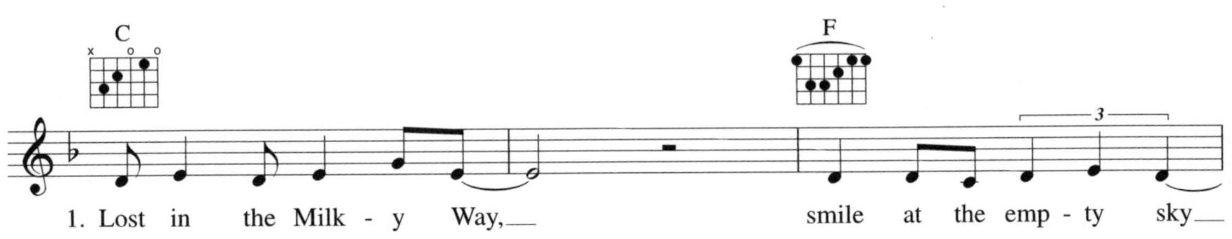

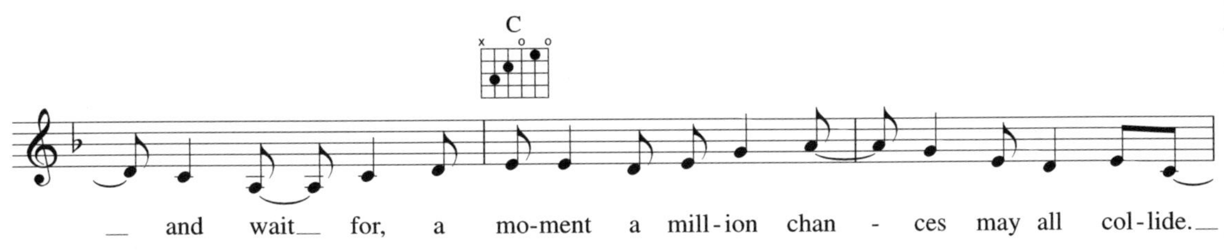

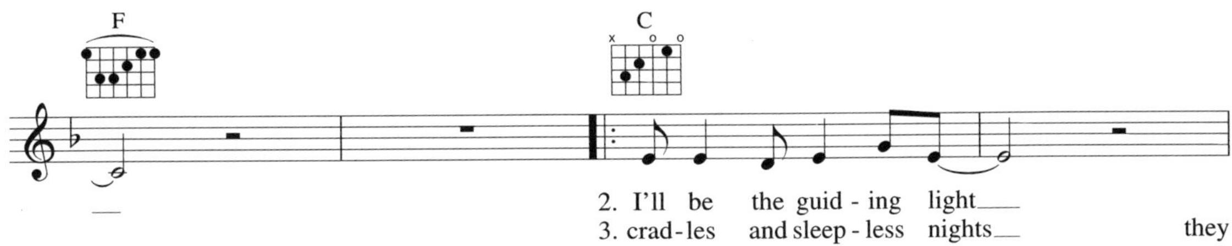

F
C
swim to me through stars___ that shine___ down and call to the sleep - ing world_
breathe in life for - ev - er. and stare at the world from deep__
F
C
___ as they fall to earth.___
___ un - der eid - er - down.___
So here's your___ life,
F
C
we'll find a____ way. We're sail - ing blind,
F
C
F
but it's cer - tain no - thing's cer - tain. I don't mind I___
C
F
C
F
___ get the feel - ing, you'll be fine, I_____ still be-lieve that in this world we've_
G
1.
___ got to find the time___ for the life of Ril -
1. cont.
C
F
B♭
F
C
F
B♭
F
- ey.__ 3. From

2.(𝄋)
G
C
F
for the first time I don't mind I get the feel - ing, you'll be fine, I
still be-lieve that in this world we've got to find the time
To Coda ⊕
for the life of Ril - ey.
Oh this world is a cra - zy ride so take
your seat and hold on tight.
D.𝄋 al Coda ⊕
So
⊕ Coda
B♭
- ley, the life of Ril - ey,
the life of Ril - ey, the life of Ril - ey.

Linger

Words by Dolores O'Riordan
Music by Dolores O'Riordan & Noel Hogan

C
Cmaj7
G
it's tear-ing me a-part, it's ru-in-ing ev-'ry-thing.
D
2. I swore, I swore I would be true
(3.) if you could get by
A6
and hon-ey, so did you, so
try-ing not to lie,
C
Cmaj7
why were you hold-ing her hand? Is that the way we stand?
things would-n't be so con-fused, and I would-n't feel so used,
C
Cmaj7
G
Were you ly-ing all the time? Was it just a game to you?
but you al-ways real-ly knew I just wan-na be with you.
D
But I'm in so deep, you know I'm such a fool

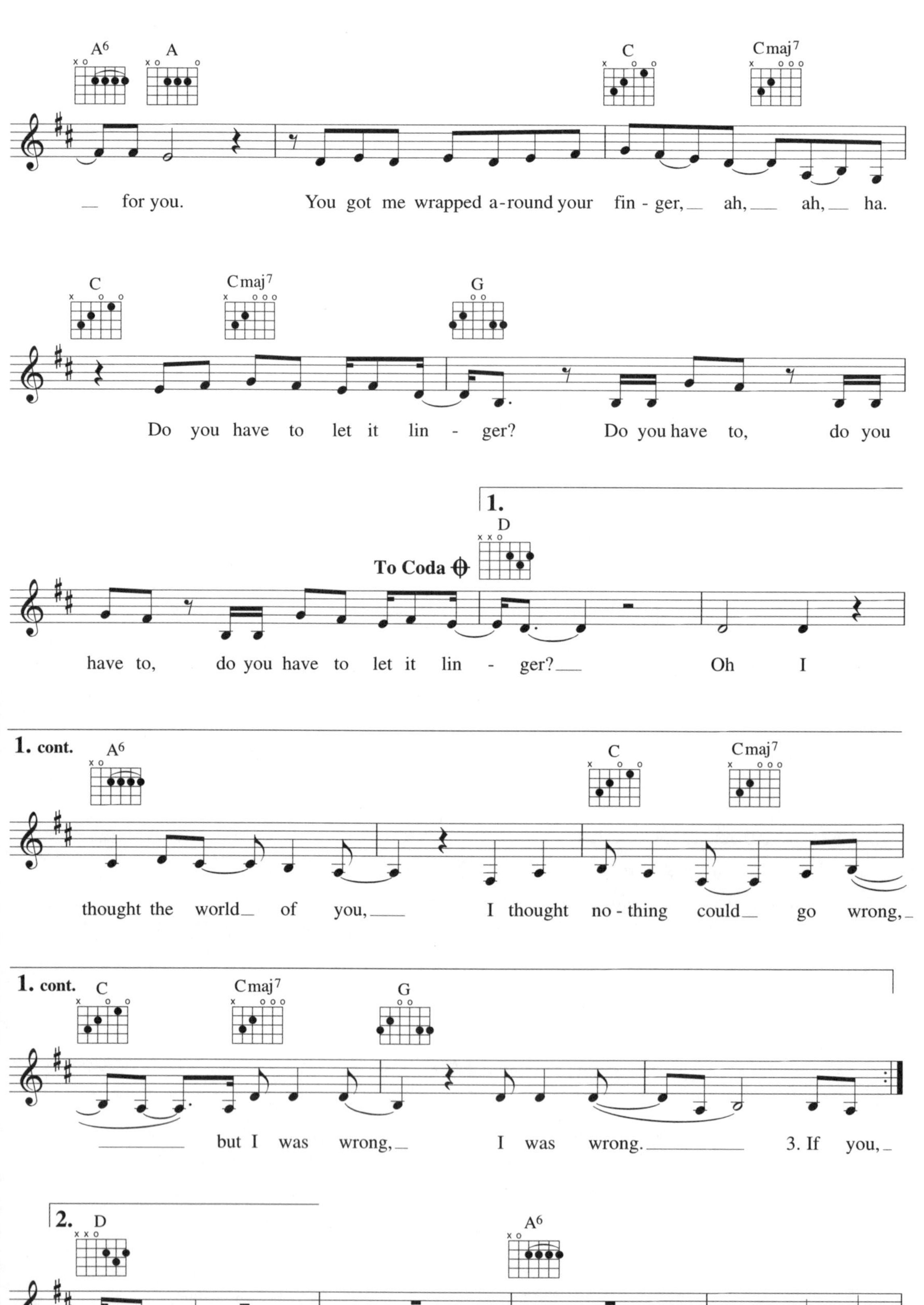
A6
A
C
Cmaj7
_ for you. You got me wrapped a-round your fin - ger, _ ah, _ ah, _ ha.
C
Cmaj7
G
Do you have to let it lin - ger? Do you have to, do you
1.
To Coda
D
have to, do you have to let it lin - ger? _ Oh I
1. cont.
A6
C
Cmaj7
thought the world _ of you, _ I thought no - thing could _ go wrong, _
1. cont.
C
Cmaj7
G
_ but I was wrong, _ I was wrong. _ 3. If you, _
2.
D
A6
- ger? _
(Instrumental)

C
Cmaj7
C
Cmaj7
G
D. 𝄋 al Coda 𝄌
And I'm in so
𝄌 Coda
D
- ger?
- ger?
You know I'm such a fool
2° vocal tacet
A6
A
for you
you got me wrapped a - round your
C
Cmaj7
C
Cmaj7
fin - ger, ah, ah, ha.
Do you have to let it lin -
G
- ger? Do you have to do you have to, do you have to let it lin -
D
Dsus4
Play 3x
D

Livin' La Vida Loca

Words & Music by Desmond Child & Robi Rosa

2. She's in - to new sen - sa - tions, new kicks in the can-dle - light.
(Verse 3 see block lyric)

She's got a new ad - dic - tion s'full ev - 'ry day and night. She'll

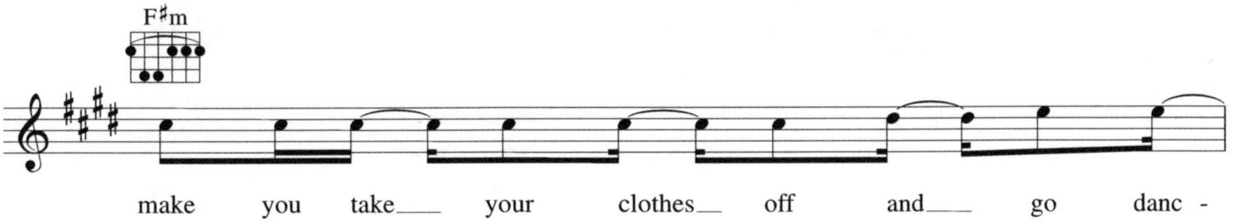

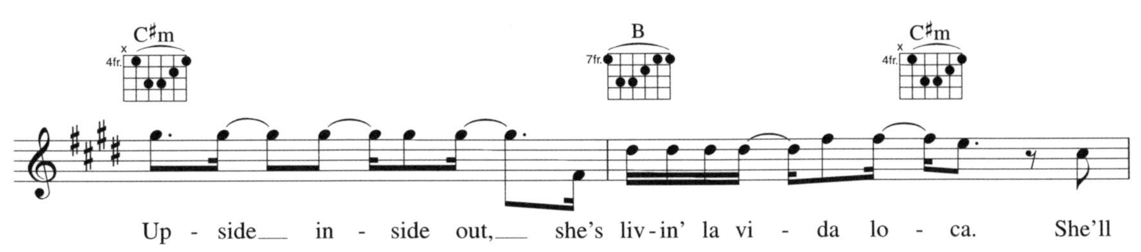

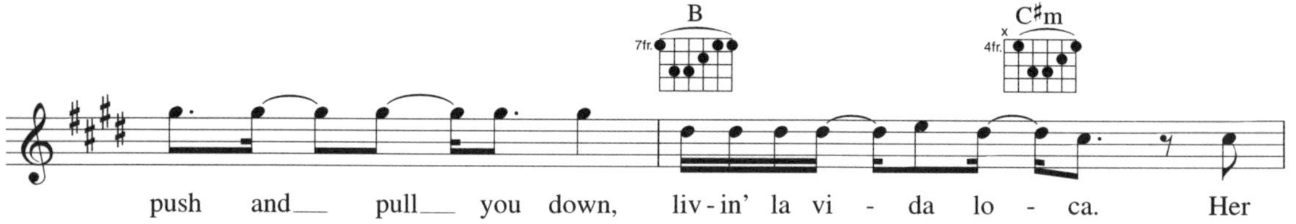
B
7fr.
C♯m
4fr.
push and___ pull___ you down, liv-in' la vi - da lo - ca. Her

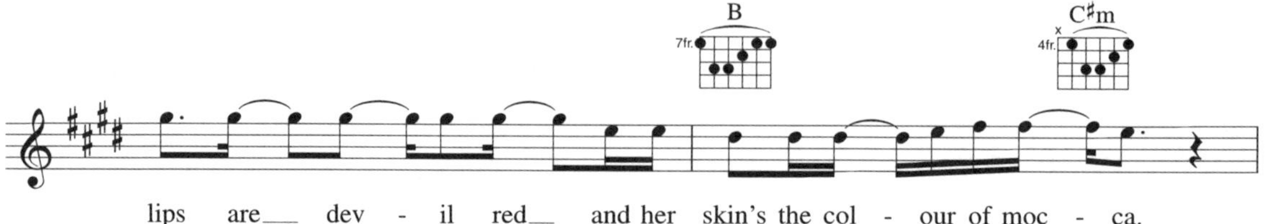
B
7fr.
C♯m
4fr.
lips are___ dev - il red___ and her skin's the col - our of moc - ca.

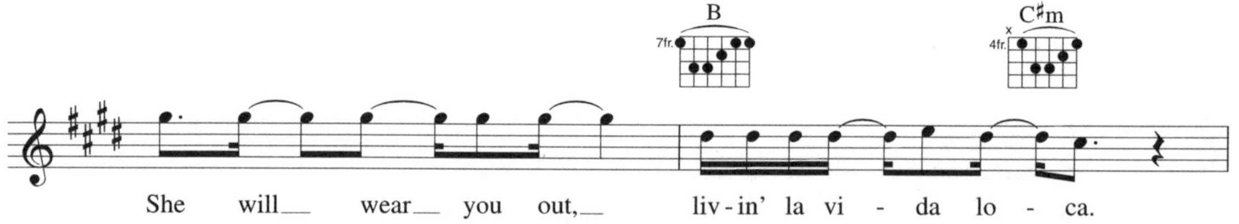
B
7fr.
C♯m
4fr.
She will___ wear___ you out,___ liv-in' la vi - da lo - ca.

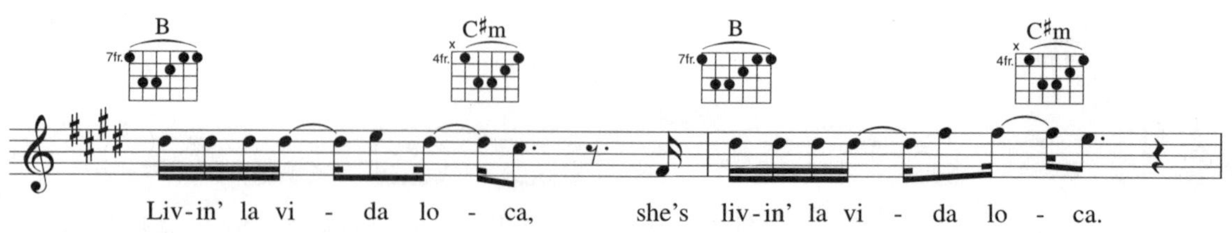
B
7fr.
C♯m
4fr.
Liv-in' la vi - da lo - ca, she's liv-in' la vi - da lo - ca.

1.
(Instrumental)

1. cont.

2.
(Instrumental)

She'll

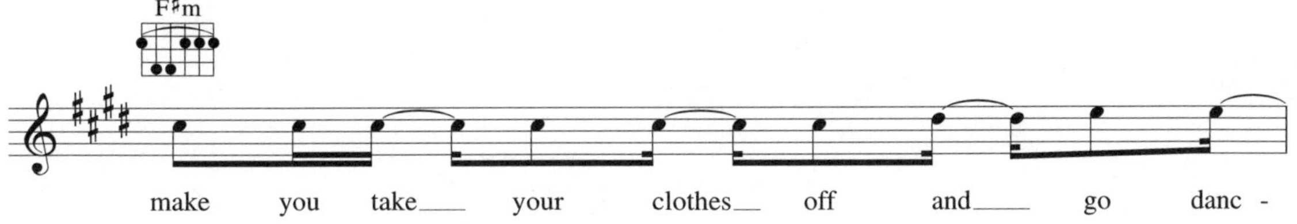
F♯m
make you take your clothes off and go danc -

G♯m
4fr.
A
5fr.
- ing in the rain. She'll make you live her cra - zy life or she'll take

B
7fr.
G♯
4fr.
a - way your pain like a bul - let to your brain.

C♯m
4fr.
B
7fr.
C♯m
4fr.
Up - side, in - side out, she's liv - in' la vi - da lo - ca. She'll

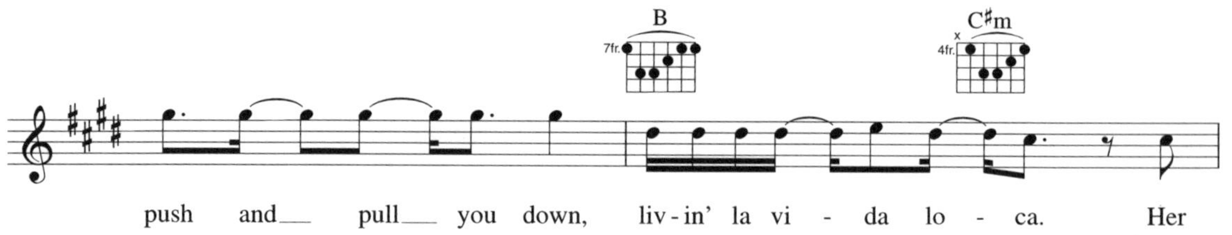
B
7fr.
C♯m
4fr.
push and pull you down, liv-in' la vi - da lo - ca. Her

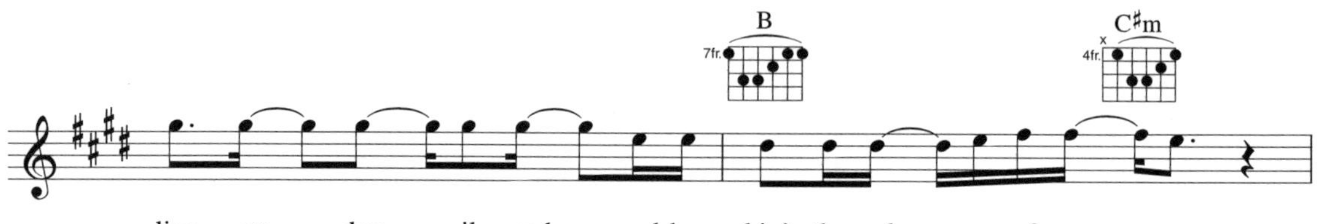
B
7fr.
C♯m
4fr.
lips are dev - il red and her skin's the col - our of moc - ca.

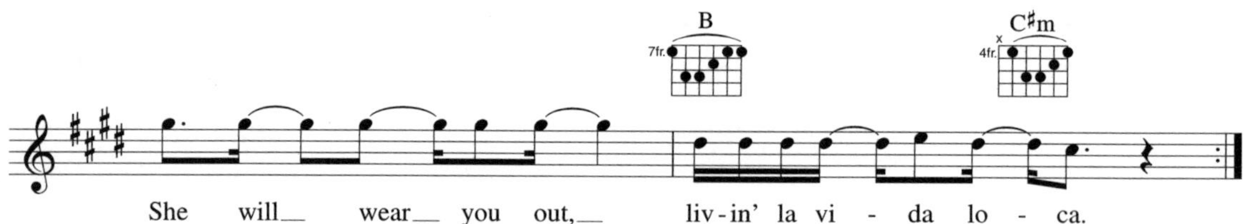
B
7fr.
C♯m
4fr.
She will wear you out, liv-in' la vi - da lo - ca.

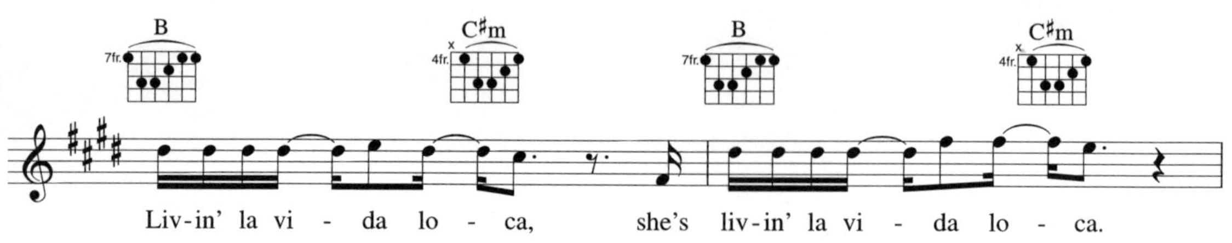
B
7fr.
C♯m
4fr.
B
7fr.
C♯m
4fr.
Liv-in' la vi - da lo - ca, she's liv-in' la vi - da lo - ca.

B
7fr.
C♯m
4fr.
(Instrumental)

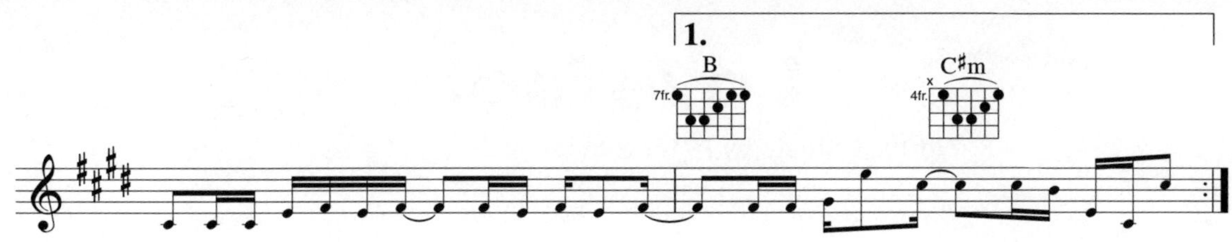

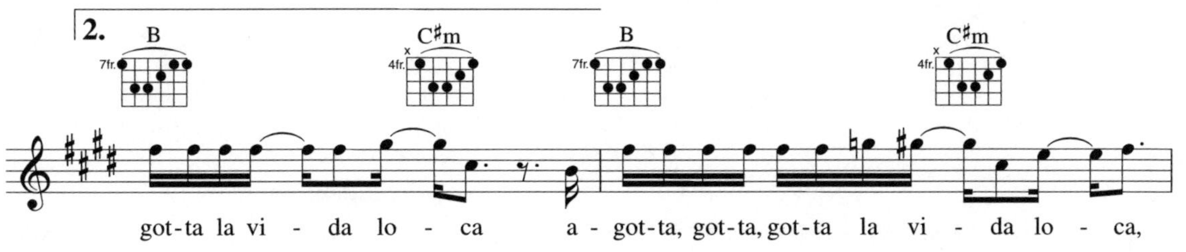

Verse 3:
Woke up in New York City
In a funky cheap hotel
She took my heart and she took my money
She must have slipped me a sleepin' pill
She never drinks the water
Makes you order French champagne
And once you've had a taste of her
You'll never be the same
Yeah, she'll make you go insane.

Lovefool

Words & Music by Peter Svensson & Nina Persson

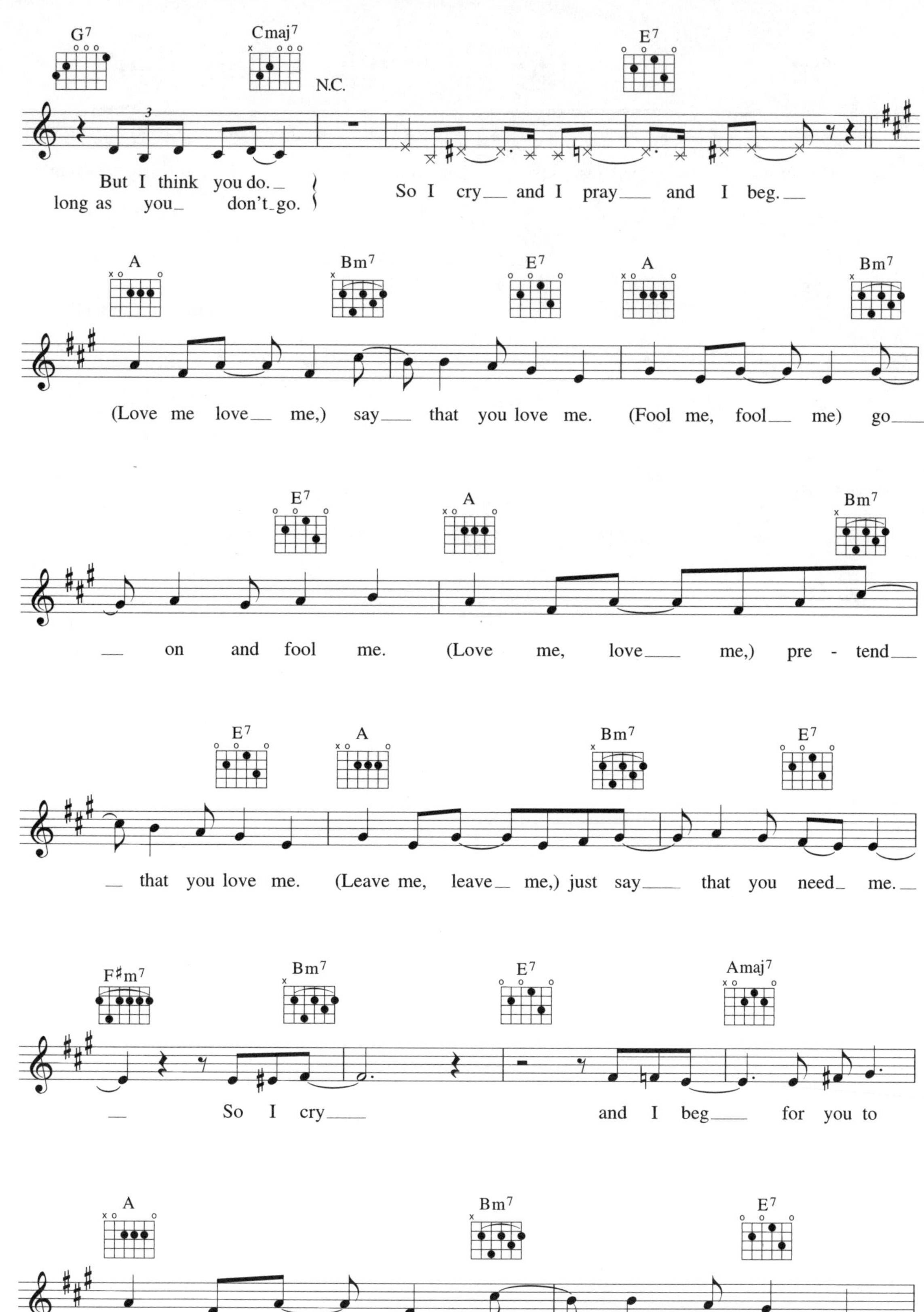
G7
Cmaj7
N.C.
E7
But I think you do.
long as you don't go.
So I cry and I pray and I beg.
A
Bm7
E7
A
Bm7
(Love me love me,) say that you love me. (Fool me, fool me) go
E7
A
Bm7
on and fool me. (Love me, love me,) pre - tend
E7
A
Bm7
E7
that you love me. (Leave me, leave me,) just say that you need me.
F♯m7
Bm7
E7
Amaj7
So I cry and I beg for you to
A
Bm7
E7
(love me, love me.) Say that you love me.

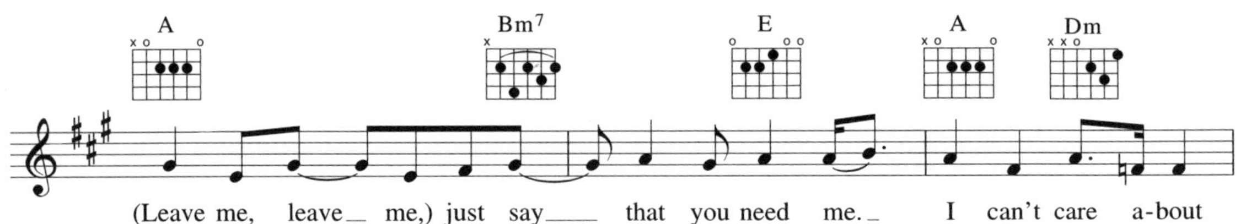
A
Bm7
E
A
Dm
(Leave me, leave me,) just say that you need me. I can't care a-bout

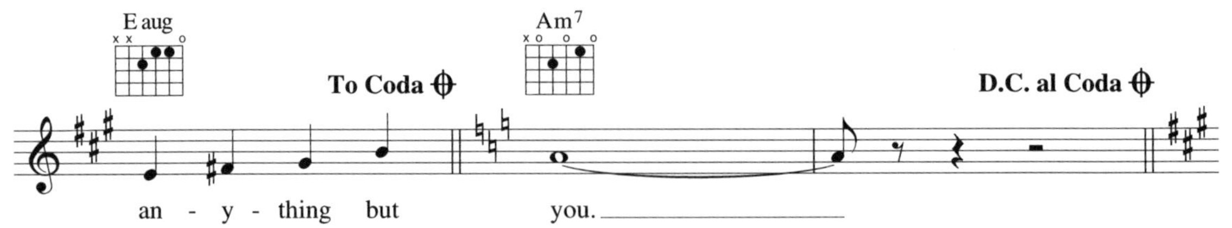
E aug
To Coda
Am7
D.C. al Coda
an - y - thing but you.

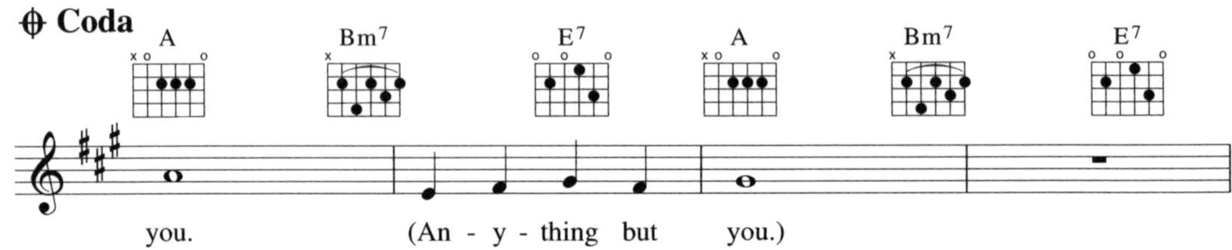
Coda
A
Bm7
E7
A
Bm7
E7
you. (An - y - thing but you.)

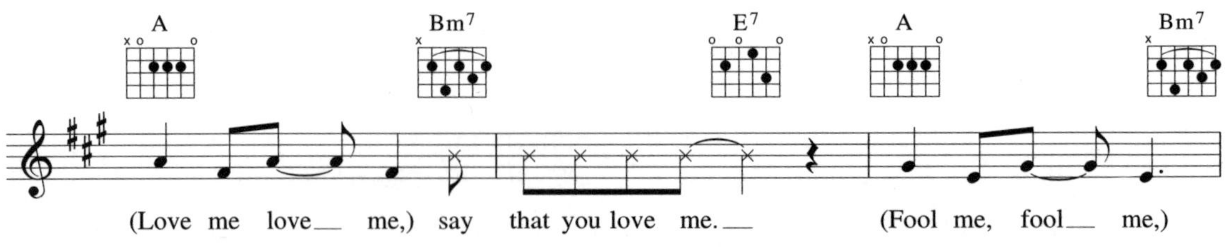
A
Bm7
E7
A
Bm7
(Love me love me,) say that you love me. (Fool me, fool me,)

E7
A
Bm7
E
go on and fool me. (Love me, love me.) I know that you need me.

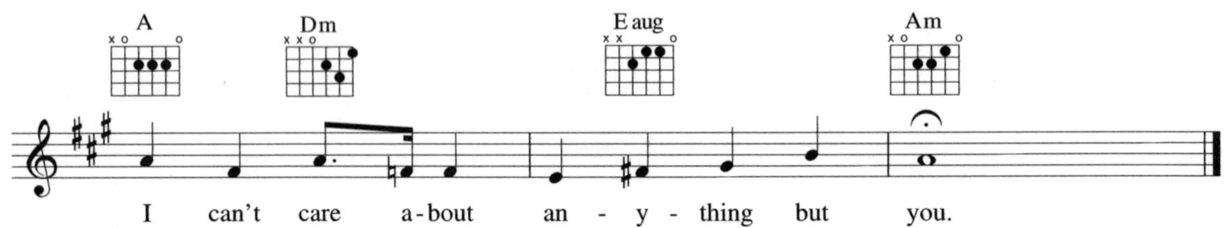
A
Dm
E aug
Am
I can't care a-bout an - y - thing but you.

Maria

Words & Music by Jimmy Destri

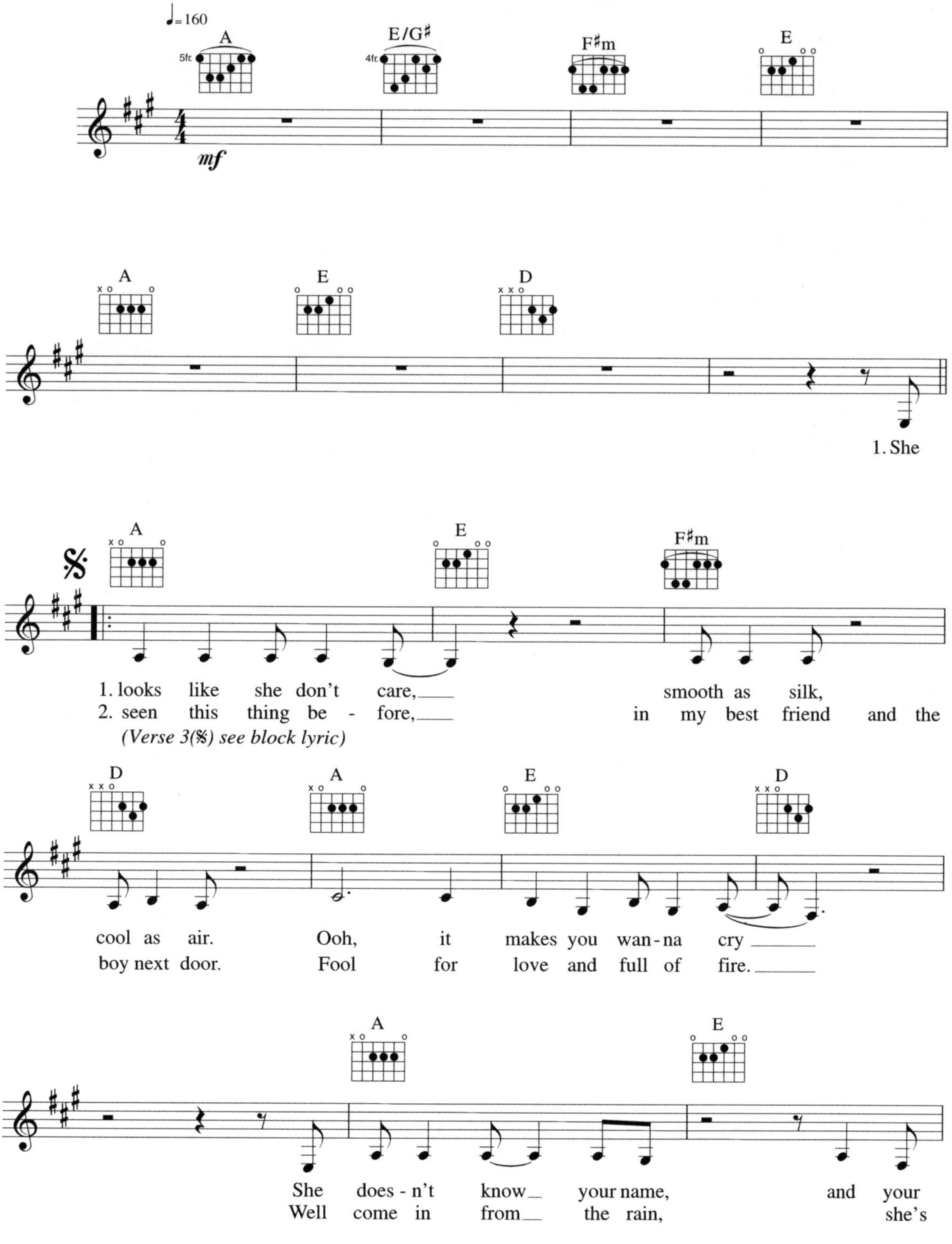

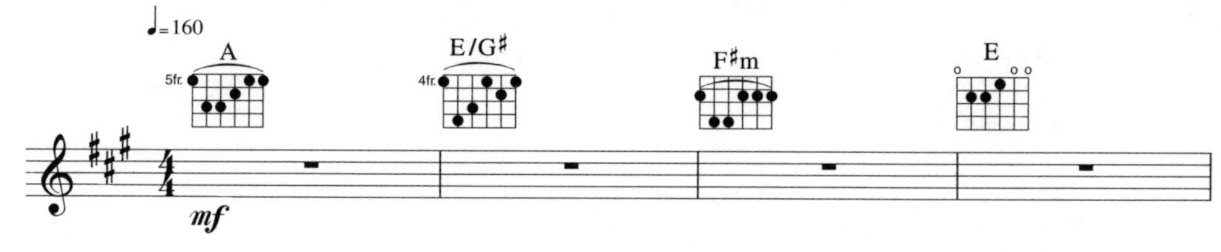

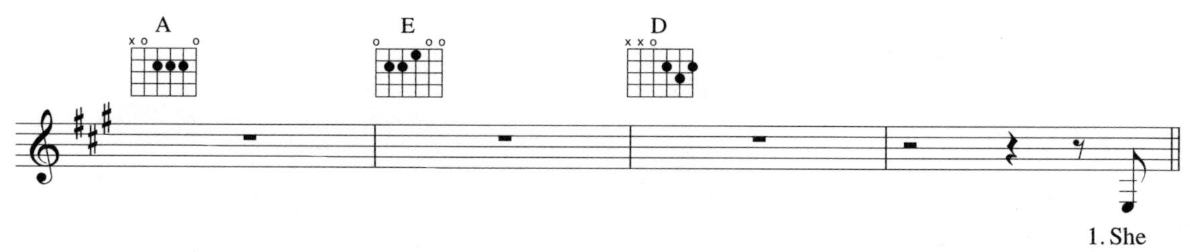

𝄋

A E F♯m

1. looks like she don't care, smooth as silk,

2. seen this thing be - fore, in my best friend and the

(Verse 3(𝄋) see block lyric)

D A E D

cool as air. Ooh, it makes you wan - na cry

boy next door. Fool for love and full of fire.

F♯m
D
A
heart beats like a sub - way train.
oc - eans run - ning down the drain.
Ooh, it
Blue, as
E
D
To Coda
makes you wan - na die.
ice and de - sire.
D
E
F♯m
Ooh don't you wan - na take her,
Don't you wan - na make her,
D
E
F♯m
you wan - na make her all your own?
Ooh don't you wan - na take her home?
A
E/G♯
4fr.
F♯m
Ma - ri - a, you've got - ta see her.
D
A
E
D
Go in - sane and out of your mind.

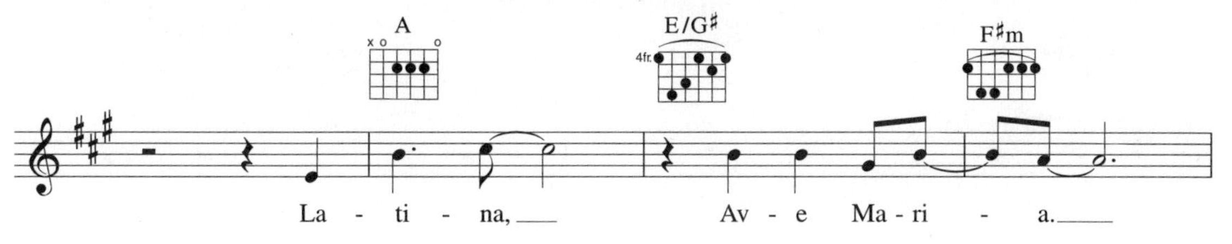
A
E/G♯
4fr.
F♯m
La - ti - na, Av - e Ma - ri - a.

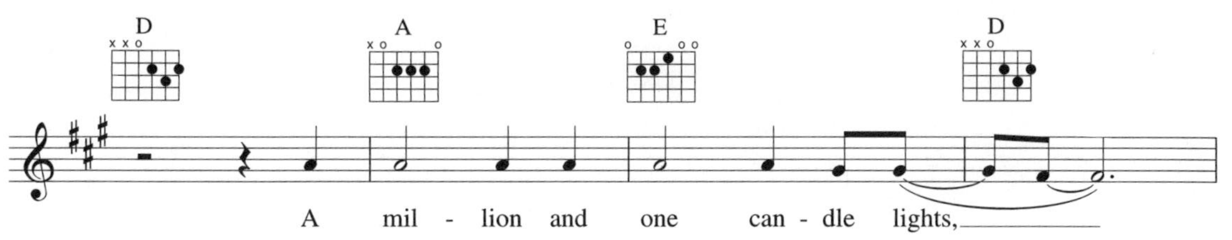
D
A
E
D
A mil - lion and one can - dle lights,

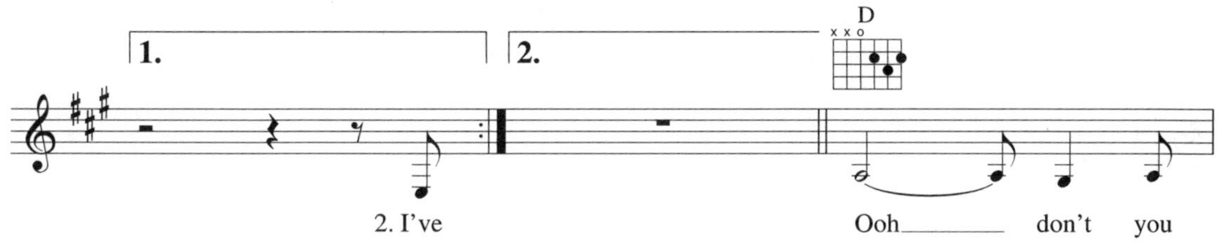
1.
2.
D
2. I've
Ooh don't you

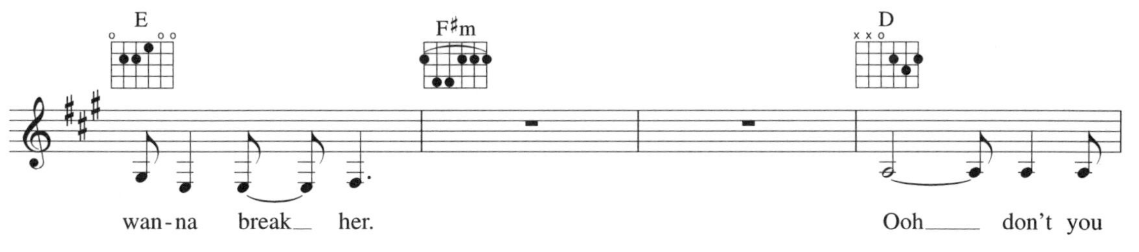
E
F♯m
D
wan-na break her.
Ooh don't you

E
F♯m
D.𝄋 al Coda
wan - na take her home?
3. She

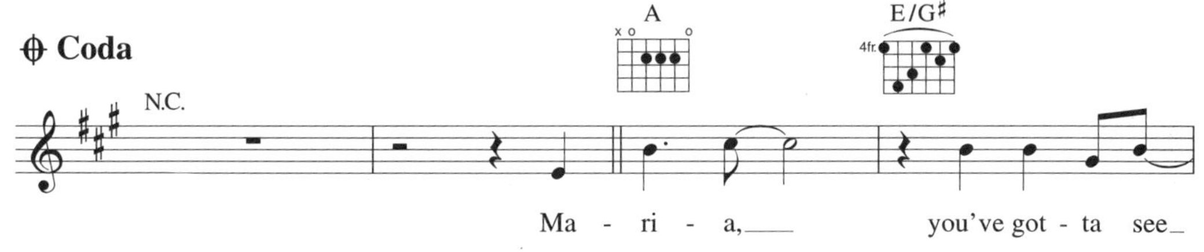
Coda
N.C.
A
E/G♯
4fr.
Ma - ri - a, you've got - ta see

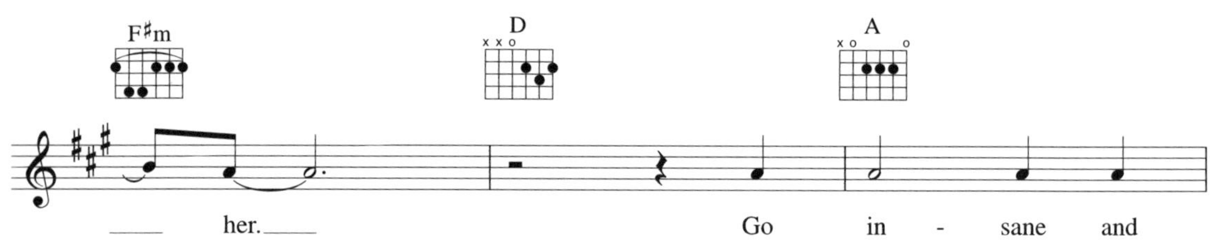
F♯m
D
A
her.
Go in - sane and

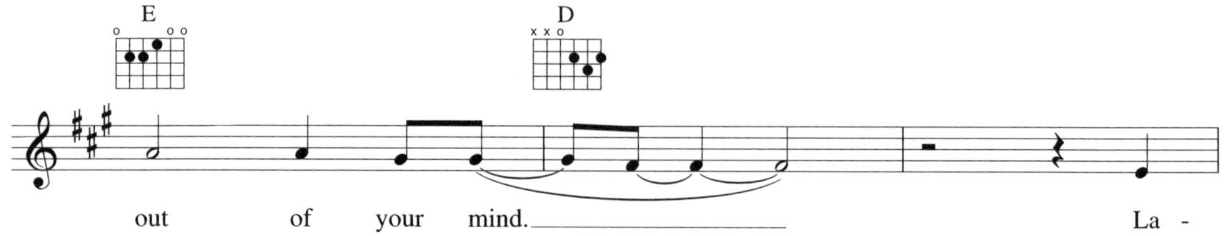
E
D
out of your mind.
La -

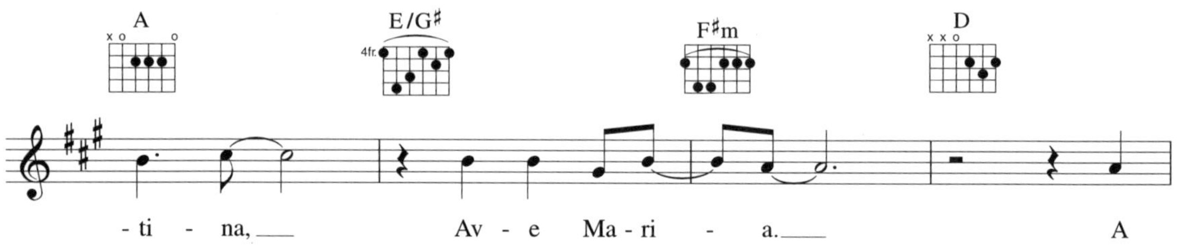
A
E/G♯
4fr.
F♯m
D
- ti - na,
Av - e Ma - ri - a.
A

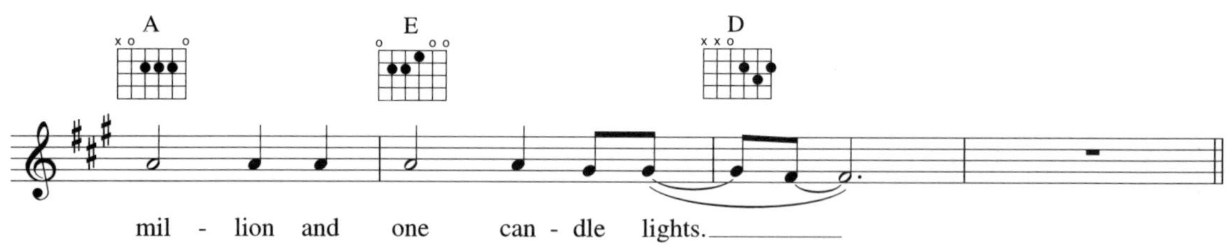
A
E
D
mil - lion and one can - dle lights.

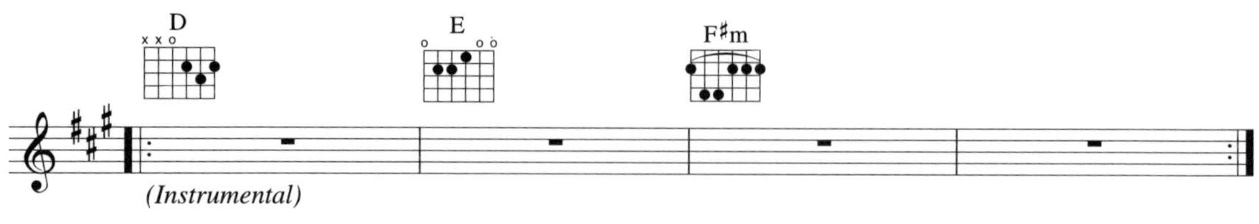
D
E
F♯m
(Instrumental)

B
F♯m

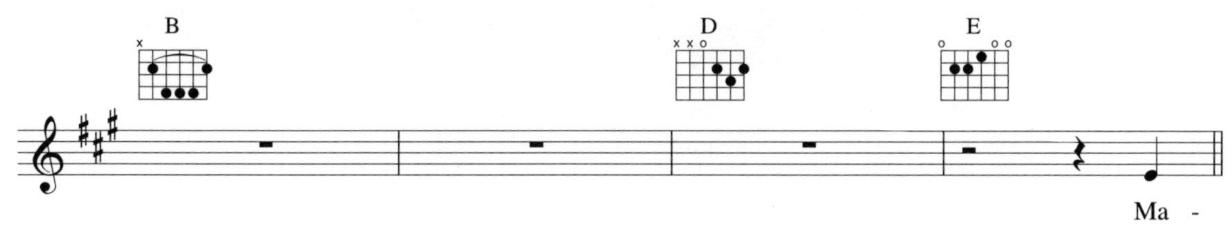

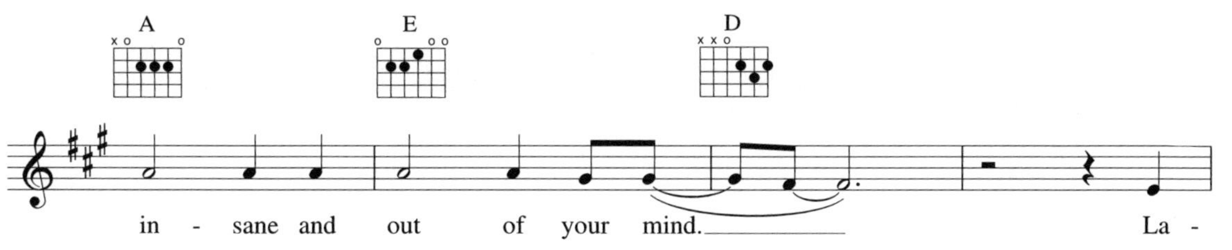

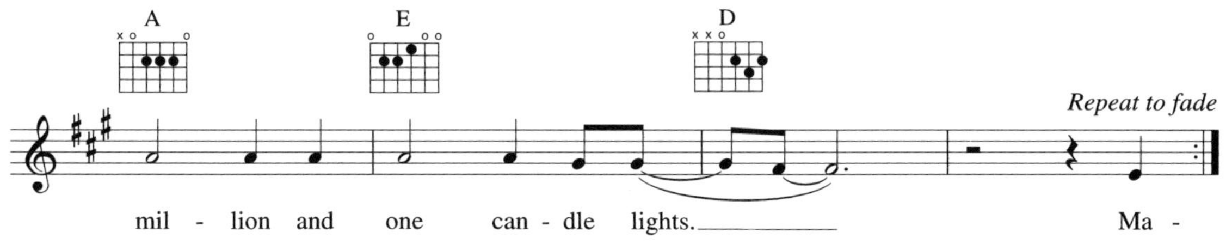

Verse 3(𝄋):
She walks like she don't care
You wanna take her everywhere
Ooh it makes you wanna cry
She's like a millionaire
Walking on imported air
Ooh it makes you wanna die.

Missing

Words by Tracey Thorn
Music by Ben Watt

Am7
F
bet - ter place.
And I miss you
like the
G
Dm7
Am7
des - erts miss the rain,
and I miss you
1.2.
F
G
Dm7
like the des - erts miss the rain.
3.
Dm7
Am
I step off the train,
I'm
G6/A
3fr.
Fmaj7/A
walk - ing down your street a - gain,
past your door,
Asus2
I guess you don't live there an - y - more.
It's

Verse 3:
Back on the train
I ask why did I come again?
Can I confess I've been hanging 'round your old address?
And the years have proved
To offer nothing since you've moved
You're long gone but I can't move on
And I miss you.

The More You Ignore Me, The Closer I Get

Words & Music by Morrissey & Boz Boorer

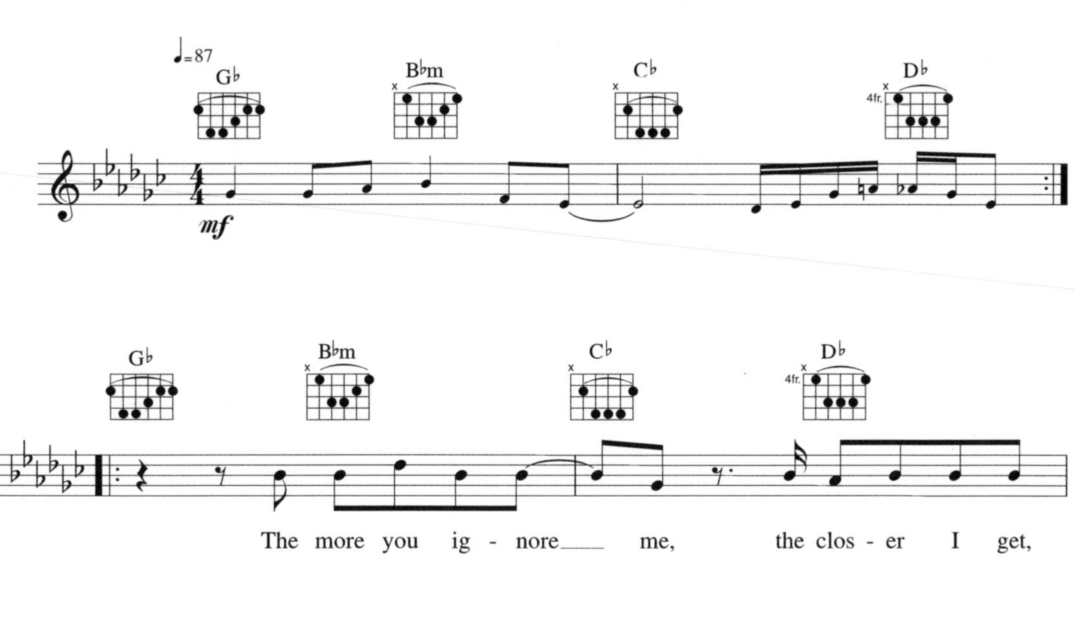

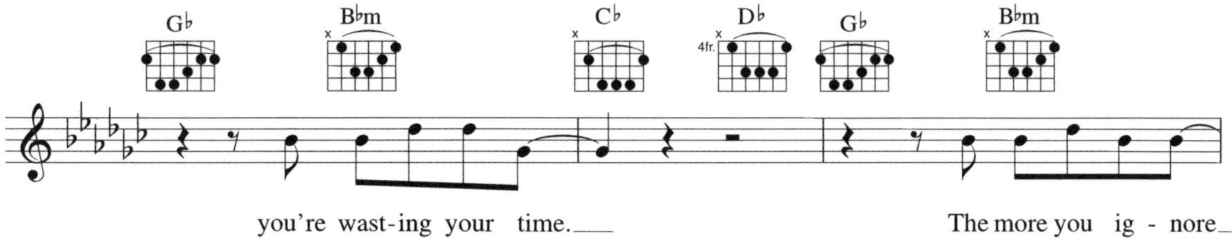

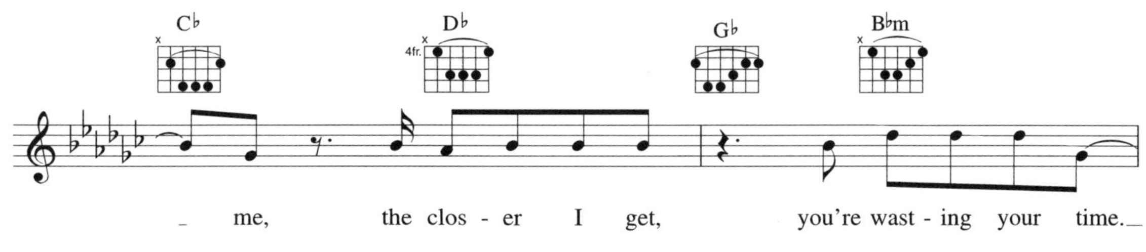

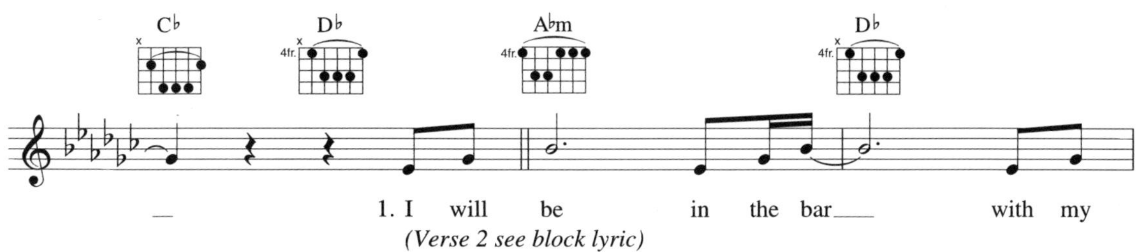

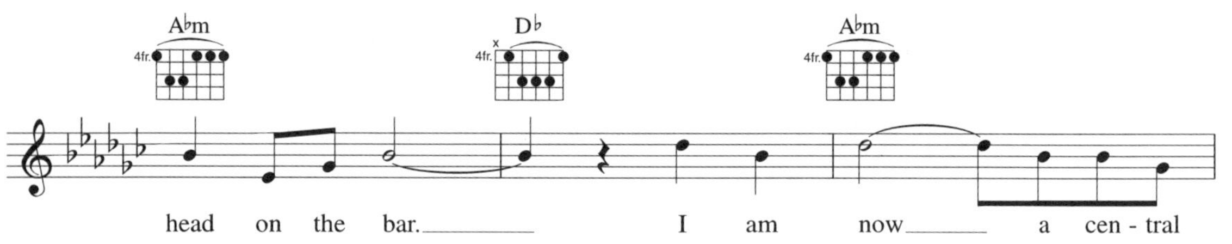

A♭m
D♭
A♭m
head on the bar. I am now a cen - tral

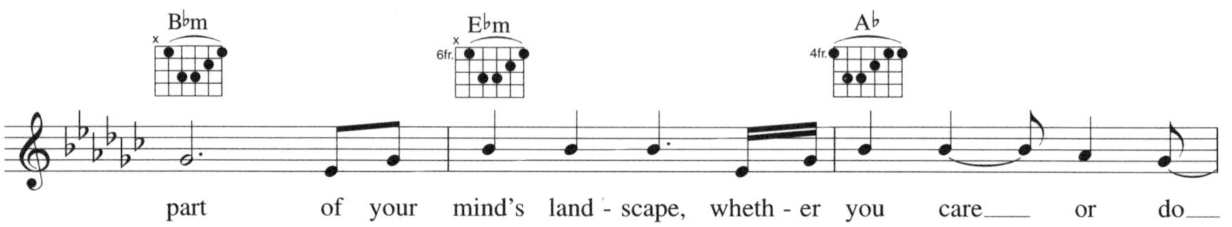

B♭m
E♭m
A♭
part of your mind's land - scape, wheth - er you care or do

D♭
not. Yeah, I've made up your mind.

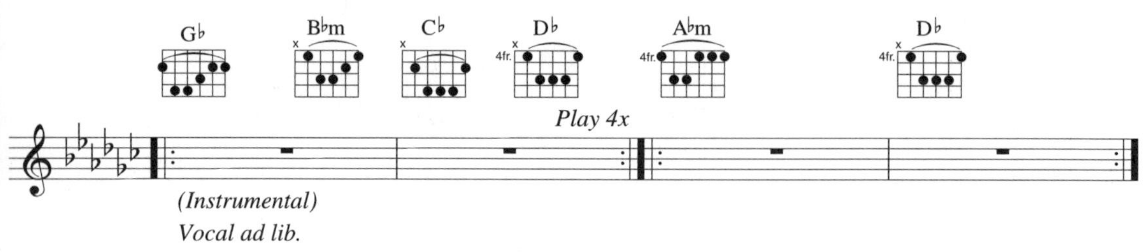

G♭
B♭m
C♭
D♭
A♭m
D♭
Play 4x
(Instrumental)
Vocal ad lib.

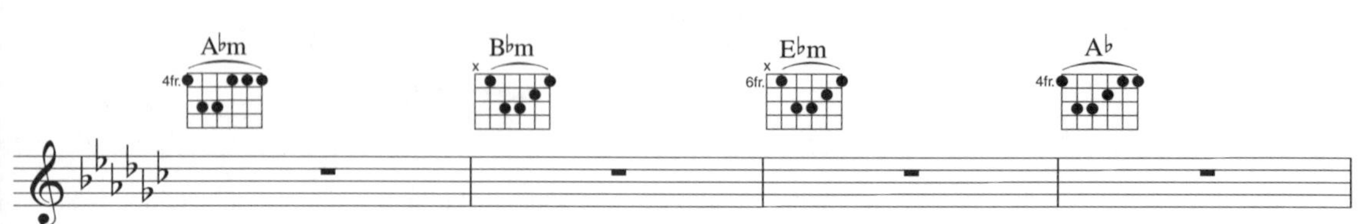

A♭m
B♭m
E♭m
A♭

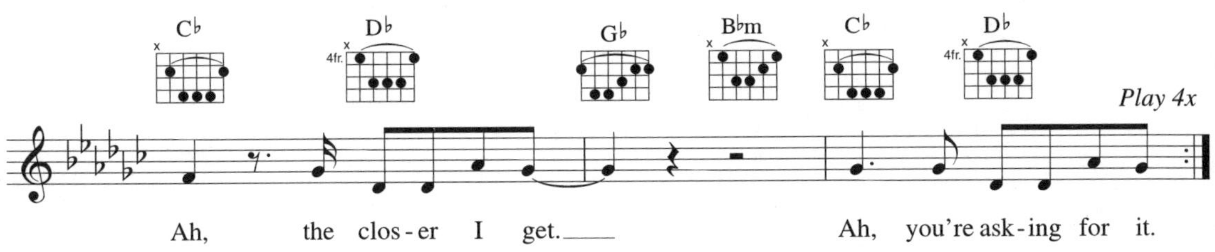

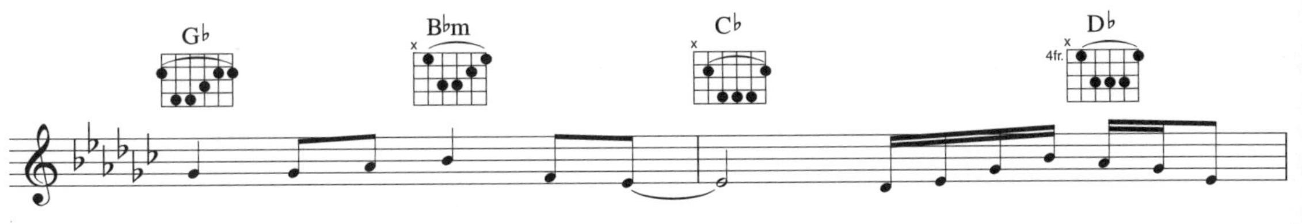

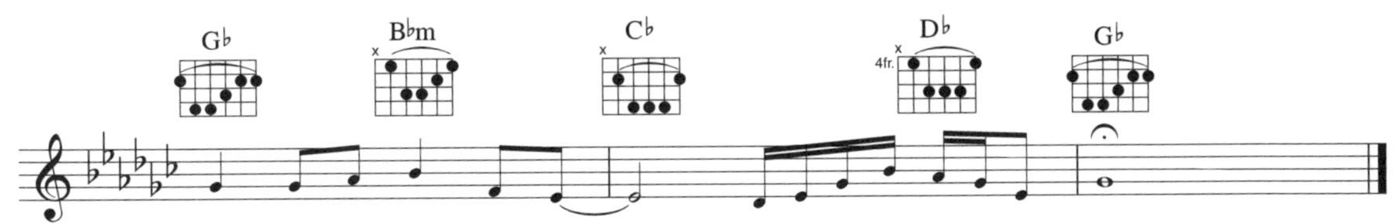

Verse 2:
Beware, I bear more grudges
Than lonely high court judges
When you sleep, I will creep into your thoughts
Like a bad debt that you can't pay
Take the easy way and give in
Yeah, and let me in.

National Express

Words & Music by Neil Hannon

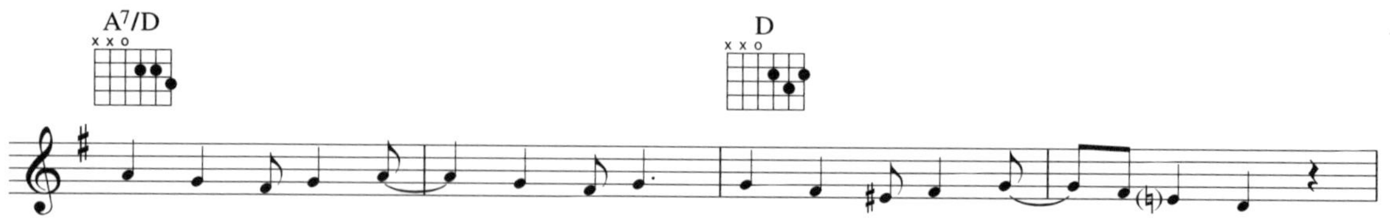

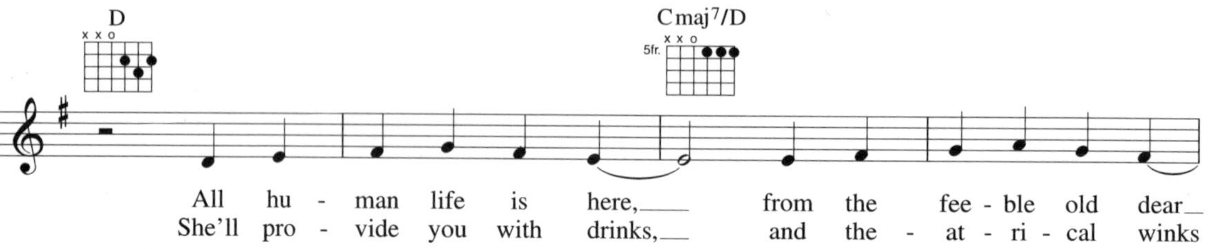

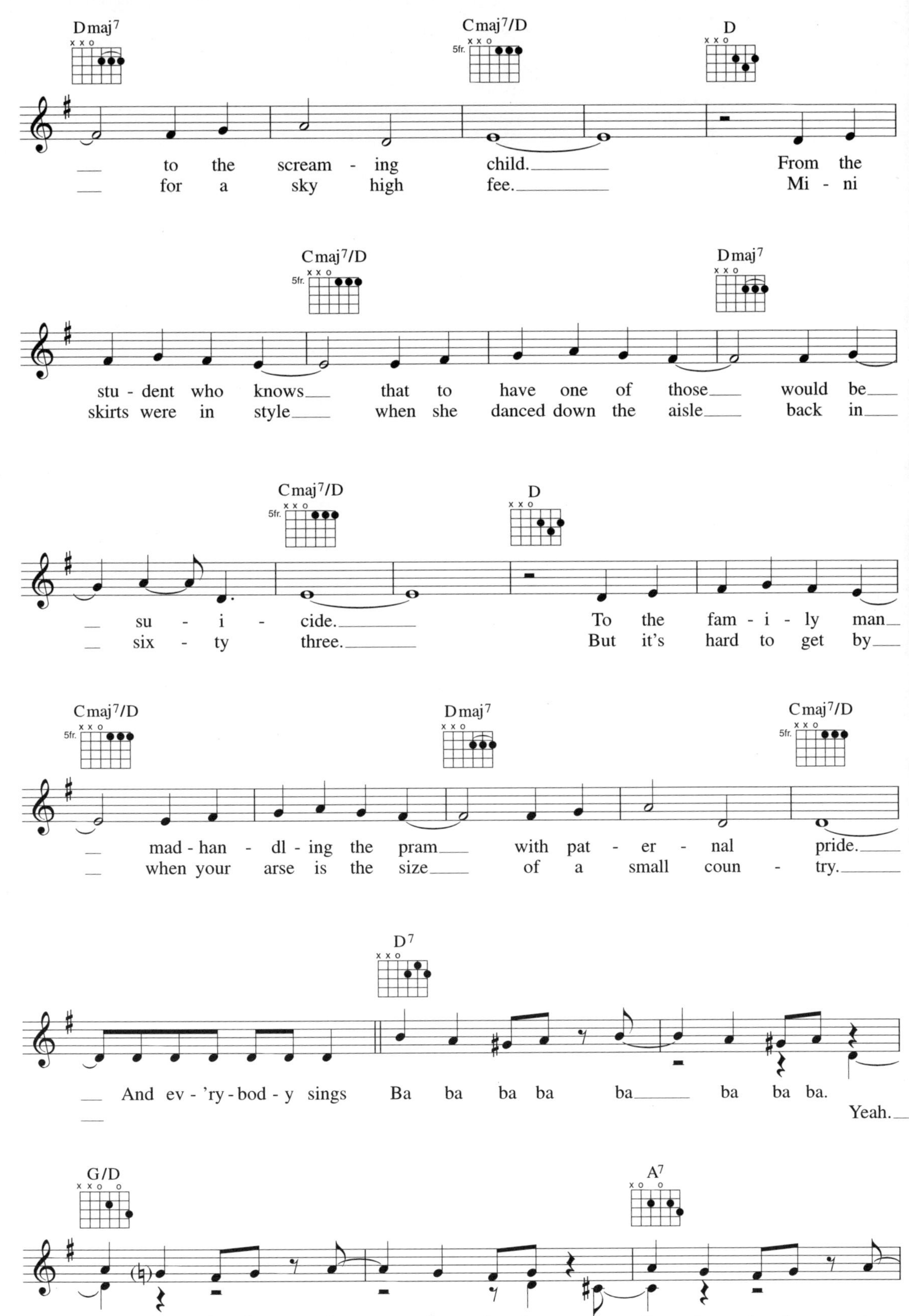
Dmaj7
Cmaj7/D
D
5fr.
to the scream - ing child.
for a sky high fee.
From the
Mi - ni
Cmaj7/D
Dmaj7
stu - dent who knows that to have one of those would be
skirts were in style when she danced down the aisle back in
Cmaj7/D
D
su - i - cide.
six - ty three.
To the fam - i - ly man
But it's hard to get by
Cmaj7/D
Dmaj7
Cmaj7/D
mad - han - dl - ing the pram with pat - er - nal pride.
when your arse is the size of a small coun - try.
D7
And ev - 'ry - bod - y sings Ba ba ba ba ba ba ba ba.
Yeah.
G/D
A7
Ba ba ba ba ba ba ba ba. Ba ba ba ba ba
Uh - huh.

D
ba ba ba. Ba ba ba ba ba ba ba ba.
Al - right. We're -
G
Ba ba ba ba ba ba ba ba ba. Ba ba ba ba ba ba ba ba.
go - - - - - - ing where the
A7
1.
D
Ba ba ba ba ba ba ba ba. Ba ba ba ba ba ba ba ba.
air is free.
2.
Bm7
F♯m
ba ba ba Ba ba ba ba ba ba ba ba.
is free.
G
D/F♯
Em
F♯m
G
A
To - mor - row be - longs to me.
A
A aug
When you're sad and feel - ing blue with no-thing bet - ter to do,

F♯m/A
A7
don't just sit there feel-ing stressed take a trip on the Na-tional Ex - press.
D
C6/D
D6
C6/D
D
C6/D
On the Na-tional Ex - press.
D6
C6/D
let's go.
D
C6/D
(Instrumental)
D6
C6/D
D
C6/D
Repeat to fade
Na - tional Ex - press
Na - tional Ex - press.

Never Ever

Words & Music by Shaznay Lewis, Esmail Jazayeri & Sean Mather

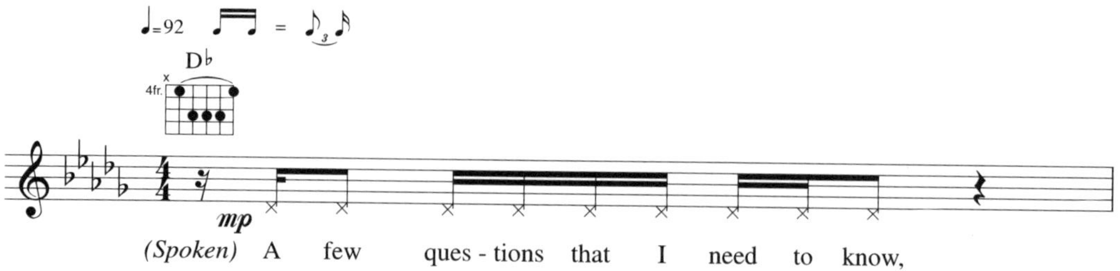

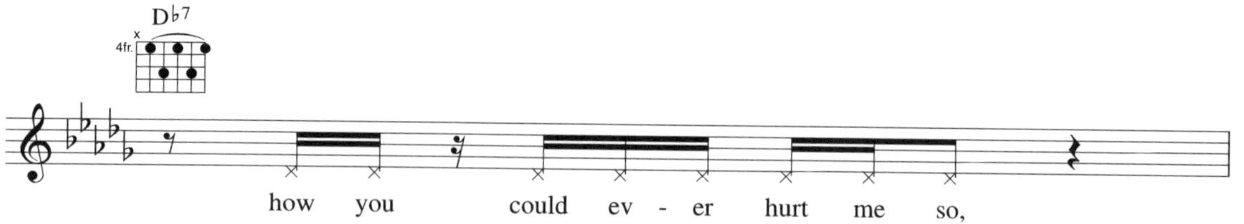

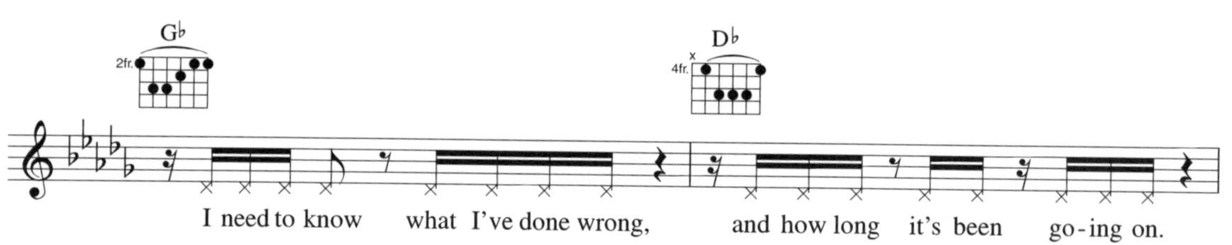

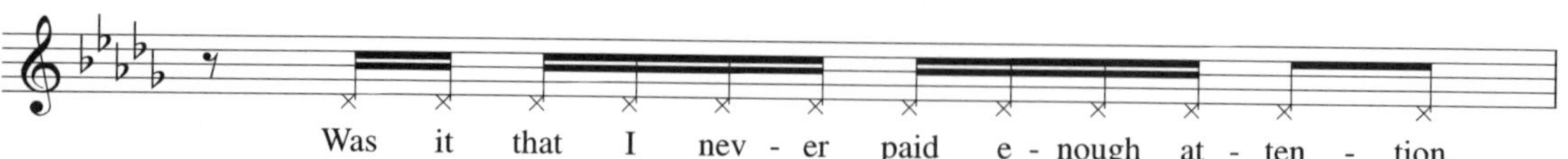

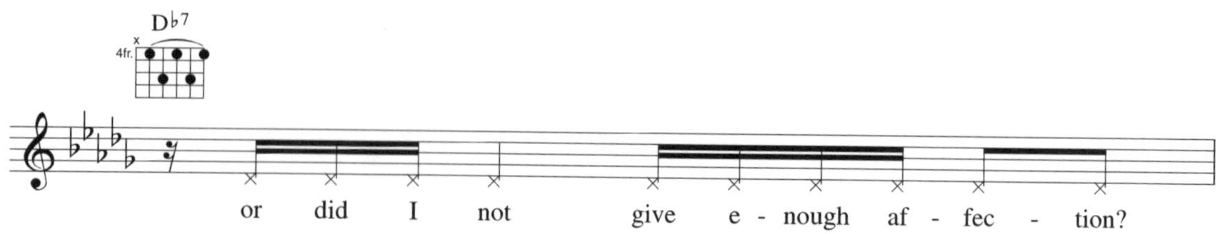

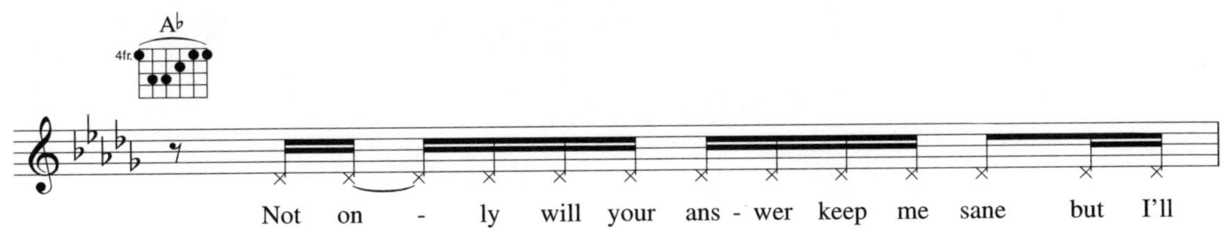
A♭
4fr.
Not on - ly will your ans - wer keep me sane but I'll

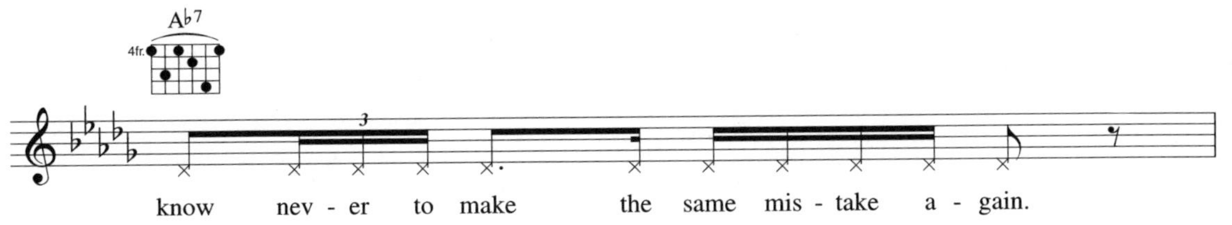
A♭7
4fr.
3
know nev - er to make the same mis - take a - gain.

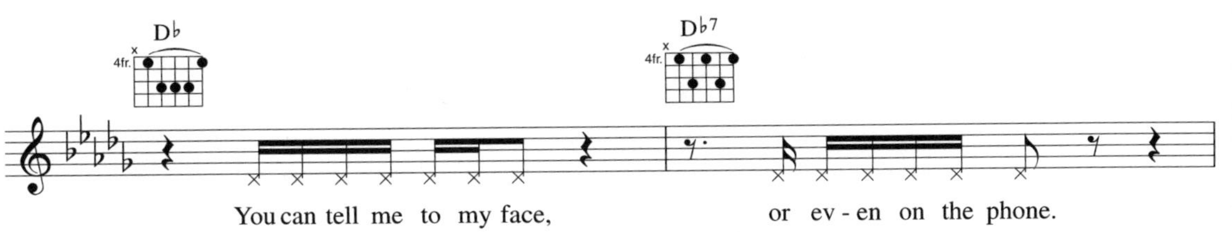
D♭
4fr.
D♭7
4fr.
You can tell me to my face, or ev - en on the phone.

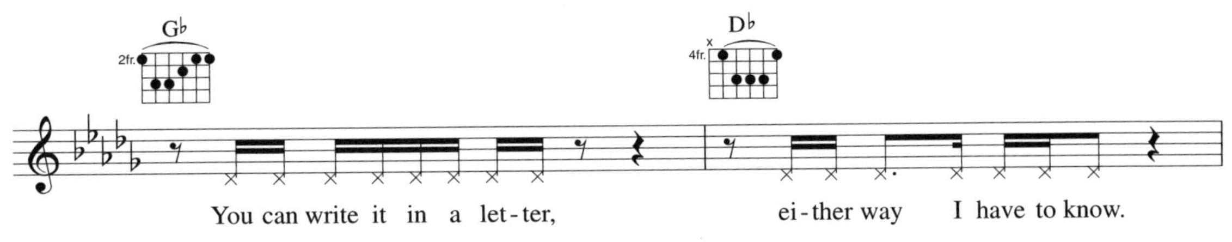
G♭
2fr.
D♭
4fr.
You can write it in a let - ter, ei - ther way I have to know.

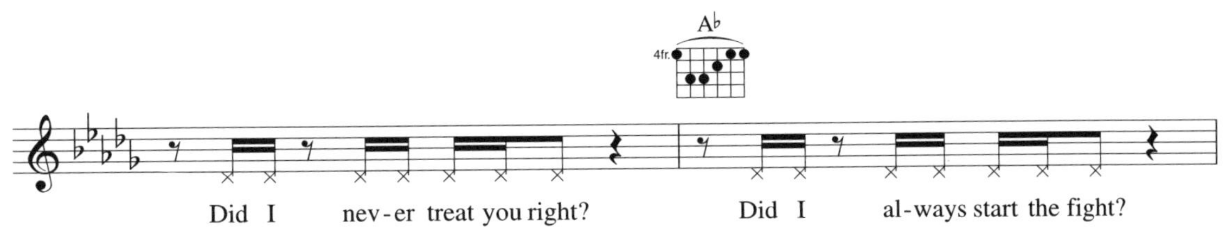
A♭
4fr.
Did I nev - er treat you right? Did I al - ways start the fight?

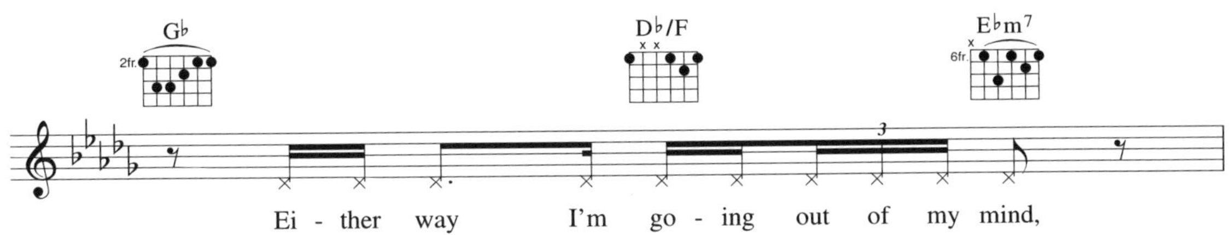
G♭
2fr.
D♭/F
E♭m7
6fr.
3
Ei - ther way I'm go - ing out of my mind,

D♭
all the ans - wers to my ques - tions, I have to find.
D♭
D♭7
mf
1. My head's spin - ning, boy I'm in a daze,
2. I'll keep search - ing, deep with - in my soul,
G♭
D♭
I feel i - so - lat - ed, don't want to com - mun - i - cate.
for all the ans - wers don't wan - na hurt no more
D♭7
I'll take a show - er, I will scour, I will run
I need peace got - ta feel at ease, need to be
A♭
A♭7
find peace of mind, the hap - py mind, I once owned yeah.
free from pain, go - ing in - sane my heart aches yeah.
D♭
Flex - in' vo - cab - u - la - ry runs right through me.
Some - times vo - cab - u - la - ry runs through my head.

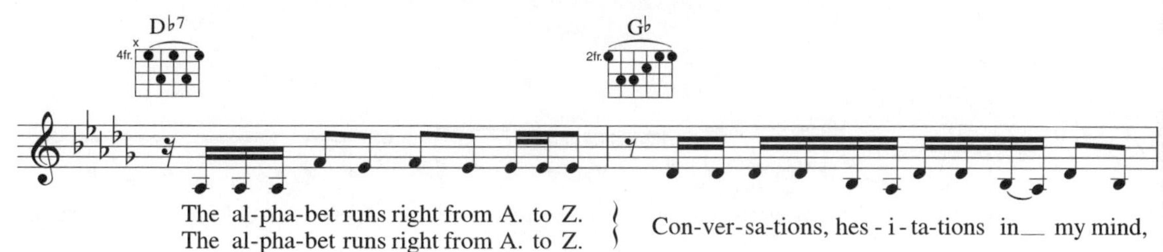
D♭7
4fr.
G♭
2fr.
The al-pha-bet runs right from A. to Z.
The al-pha-bet runs right from A. to Z.
Con-ver-sa-tions, hes - i - ta-tions in__ my mind,

D♭
4fr.
you got my con-science ask - ing ques - tions that I can't find.

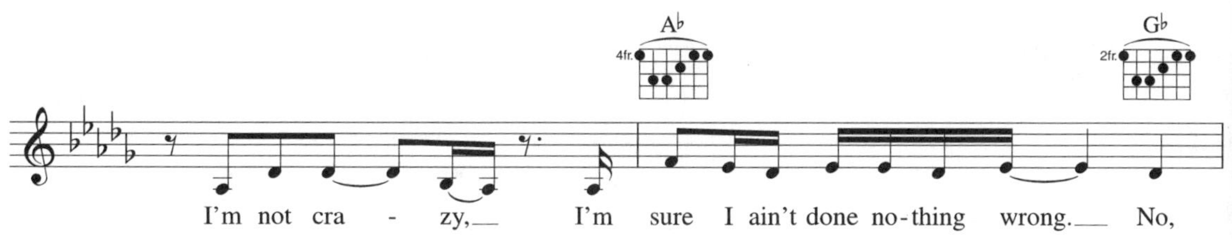
A♭
4fr.
G♭
2fr.
I'm not cra - zy,__ I'm sure I ain't done no-thing wrong.__ No,

D♭/F
E♭m7
6fr.
D♭
4fr.
I'm just wait - ing,__ 'cause I heard that this feel-ing won't last__ that long.______

D♭
4fr.
D♭7
4fr.
Nev-er ev-er have I ev-er felt so low,
when you gon-na take me out of this black hole?

G♭
2fr.
Nev - er ev - er have I ev - er felt so sad.

D♭
4fr.
The way I'm feel-ing, yeah you got me feel-ing real-ly bad. Nev-er ev-er have I had to find,

A♭
4fr.
G
3fr.
I've had to dig a - way to find my own peace of mind.

G♭
2fr.
D♭/F
E♭m7
6fr.
To Coda
I've nev - er ev - er had my con - science to fight,

D♭
4fr.
the way I'm feel - ing yeah it just don't feel right.

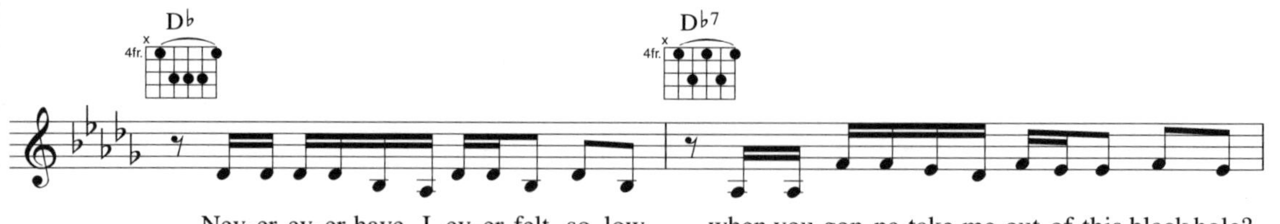
D♭
4fr.
D♭7
4fr.
Nev-er ev-er have I ev-er felt so low, when you gon-na take me out of this black hole?

G♭
2fr.
Nev - er ev - er have I ev - er felt so sad.

D♭
4fr.
The way I'm feel - ing, yeah you got me feel - ing real - ly bad.

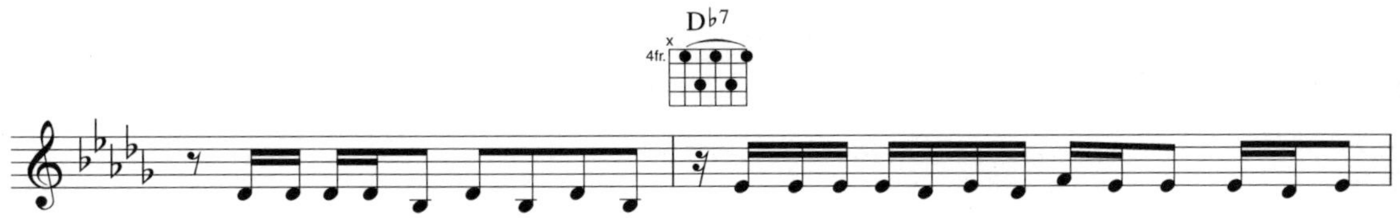
D♭7
4fr.
Nev-er ev-er have I had to find, I've had to dig a-way to find my own peace of mind.

A♭
4fr.
I've nev - er ev - er had my con - science to fight,

A♭7
4fr.
D.𝄋 al Coda ⊕
the way I'm feel - ing yeah it just don't feel right.

⊕ Coda
D♭
4fr.
the way I'm feel - ing yeah it just don't feel (right.)
You can tell

N.C.
Repeat ad lib to fade
me to___ my face,_____ you can tell___ me on___ the phone._____

No Matter What

Music by Andrew Lloyd Webber
Words by Jim Steinman

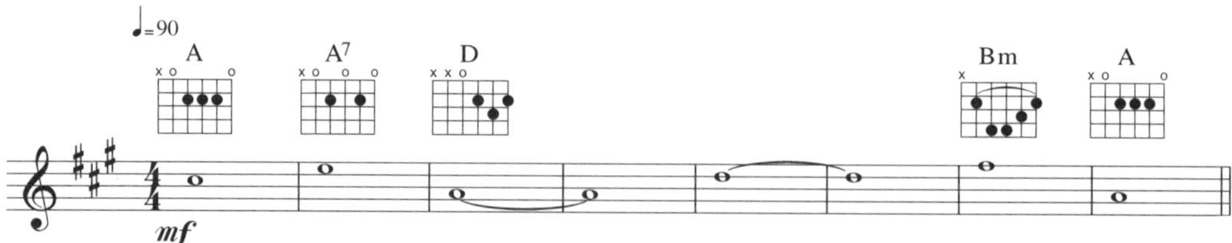

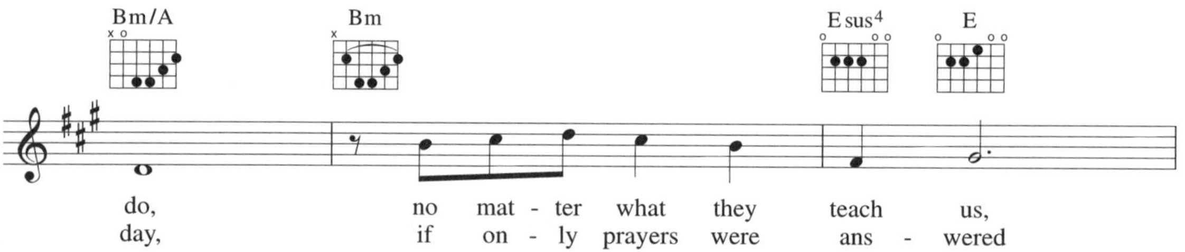

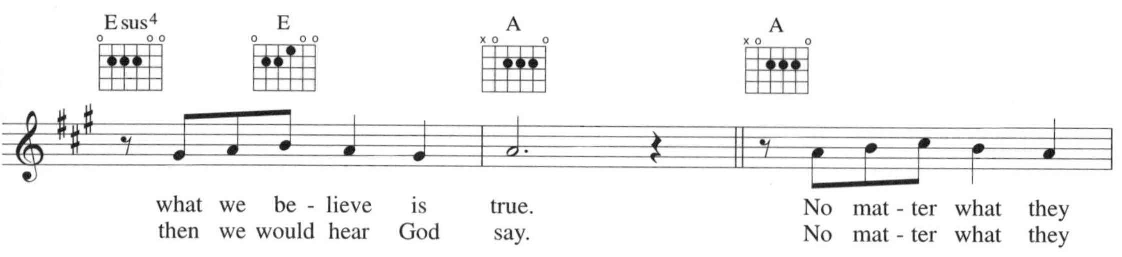

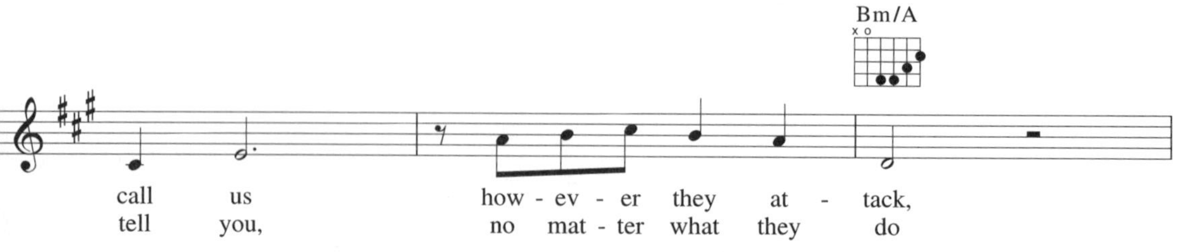

Bm
Esus4
E
Esus4
E
no mat - ter where they take us, we'll find our own way back.
no mat - ter what they teach you, what you be - lieve is true.
A
A
A7
I can't de - ny what I be - lieve,
And I will keep you safe and strong
D
Bm
I can't be what I'm not. I know our love's for -
and shelt - ered from the storm. No mat - ter where it's
1.
Esus4
E
Esus4
E
A
ev - er, I know no mat - ter what.
bar - ren, a dream is be - ing born.
2.
A
C
Dm
(Instrumental)
G
C

C
Dm
No mat-ter who they fol - low, no mat-ter where they lead,
Gsus4
G
Gsus4
G
C
no mat-ter how they judge us, I'll be ev-ery-one you need. No
C
C7
F
mat-ter if the sun don't shine, or if the skies are blue.
Dm
Gsus4
G
Gsus4
G
C
No mat-ter what the end-ing my life be-gan with you. I
C
C7
F
C/E
rall.
can't de-ny what I be-lieve, I can't be what I'm not.
Dm
G
I know this love's for ev-er, that's all the mat-ters now no mat-ter
C
Am7
C
Am7
a tempo
Repeat to fade
what. No, no mat - ter what. No, no mat -

Nothing Else Matters

Words & Music by James Hetfield & Lars Ulrich

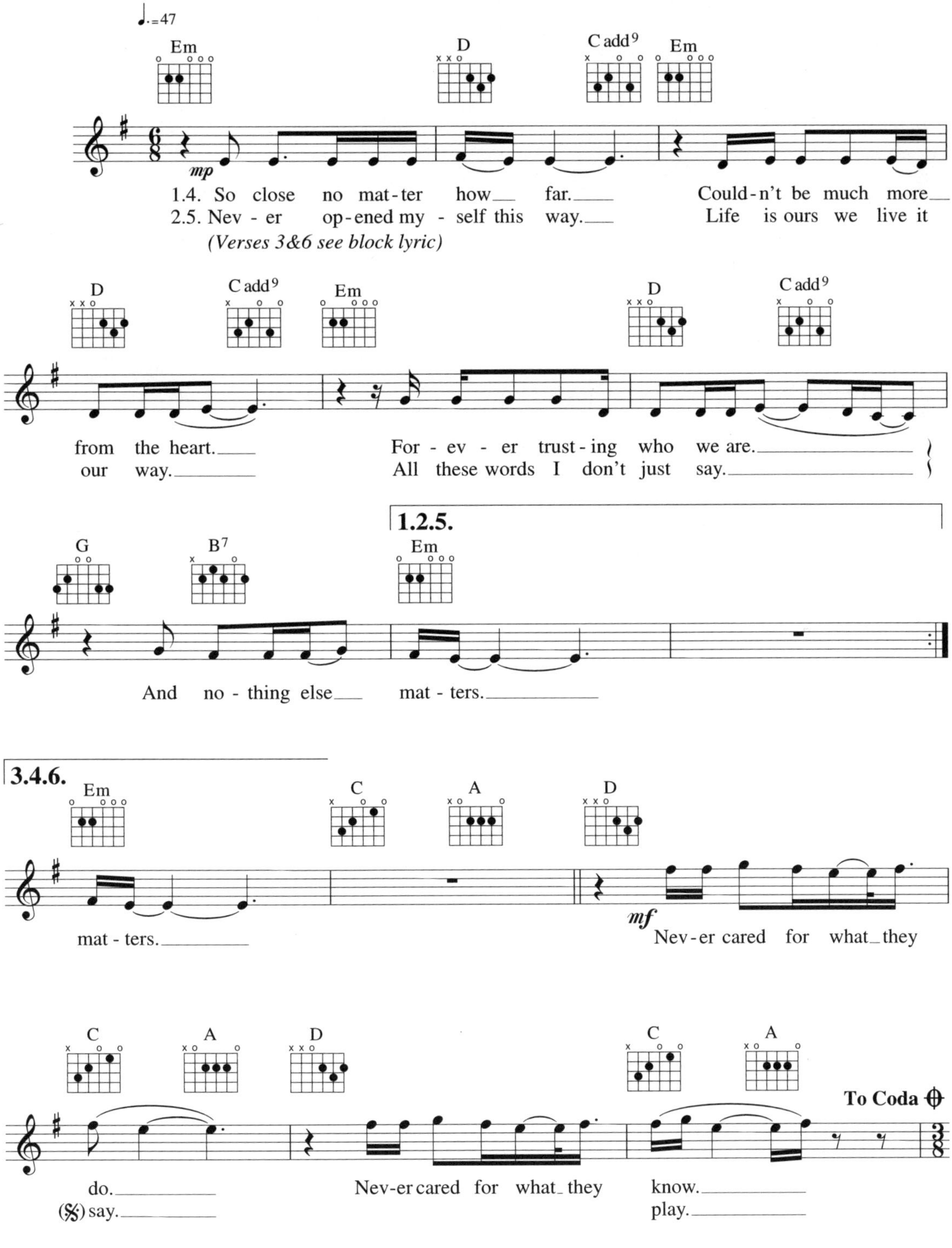

♩. = 47
Em
D
C add9
Em
mp
1.4. So close no mat-ter how far. Could-n't be much more
2.5. Nev - er op-ened my - self this way. Life is ours we live it
(Verses 3&6 see block lyric)
D
C add9
Em
D
C add9
from the heart. For - ev - er trust - ing who we are.
our way. All these words I don't just say.
1.2.5.
G
B7
Em
And no - thing else mat - ters.
3.4.6.
Em
C
A
D
mf
mat - ters. Nev-er cared for what they
C
A
D
C
A
To Coda
do. Nev-er cared for what they know.
(𝄋) say. play.

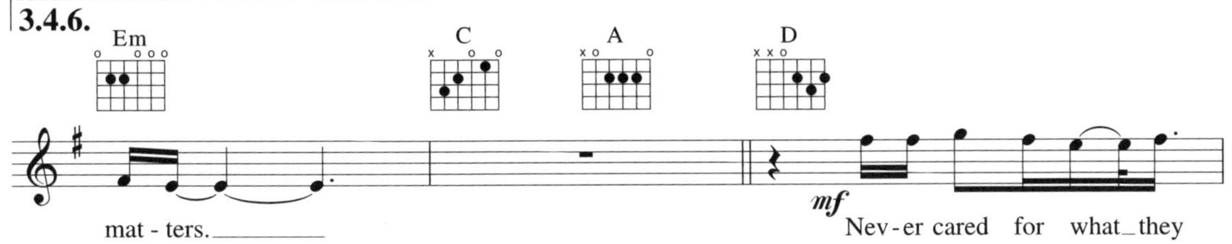

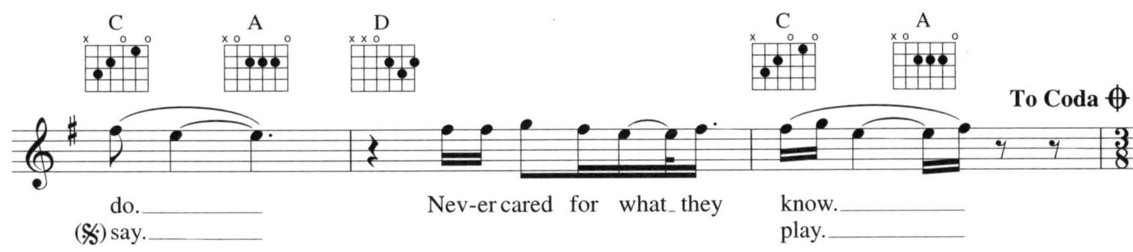

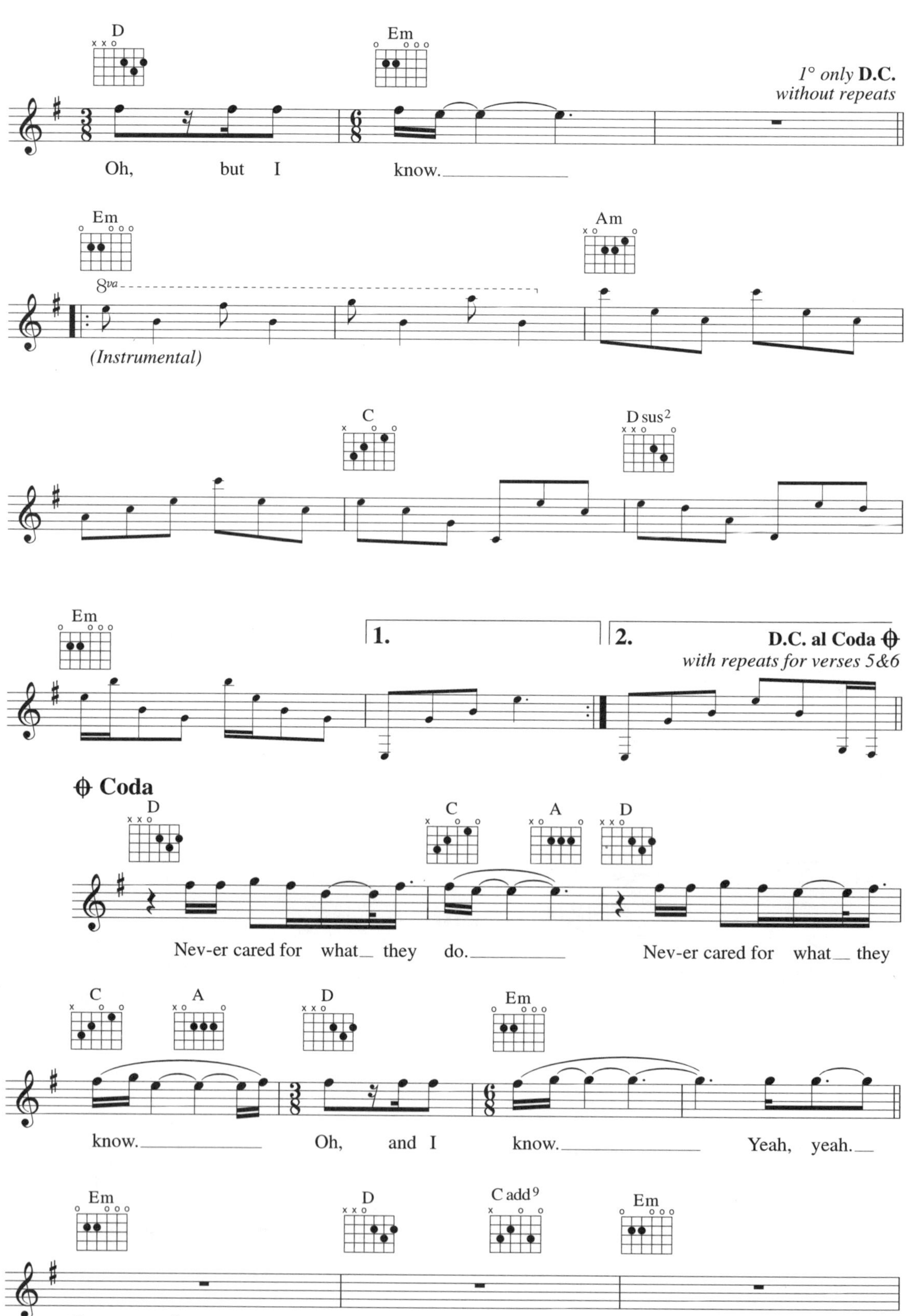
D
Em
1° only D.C.
without repeats
Oh, but I know.
Em
Am
8va
(Instrumental)
C
D sus2
Em
1.
2.
D.C. al Coda
with repeats for verses 5&6
Coda
D
C
A
D
Nev-er cared for what they do.
Nev-er cared for what they
C
A
D
Em
know.
Oh, and I know.
Yeah, yeah.
Em
D
C add9
Em
(Instrumental)

Verse 3&6:
Trust I seek and find in you
Ev'ry day for us something new
Open mind for a diff'rent view
And nothing else matters.

Novocaine For The Soul

Words & Music by Mark Everett & Mark Goldenberg

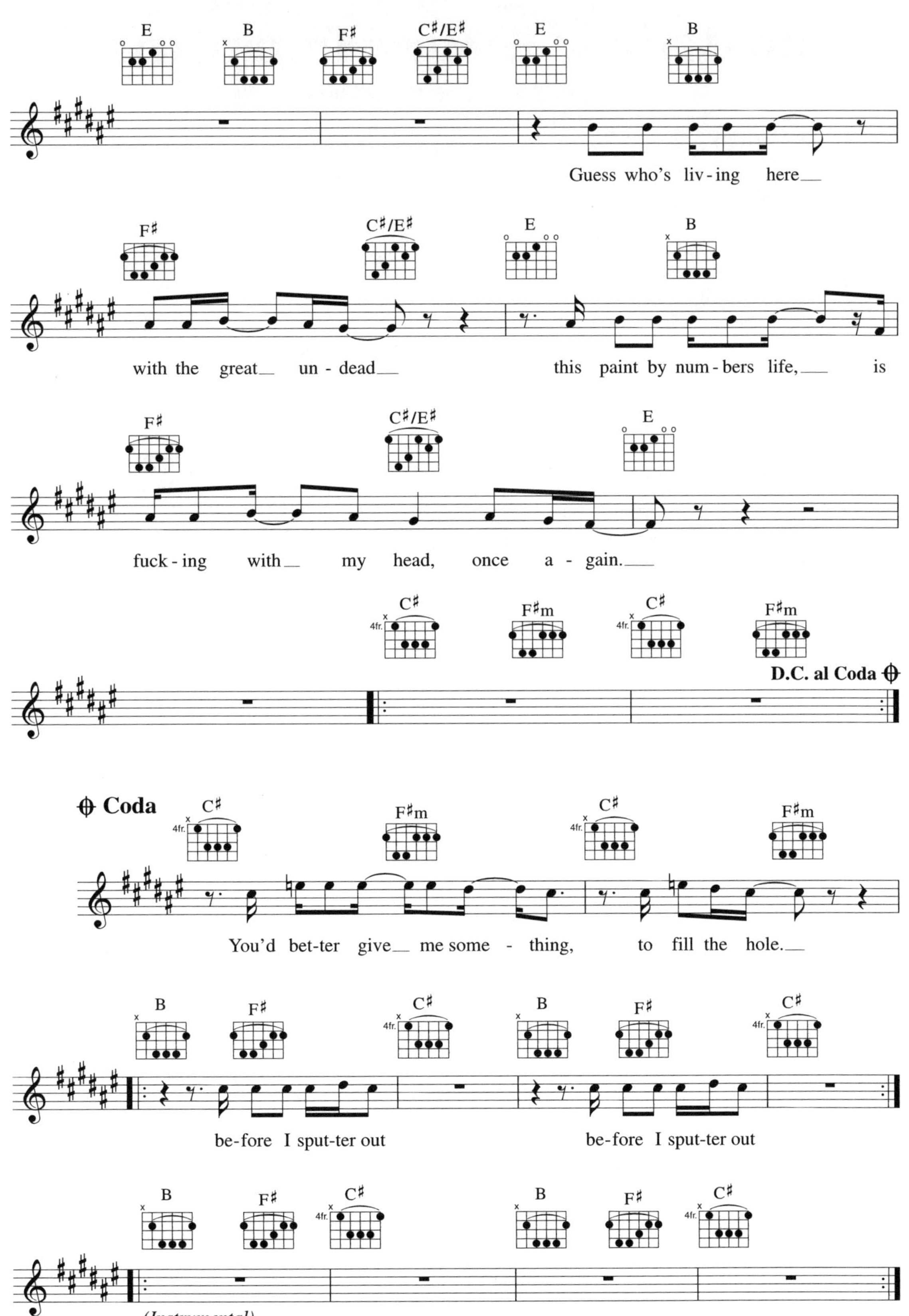
E B F♯ C♯/E♯ E B
Guess who's liv-ing here
F♯ C♯/E♯ E B
with the great un - dead this paint by num-bers life, is
F♯ C♯/E♯ E
fuck-ing with my head, once a - gain.
C♯ F♯m C♯ F♯m
D.C. al Coda
Coda
C♯ F♯m C♯ F♯m
You'd bet-ter give me some - thing, to fill the hole.
B F♯ C♯ B F♯ C♯
be-fore I sput-ter out be-fore I sput-ter out
B F♯ C♯ B F♯ C♯
(Instrumental)
4fr.

Nothing Ever Happens

Words & Music by Justin Currie

F
2.3.
F
lone - ly to - mor - row.
And no - thing
B♭
F
B♭
ev - er hap - pens,
No - thing hap - pens at all.
Dm
B♭
The need - le re - turns to the start of the song and we
C
B♭
To Coda
F
all sing a - long like be - fore.
And we'll all be
B♭
F
lone - ly to - night, and lone - ly to - mor - row.
G
Dm7
F
G
F
G
F
D.C. al Coda
4. And

2. Gentlemen time please, you know we can't serve anymore
Now the traffic lights change to stop when there's nothing to go
And by five o'clock everything's dead
And every third car is a cab
And ignorant people sleep in their beds
Like the doped white mice in the college lab.

3. Telephone exchanges click while there's nobody there
The Martians could land in the car park and no one would care
Closed-circuit cameras in department stores
Shoot the same movie every day
And the stars of these films neither die nor get killed
Just survive constant action replay.

4. And bill hoardings advertise products that nobody needs
While angry of Manchester writes to complaint about
All the repeats on T.V.
And computer terminals report some gains
On the values of copper and tin
While American businessmen snap up Van Goghs
For the price of a hospital wing.

One

Words & Music by U2

Fmaj7
G
Am
Did I dis - ap - point -
D
Fmaj7
G
— you — or leave a bad — taste in your mouth?
Am
D
Fmaj7
You act like you ne- ver had — love, and you — want me — to go — with- out.
G
Gsus4
G
C
Am
— Well — it's too late — to - night, —
Fmaj7
C
3
to drag the past out in to the light. We're one, but we're
Am
Fmaj7
not the same, — we got to car - ry — each oth - er, car -
C
Am
D
Fmaj7
ry each oth - er. One. ———

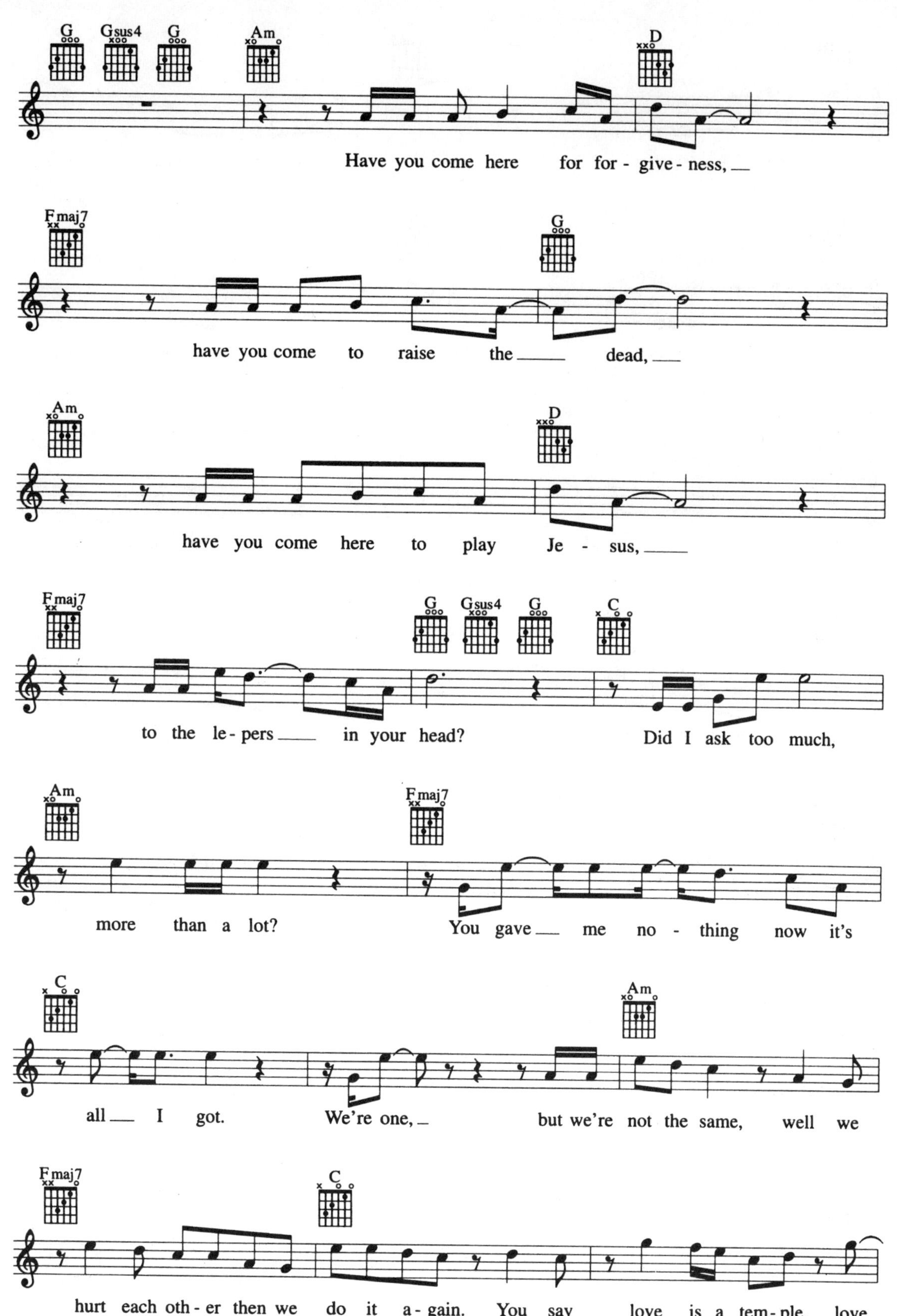
G Gsus4 G Am D
Have you come here for for - give - ness, —
Fmaj7 G
have you come to raise the — dead, —
Am D
have you come here to play Je - sus, —
Fmaj7 G Gsus4 G C
to the le - pers — in your head? Did I ask too much,
Am Fmaj7
more than a lot? You gave — me no - thing now it's
C Am
all — I got. We're one, — but we're not the same, well we
Fmaj7 C
hurt each oth - er then we do it a - gain. You say love is a tem - ple, love -

Am
C
the high - er law,
love is a tem - ple, love
Am
C
the high - er law.
You ask me to en - ter, but
G
then you make me crawl,
and I can't be hold - ing on
Fmaj7
to what you got,
when all you got is hurt.
C
Am
Fmaj7
One love,
one blood,
one life you got to
C
Am
do what you should.
One life
with each oth - er,
Fmaj7
C
sis - ters,
bro - thers.
One life, but we're

Am
Fmaj7
not the same, we got to car - ry each oth - er, car -
C
Am
Fmaj7
ry each oth - er. One, one.
C
Am
Fmaj7
8va
(Instrumental)
C
Am
(8va)
Ooh, oh,
Fmaj7
C
ba - by, ba - by, ba - by, ha,
Am
Fmaj7
C
ha, ha,
Am
Fmaj7
C
ah.

Perfect 10

Words & Music by Paul Heaton & Dave Rotheray

E7
with a big fat eight_ you wan-na see the smile_ on my face._
A7
And ev-en at my door,_ with a poor, poor four___
E7
there ain't no man can re-place._ 'Cause we love our love_
A Bm7 D
_ in dif-fer-ent siz - es, I love her bo - dy e-spe-cially the lies._
A
___ Time takes its toll,___ but not on the eyes._
Bm7 E7 1. A
___ Prom-ise me this,___ take me to - night.______

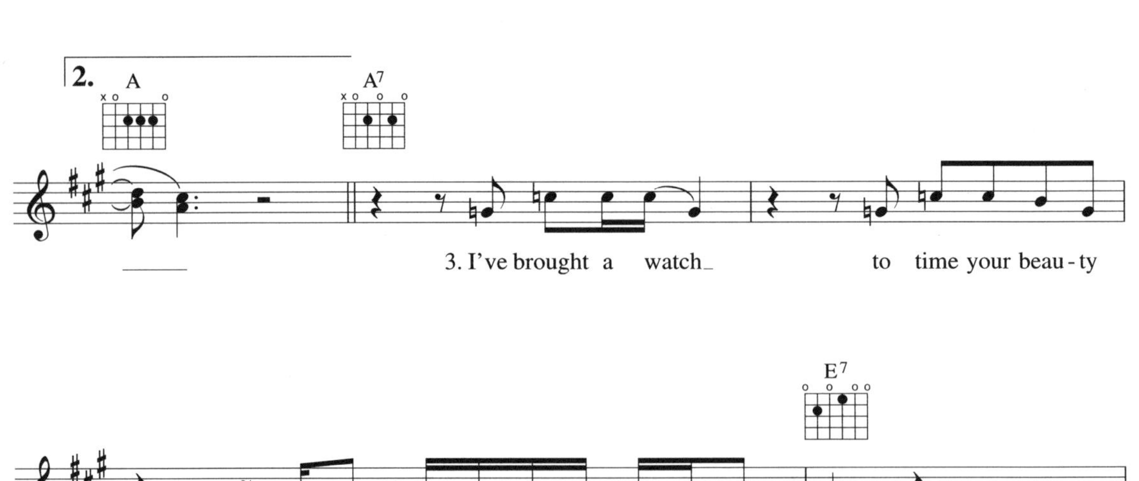
2.
A
A7
3. I've brought a watch to time your beau - ty

E7
and I've had to fit a sec - ond hand.

A7
I've bought a cal - en - dar and ev - 'ry month

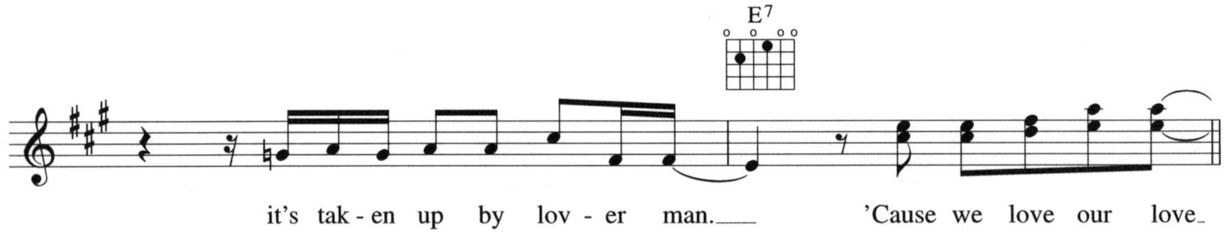
E7
it's tak - en up by lov - er man. 'Cause we love our love

A
Bm7
D
in dif - fer - ent siz - es, I love her bo - dy e - spe - cially the lies.

A
Bm7
Time takes its toll but not on the eyes. Pro - mise me this

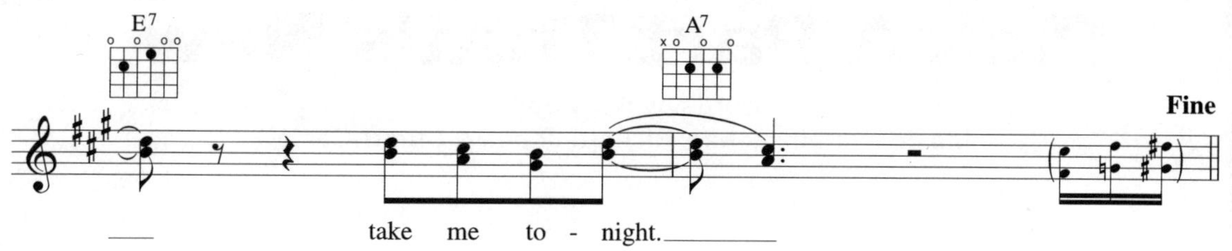

Verse 2:
If he's extra large
Well I'm in charge
I can work this thing on top
And if he's XXL
Well what the hell
Every penny don't fit the slot
The anorexic chicks
The model six
They don't hold no weight with me
Well eight or nine
Well that's just fine
But I like to hold something I can see.

'Cause we love our love *etc.*

Pick A Part That's New

Words by Kelly Jones
Music by Kelly Jones, Richard Jones & Stuart Cable

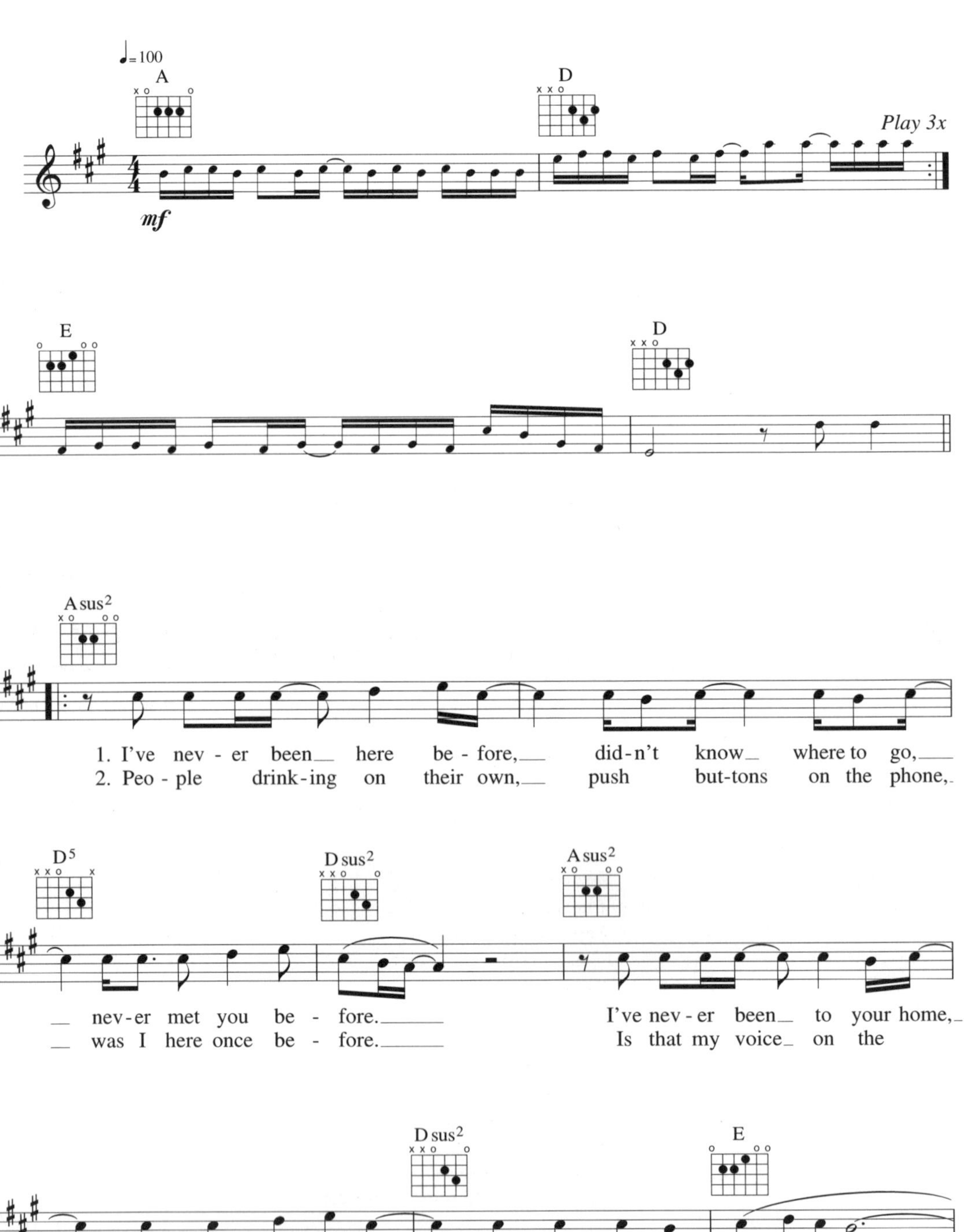

D5
walk-ing feels fa - mi - liar.
con - fu - sion's fa - mi - liar.

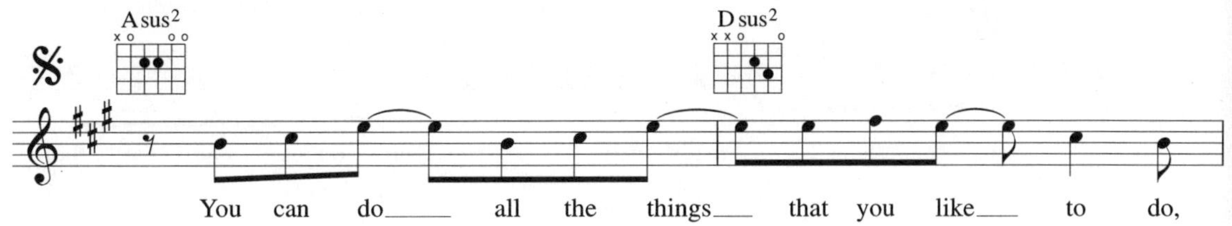
Asus2
Dsus2
You can do all the things that you like to do,

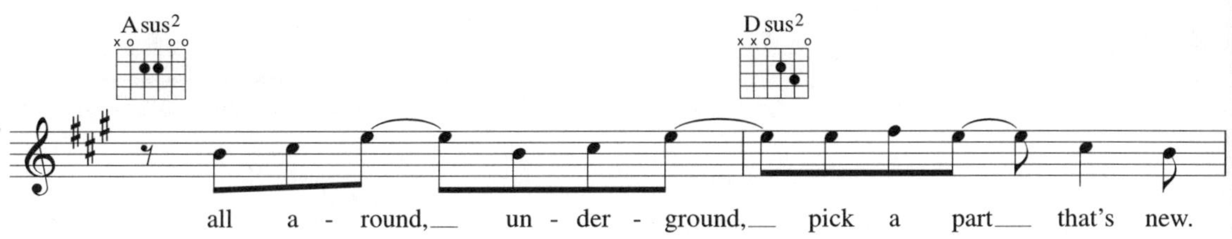
Asus2
Dsus2
all a - round, un - der - ground, pick a part that's new.

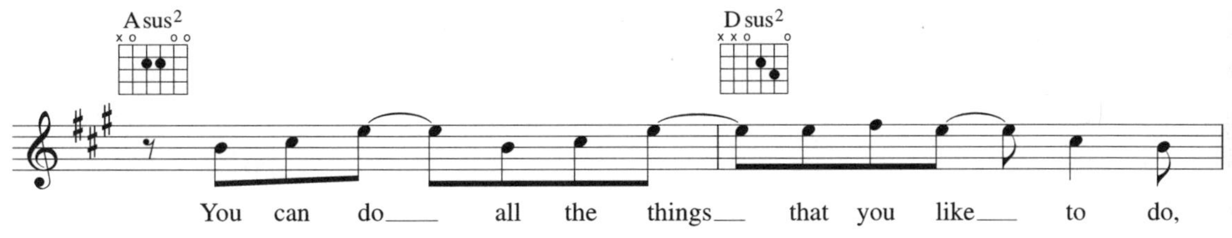
Asus2
Dsus2
You can do all the things that you like to do,

Asus2
Dsus2
E
D5
To Coda
all a - round, up-side down, pick a part that's new.

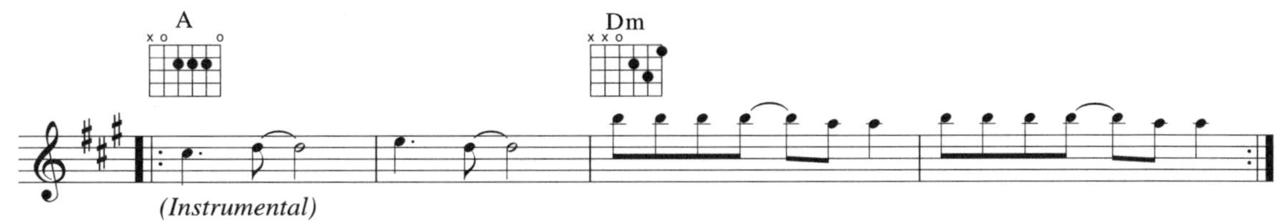
A
Dm
(Instrumental)

E
D5
D.𝄋 al Coda ⊕
⊕ Coda
Dsus2
Asus2
anything that's new. You can do all the things
that you like to do, all around, underground,
pick a part that's new. You can do all the things that you like to do,
E
all around, upside down pick a part that's new.
So what's new to you? What's new to you?
A5
What's new to you?

Road Rage

Words & Music by Cerys Matthews, Mark Roberts,
Aled Richards, Paul Jones & Owen Powell

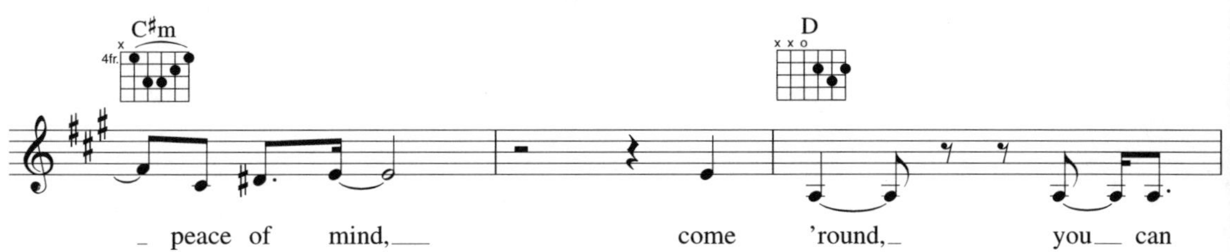

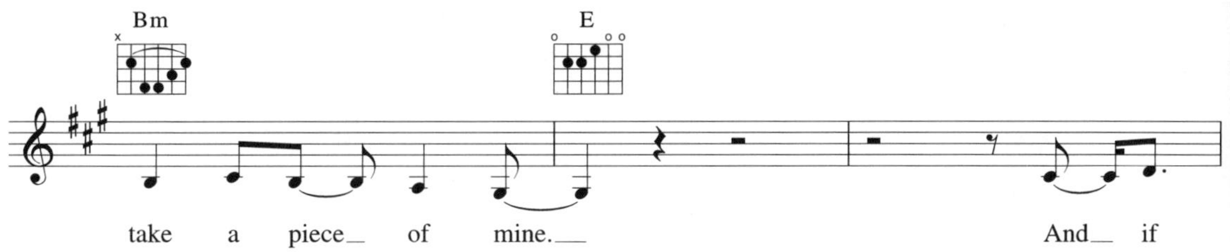

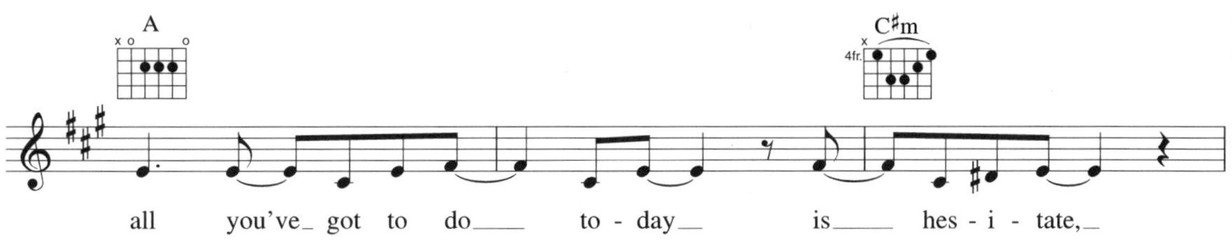

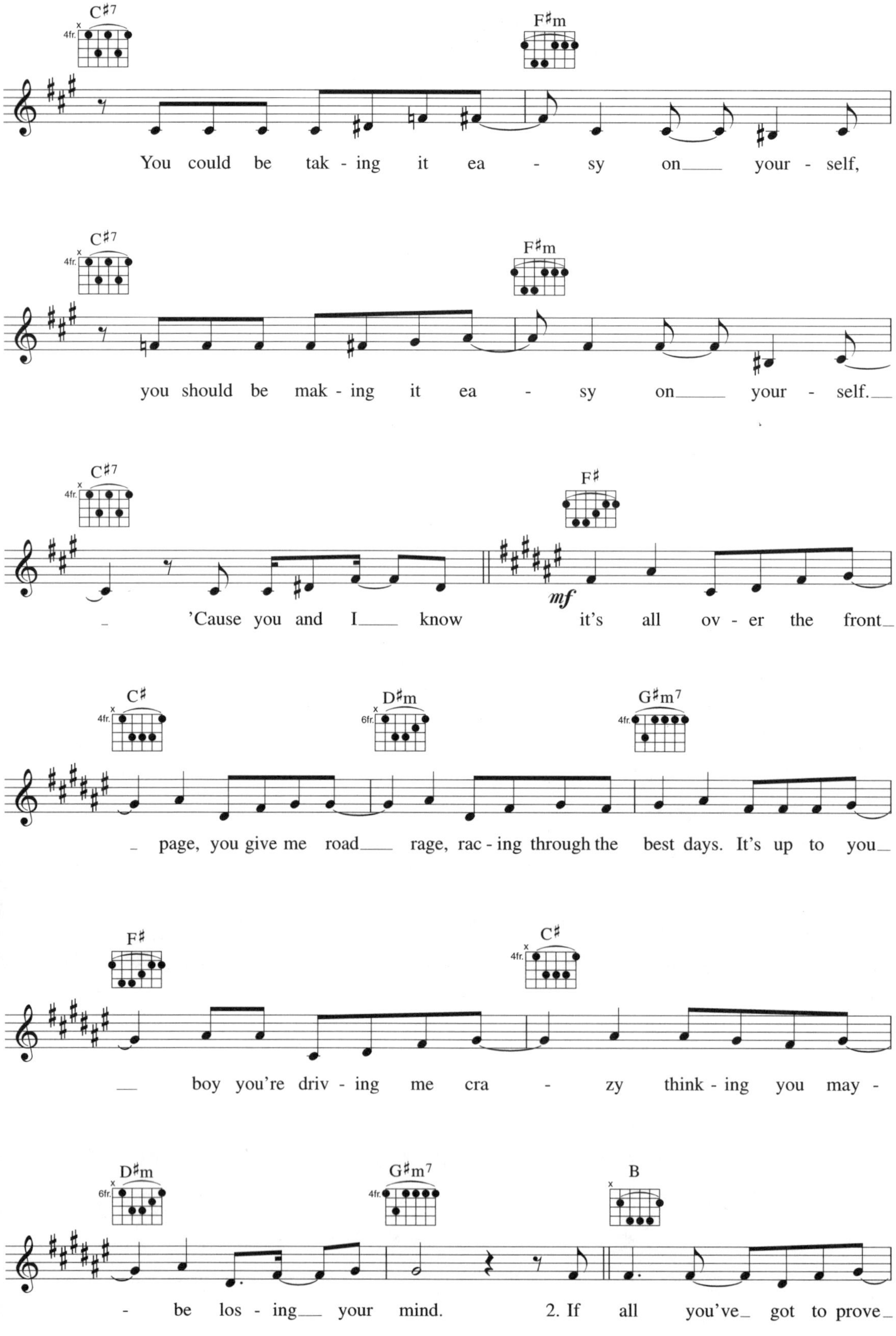

C♯7 F♯m

You could be tak - ing it ea - sy on___ your - self,

C♯7 F♯m

you should be mak - ing it ea - sy on___ your - self.__

C♯7 F♯

mf

_ 'Cause you and I___ know it's all ov - er the front_

C♯ D♯m G♯m7

_ page, you give me road___ rage, rac - ing through the best days. It's up to you_

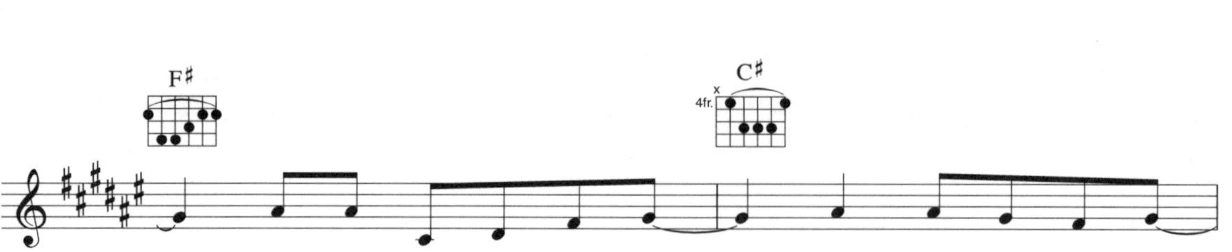

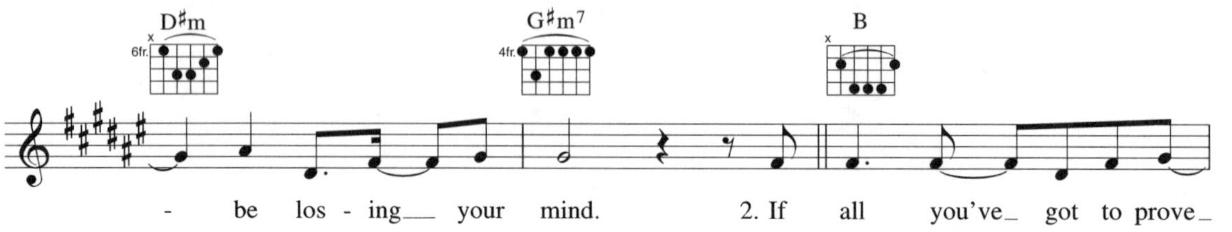

D♯m
6fr.
to - day is your in - no - cence, calm

E
C♯m
4fr.
F♯
down, you're as guil - ty as can be.

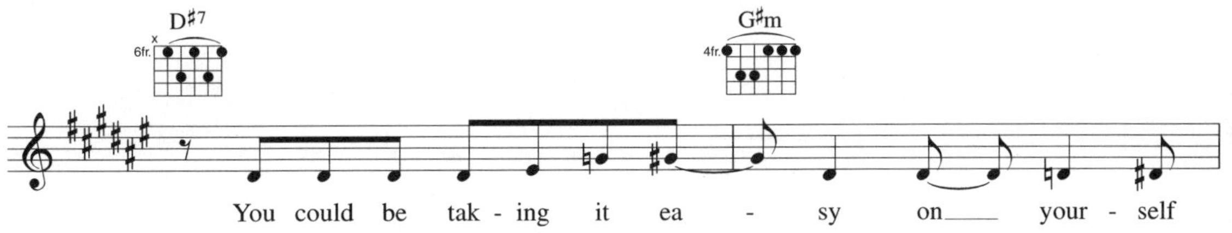
D♯7
6fr.
G♯m
4fr.
You could be tak - ing it ea - sy on your - self

D♯7
6fr.
G♯m
4fr.
you should be mak - ing it ea - sy on your - self.

D♯7
6fr.
A♭
4fr.
'Cause you and I know it's all ov - er the front

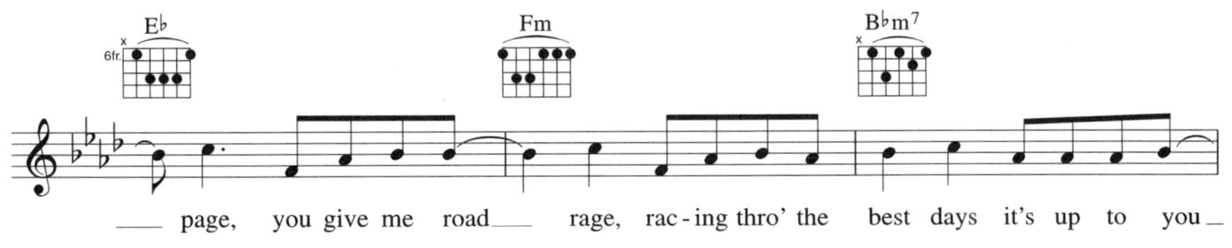
E♭
6fr.
Fm
B♭m7
page, you give me road rage, rac - ing thro' the best days it's up to you

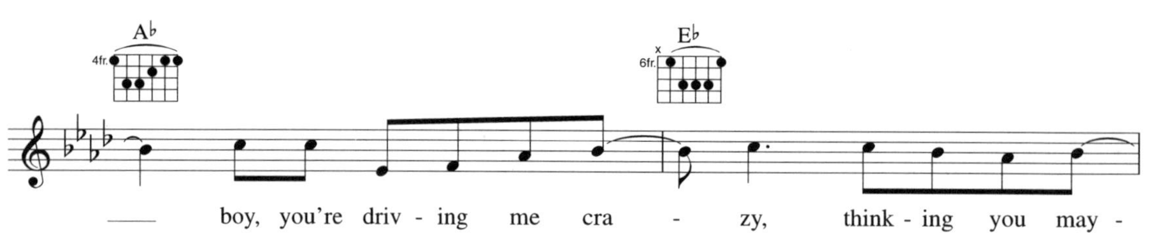
A♭
4fr.
E♭
6fr.
boy, you're driv - ing me cra - zy, think - ing you may -

Fm
B♭m7
E♭
6fr.
- be los - ing your mind. You're los - ing your mind.

A♭
4fr.
B♭m7
E♭
6fr.
You, you've been rac-ing thro' the best days.

A♭
4fr.
D♭
4fr.
Space days, road rage, fast lane. 3. And if all you've got to do

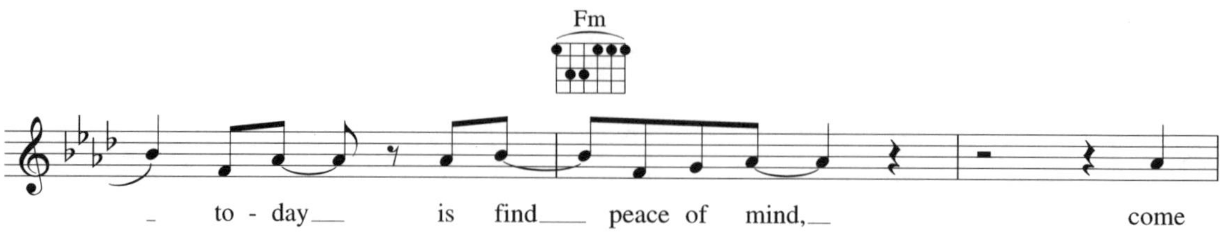
Fm
to - day is find peace of mind, come

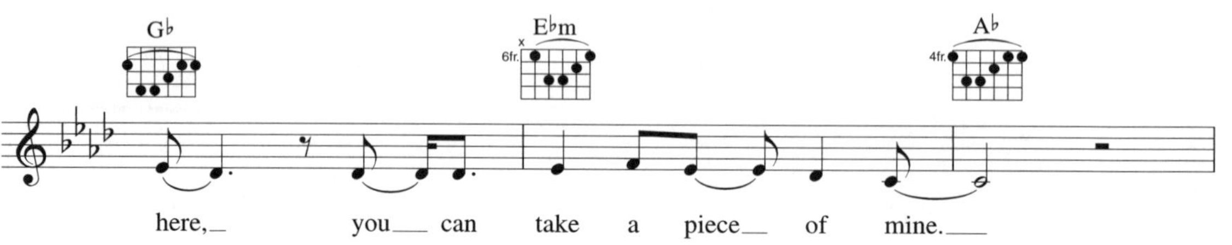
G♭
E♭m
6fr.
A♭
4fr.
here, you can take a piece of mine.

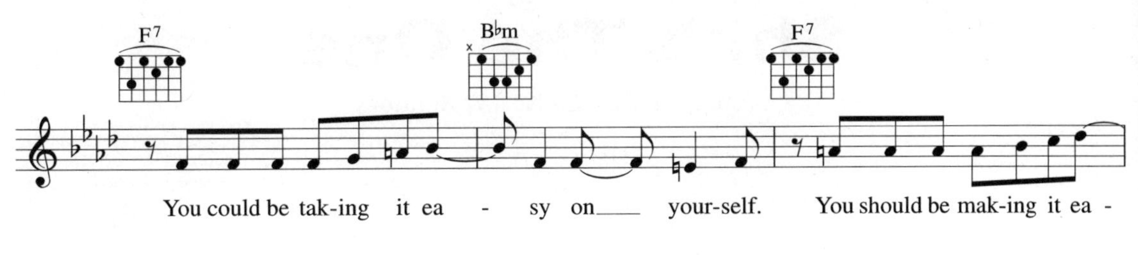
F7
B♭m
F7
You could be tak-ing it ea - sy on___ your-self. You should be mak-ing it ea -

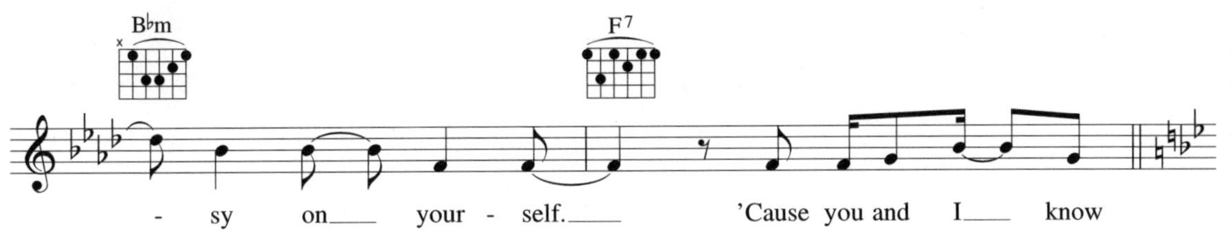
B♭m
F7
- sy on___ your - self.___ 'Cause you and I___ know

B♭
F
Gm
3fr.
it's all ov - er the front___ page, you give me road___ rage, rac-ing thro' the
we all live in the space___ age, com-ing down with road rage, rac-ing thro' the

Cm7
3fr.
B♭
F7
best days. It's up to you___ boy, you're driv-ing me cra - zy think-ing you may -

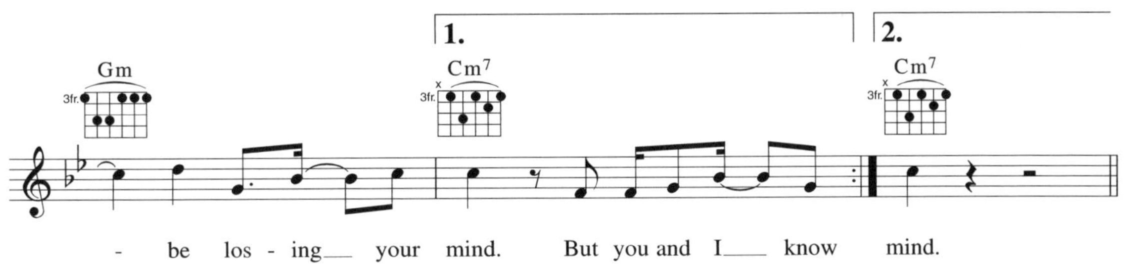
1.
2.
Gm
3fr.
Cm7
3fr.
Cm7
3fr.
- be los - ing___ your mind. But you and I___ know mind.

B♭
F
Gm
3fr.
Cm7
3fr.
Repeat to fade
It's not ov - er, it's not ov - er,___ it's not ov - er.

She's The One

Words & Music by Karl Wallinger

1. cont.
B♭
E♭maj7
2. B♭
B♭7
We were young
E♭
When you get to where you wan - na go, and you

B♭
know the things you wan - na know, you're smil - - - -

B♭7
E♭
- ing.
When you said what you wan - na say and you

Cm7
know the way you wan - na play, it. You'll be so high you'll be
2°say,
E♭/F
F
B♭
fly - ing. 2. Though the sea will be strong,
3. I was her she was me,

E♭maj7
B♭
I know we'll carry on.
we were one we were free
E♭maj7
Cm7
'Cause if there's some-bo-dy call-ing me on
And if there's some-bo-dy call-ing me on
F
B♭
E♭maj7
she's the one.
she's the one.
If there's some-bo-
If there's some-bo-
1.
Cm7
F
B♭
B♭7
-dy call-ing me on she's the one.
-dy call-ing me on she's the one.
2.
B♭
B♭7
Cm7
If there's some-bo-dy call-ing me on
F
Gm
she's the one, yes, she's the one.

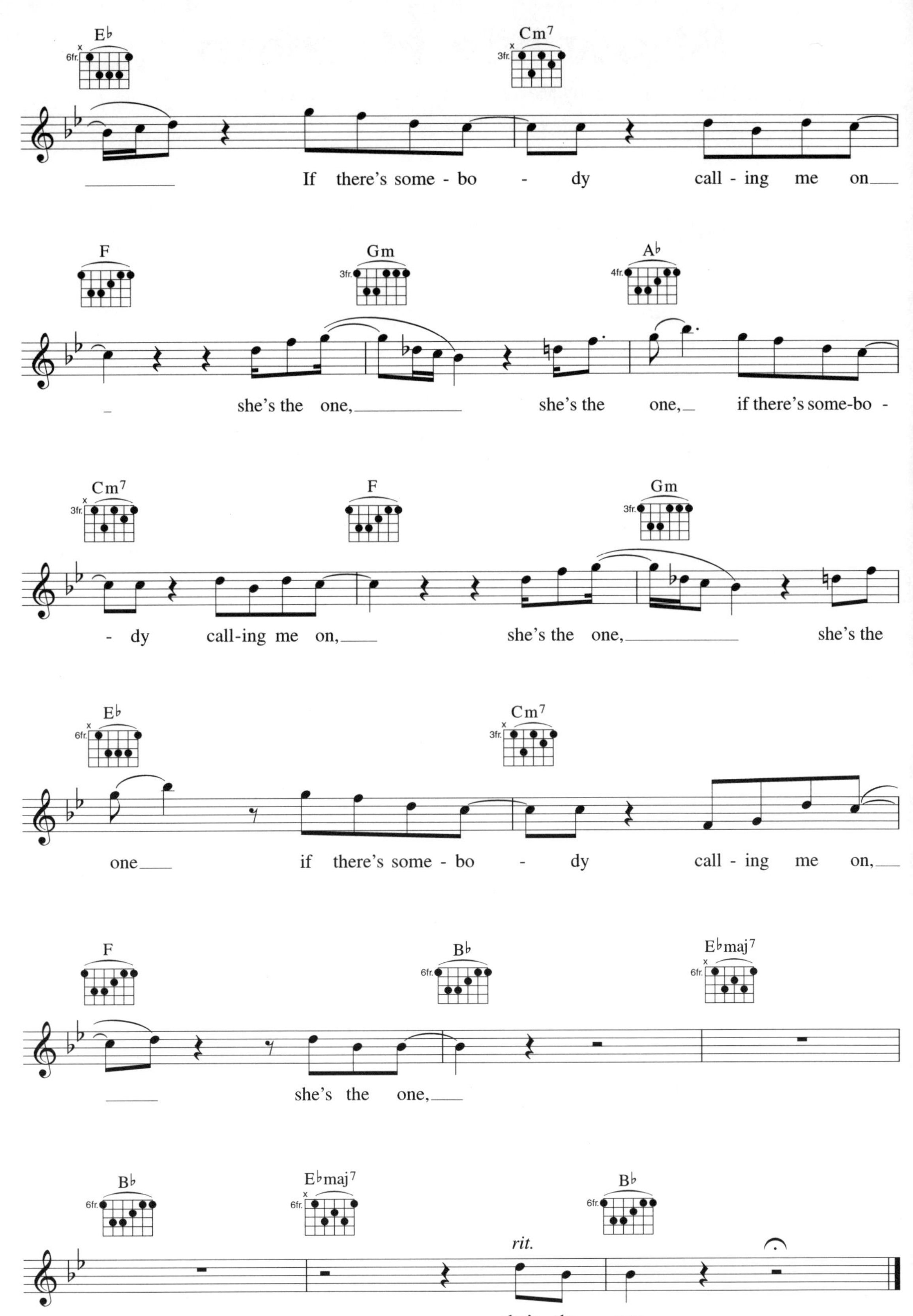
E♭
Cm7
If there's some - bo - dy call - ing me on
F
Gm
A♭
she's the one, she's the one, if there's some-bo -
Cm7
F
Gm
- dy call-ing me on, she's the one, she's the
E♭
Cm7
one if there's some - bo - dy call - ing me on,
F
B♭
E♭maj7
she's the one,
B♭
E♭maj7
B♭
rit.
she's the one.

Show Me Heaven

Words & Music by Maria McKee, Jay Rifkin & Eric Rackin

D♭
4fr.
E♭
6fr.
A♭
4fr.
B♭m7
Hold my hand don't let me fall,

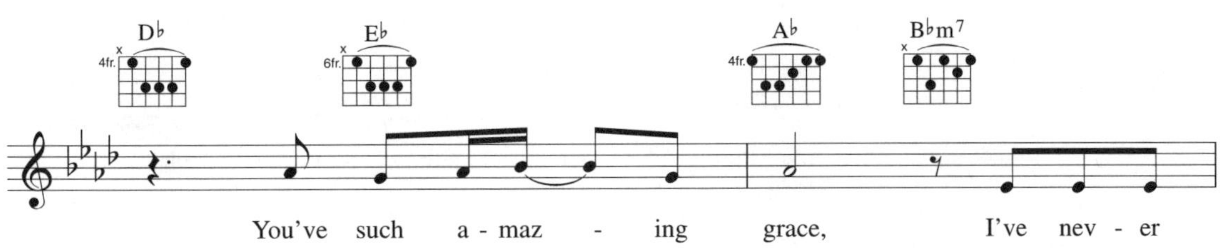
D♭
4fr.
E♭
6fr.
A♭
4fr.
B♭m7
You've such a - maz - ing grace, I've nev - er

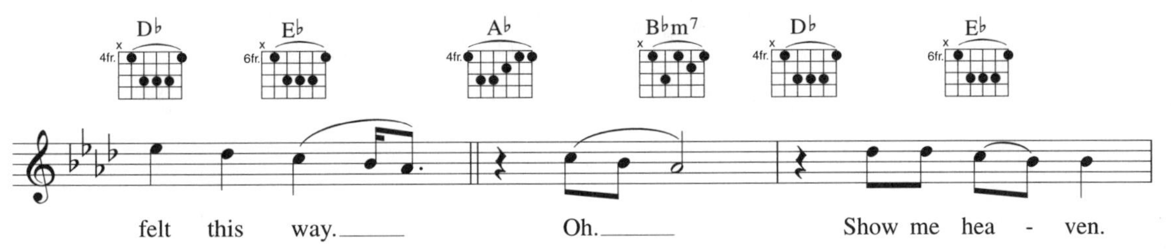
D♭
4fr.
E♭
6fr.
A♭
4fr.
B♭m7
D♭
4fr.
E♭
6fr.
felt this way. Oh. Show me hea - ven.

A♭
4fr.
B♭m7
D♭
4fr.
E♭
6fr.
A♭
4fr.
B♭m7
Cov - er me. Leave me breath - less. Oh, oh, oh

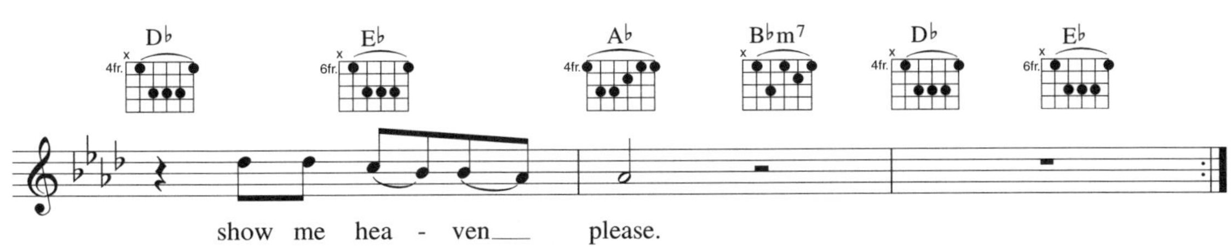
D♭
4fr.
E♭
6fr.
A♭
4fr.
B♭m7
D♭
4fr.
E♭
6fr.
show me hea - ven please.

Verse 2:
Here I go I'm shaking just like the breeze
Hey babe I need your hand to steady me
I'm not denying I'm frightened as much as you
Though I'm barely touching you
I've shivers down my spine and it feels divine.

Sit Down

Words & Music by Tim Booth, Larry Gott, Jim Glennie & Gavan Whelan

B/E
E
trol, I be - lieve this wave will break my

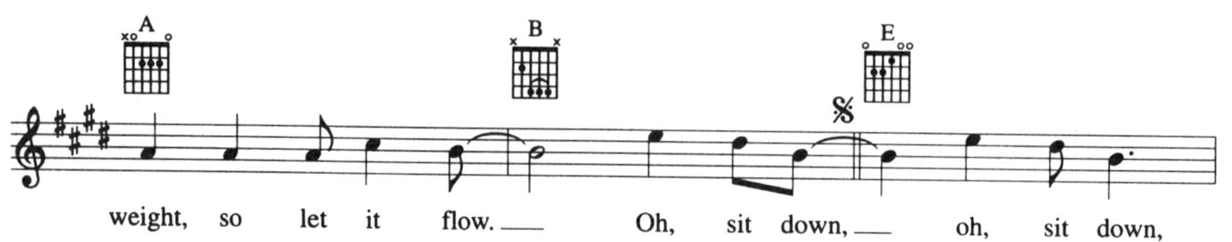
A
B
E
weight, so let it flow. Oh, sit down, oh, sit down,

A
B
oh, sit down, sit down next to me, sit down,

E
A
B
To Coda
down, down, down, down, in sym - pa - thy.

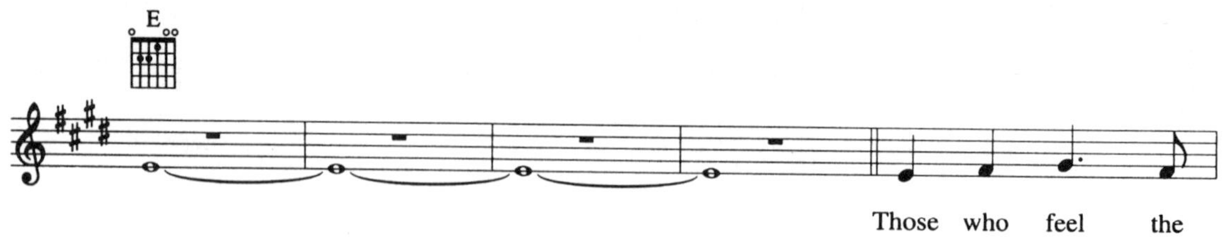
E
Those who feel the

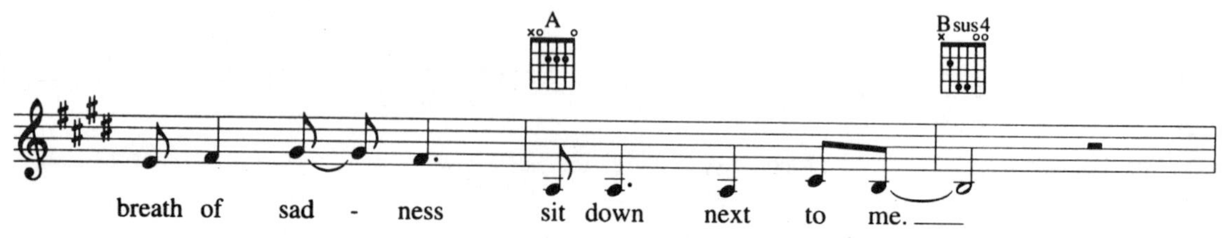
A
Bsus4
breath of sad - ness sit down next to me.

Verse 2:
Now I'm relieved to hear
That you've been to some far out places
It's hard to carry on
When you feel all alone.
Now I've swung back down again
It's worse than it was before,
If I hadn't seen such riches
I could live with being poor.

Staying Out For The Summer

Words & Music by Nigel Clark, Mathew Priest & Andy Miller

Am C G
See I work in a fact - 'ry, I don't wan - na be late.
2. I've had e - nough of lin - ing pock-ets I've never met.
Am C G Am C G
I got my debts to pay for,
They've got me work - ing all hours
Am C G Dm7
gon - na have to wait.
I ain't gained no-thing yet
G Dm7
If I ev - er see you a - gain I will tell you why.
G
I was low and in - se - cure. I
Dm7 G
1.
did - n't want to make you cry. Well my good's

1. cont.
Dm7 G Dm7 G Dm7 G
turned bad and it's just my luck that you're not on my side.
1. cont.
Dm7 G
So what hap - pens now where did you go
1. cont.
Am C G
with these feel - ings I hide. I'm stay-ing out for the sum - mer.
1. cont.
Am C G Am C G
1. cont.
Am C G
2.
Am
make you cry.
G Dm7
Well my good's turned bad and it's just

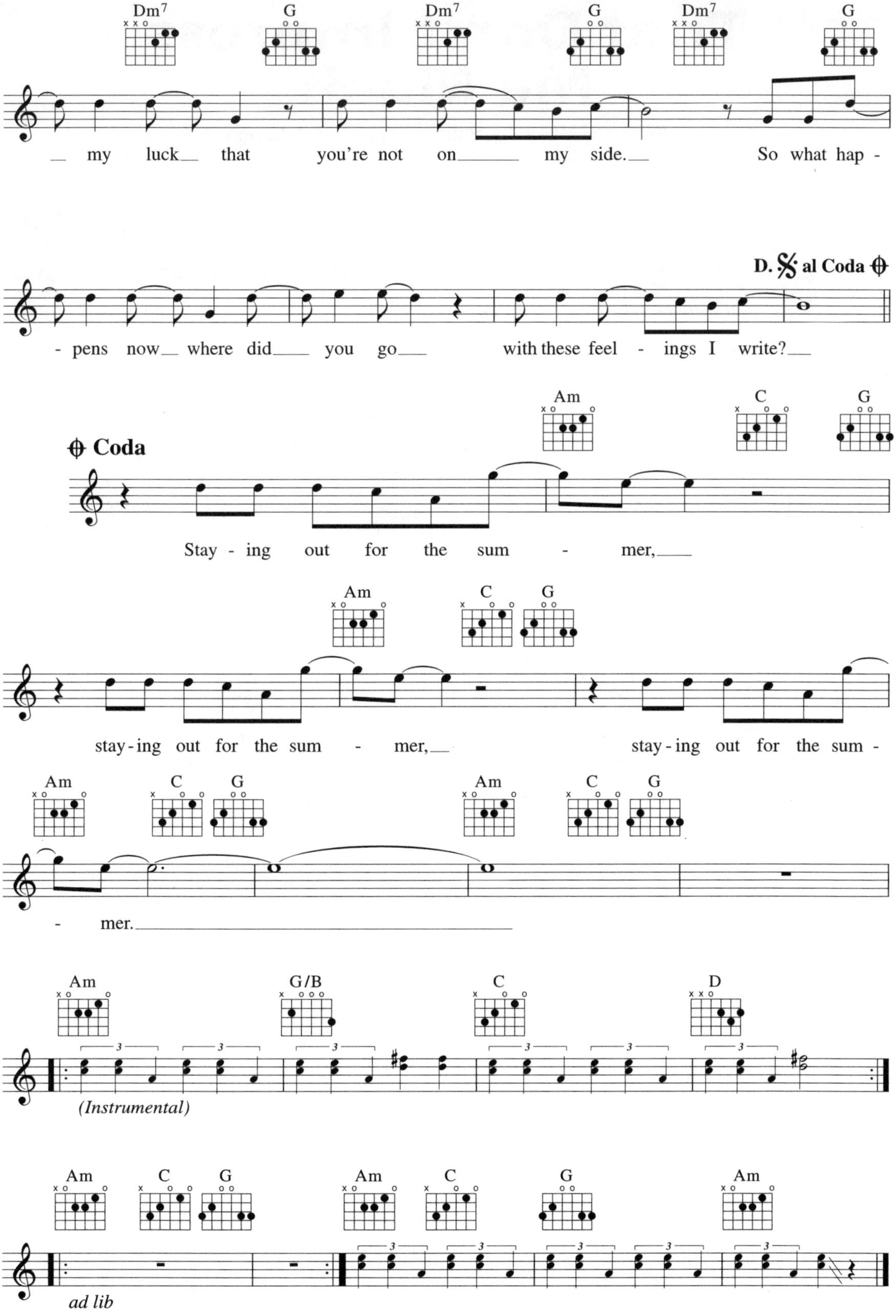

— my luck — that you're not on — my side. — So what hap -

D.S. al Coda

- pens now — where did — you go — with these feel - ings I write? —

Coda

Am C G

Stay - ing out for the sum - mer, —

Am C G

stay - ing out for the sum - mer, — stay - ing out for the sum -

Am C G Am C G

- mer. —

Am G/B C D

(Instrumental)

Am C G Am C G Am

ad lib

That Don't Impress Me Much

Words & Music by Shania Twain & R.J. Lange

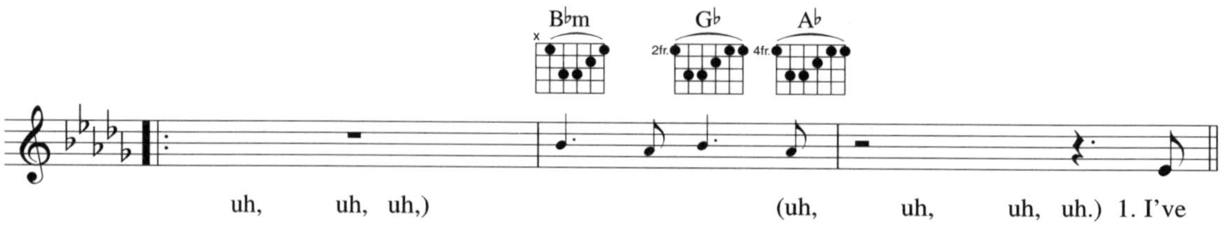

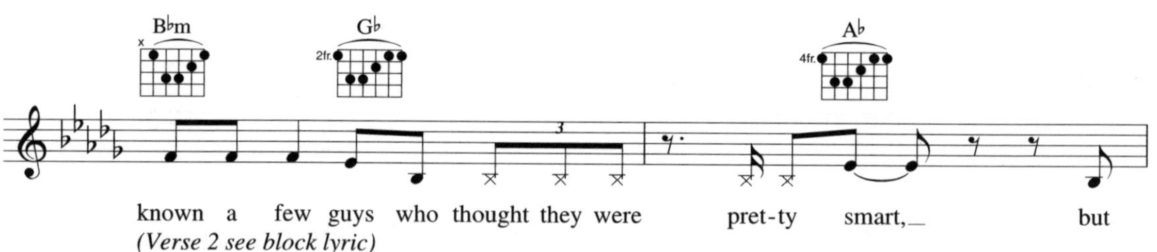

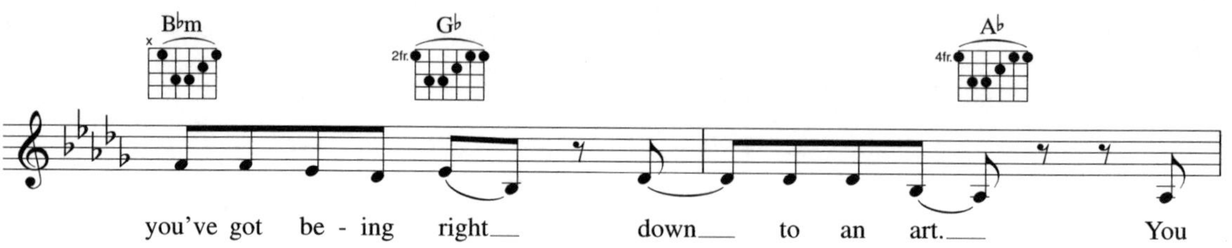

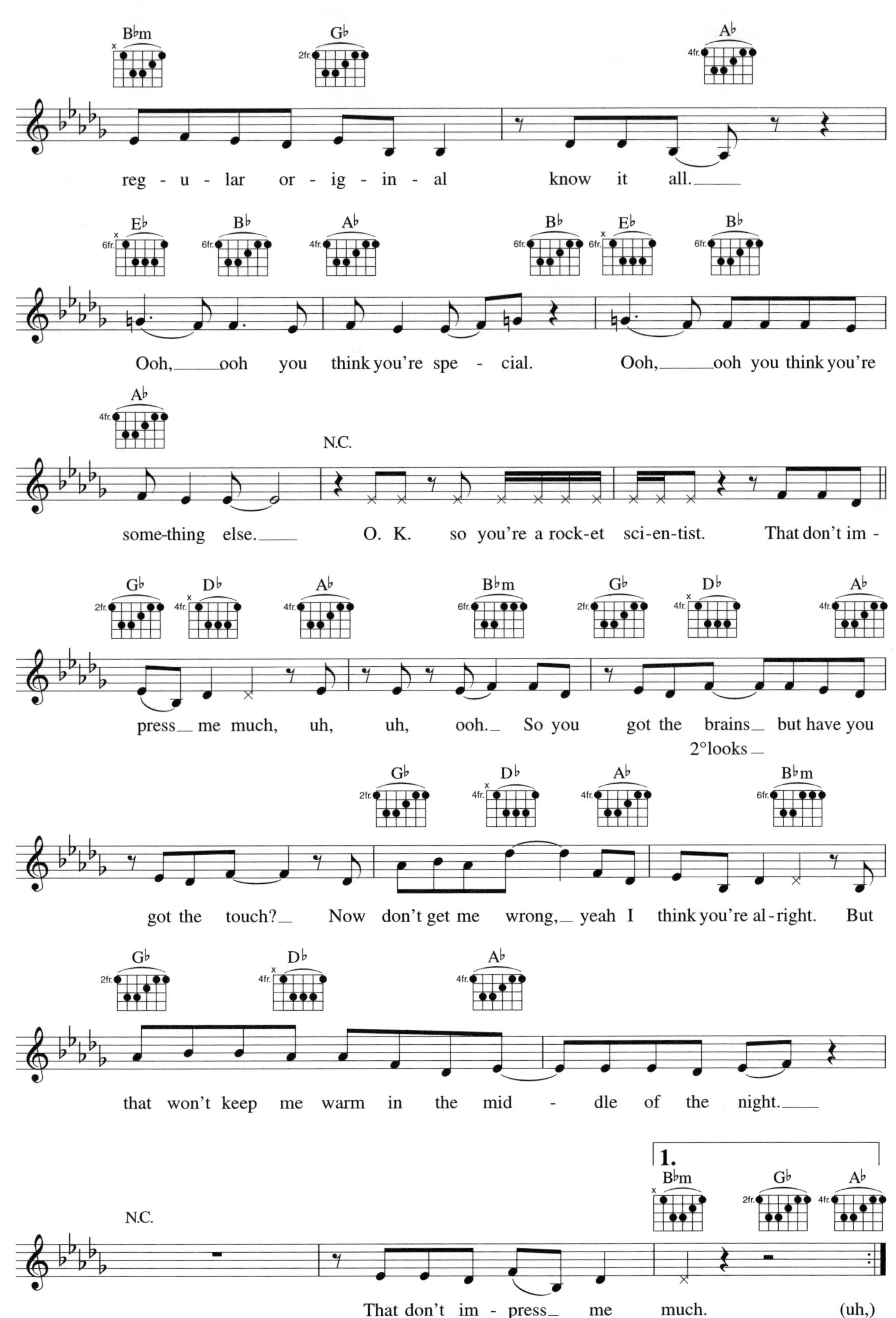
B♭m G♭ A♭
reg - u - lar or - ig - in - al know it all.
E♭ B♭ A♭ B♭ E♭ B♭
Ooh, ooh you think you're spe - cial. Ooh, ooh you think you're
A♭ N.C.
some-thing else. O. K. so you're a rock-et sci-en-tist. That don't im -
G♭ D♭ A♭ B♭m G♭ D♭ A♭
press me much, uh, uh, ooh. So you got the brains but have you
2°looks
G♭ D♭ A♭ B♭m
got the touch? Now don't get me wrong, yeah I think you're al-right. But
G♭ D♭ A♭
that won't keep me warm in the mid - dle of the night.
N.C.
1.
B♭m G♭ A♭
That don't im - press me much. (uh,)

2.
B♭m
G♭
1.2.3.
A♭
4.
A♭
(1° only) much.
(Instrumental)
You're
N.C.
one of those guys who likes to shine his ma - chine, you make me
B♭m
G♭
A♭
take off my shoes be - fore you let me get in.
B♭m
G♭
A♭
I can't be - lieve you kiss your car good - night, now
B♭m
G♭
A♭
come on ba - by tell me, you must be jok - in' right?
E♭
B♭
A♭
B♭
E♭
B♭
Ooh ooh you think you're some-thing spe - cial. Ooh, ooh you think you're
A♭
N.C.
some-thing else. O. K. so you got a car. That don't im -

Verse 2:
I never knew a guy who carried a mirror in his pocket
And a comb up his sleeve just in case
And all that extra-hold gel in your hair oughta lock it
'Cause heaven forbid it should fall outta place
Ooh, ooh you think you're special
Ooh, ooh you think you're something else
O.K. so you're Brad Pitt.
That don't impress me much *etc.*

Ten Storey Love Song

Words & Music by John Squire

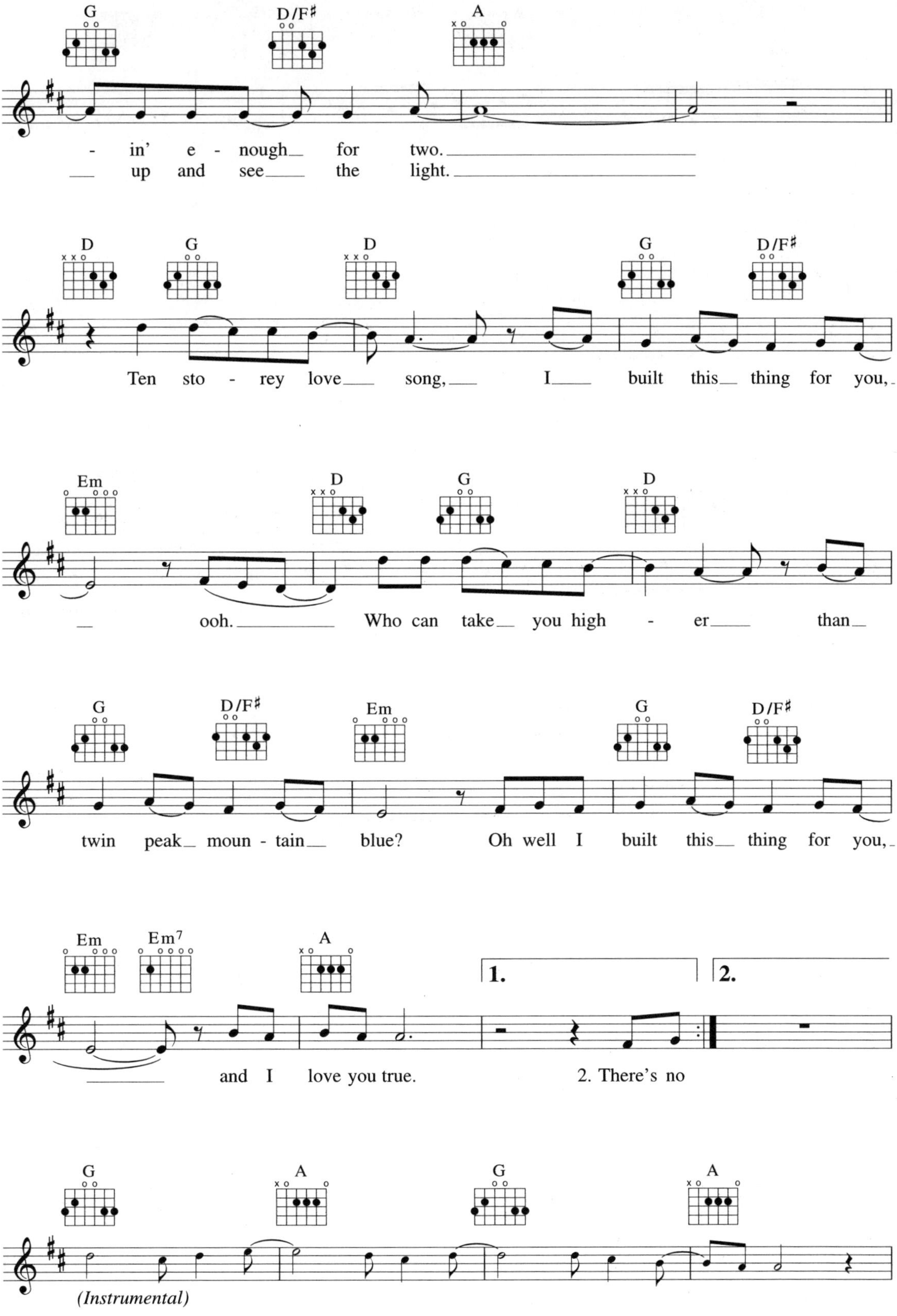

G D/F♯ A

- in' e - nough for two.
up and see the light.

D G D G D/F♯

Ten sto - rey love song, I built this thing for you,

Em D G D

ooh. Who can take you high - er than

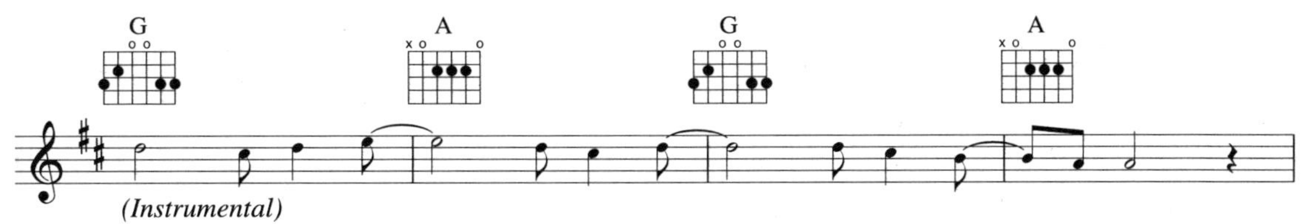

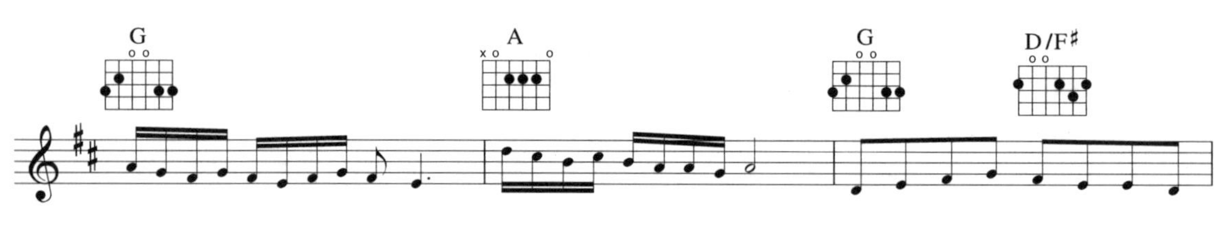
G
A
G
D/F♯

Em
Em7
A

D
G
D
G
D/F♯
Ten sto - rey love song, I built this thing for you,

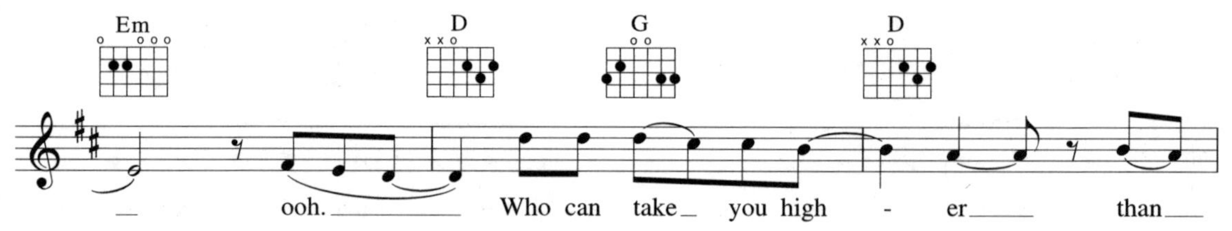
Em
D
G
D
ooh. Who can take you high - er than

G
D/F♯
Em
G
D/F♯
twin peak moun - tain blue? Oh well I built this thing for you,

Em
Em7
A
D
and I love you true.

Turn

Words & Music by Fran Healy

E
(D)
I want to sing, to sing my song
I want to sing, to sing my song
B
(A)
A
(G)
I want to live in a world where I be - long.
I want to live in a world where I'll be strong.
F♯m
(Em)
I want to live, I will sur - vive,
B
(A)
B/A
(A/G)
and I be - lieve that it won't be ve - ry long,
B/G♯
(A/F♯)
B/F♯
(A/E)
A
(G)
B
(A)
If we turn, turn turn,
E
(D)
A
(G)
B
(A)
turn, turn. Turn, turn, turn.
E
(D)
A
(G)
B
(A)
If we turn, turn, turn,

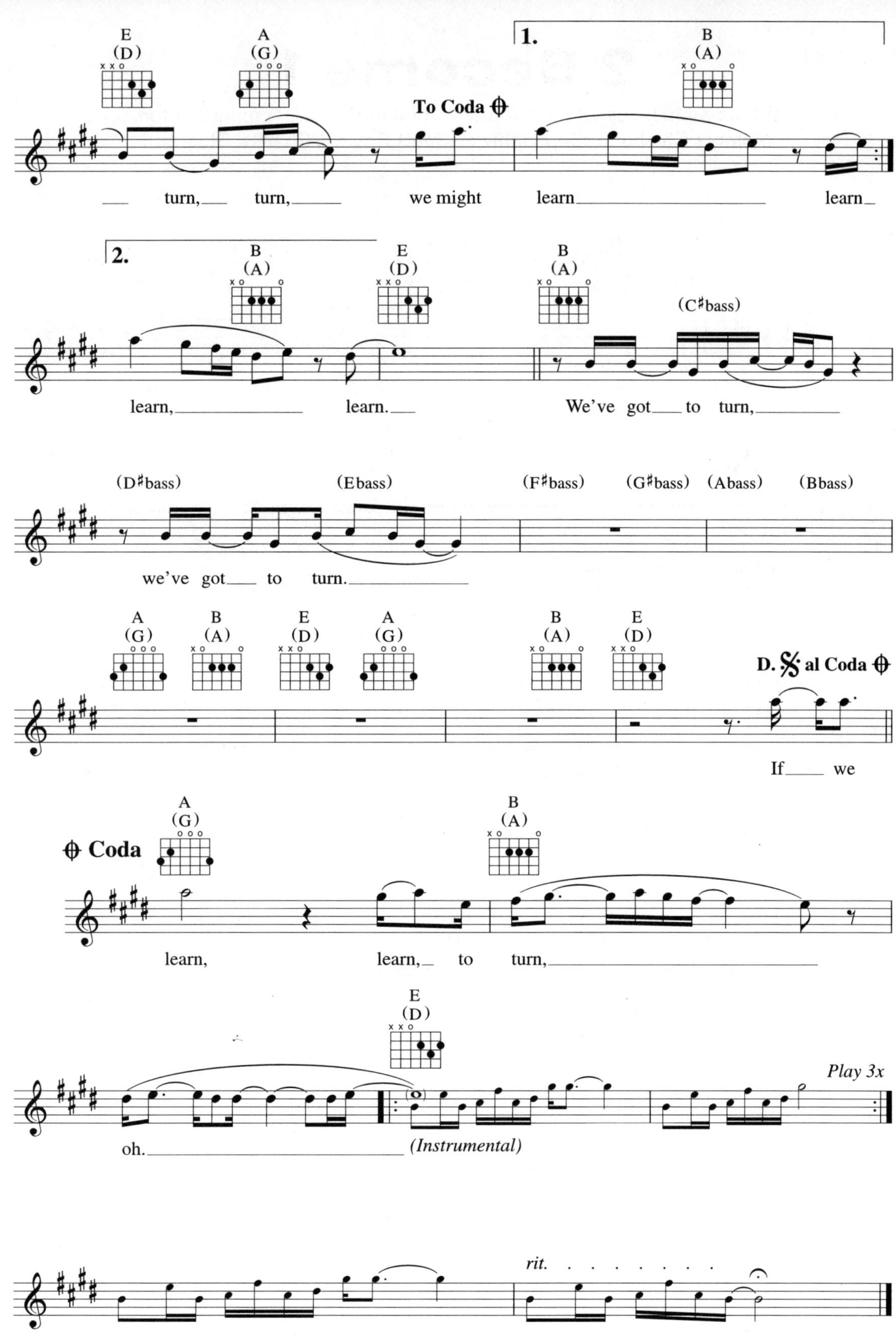
E (D)
A (G)
To Coda
1.
B (A)
turn, turn, we might learn learn
2.
B (A)
E (D)
B (A)
(C♯bass)
learn, learn. We've got to turn,
(D♯bass)
(Ebass)
(F♯bass)
(G♯bass)
(Abass)
(Bbass)
we've got to turn.
A (G)
B (A)
E (D)
A (G)
B (A)
E (D)
D.S. al Coda
If we
Coda
A (G)
B (A)
learn, learn, to turn,
E (D)
Play 3x
oh. (Instrumental)
rit.

2 Become 1

Words & Music by Victoria Aadams, Melanie Brown, Emma Bunton,
Melanie Chisholm, Geri Halliwell, Matt Rowe & Richard Stannard

G♭ A♭m11 C♭ B♭m
we can a - chieve it. Come a lit - tle bit clos - er ba - by,
take it or leave it. Are you as good as I re-mem - ber by - by,
A♭m C♭/D♭ C♭ B♭m
get it on, get it on, 'cause to - night is the night when
get it on, get it on, 'cause to - night is the night when
A♭m C♭/D♭ G♭ D♭
two be-come one.
two be-come one.
I need some love like I nev-er need-ed love be - fore,
C♭ D♭ G♭ D♭
(wan-na make love to you ba - by.) I had a lit-tle love now I'm back for
C♭ D♭
more (wan - na make love to you ba - by.)
E G♭ A C♭ G♭
Set your spi-rit free, it's the on - ly way to be.

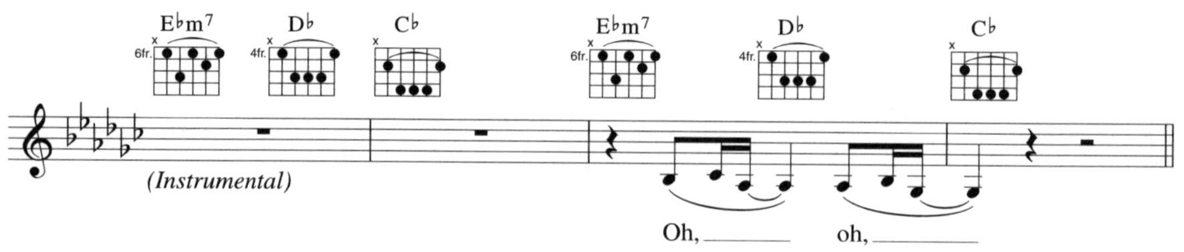
E♭m7
D♭
C♭
E♭m7
D♭
C♭
6fr.
4fr.
(Instrumental)
Oh, oh,

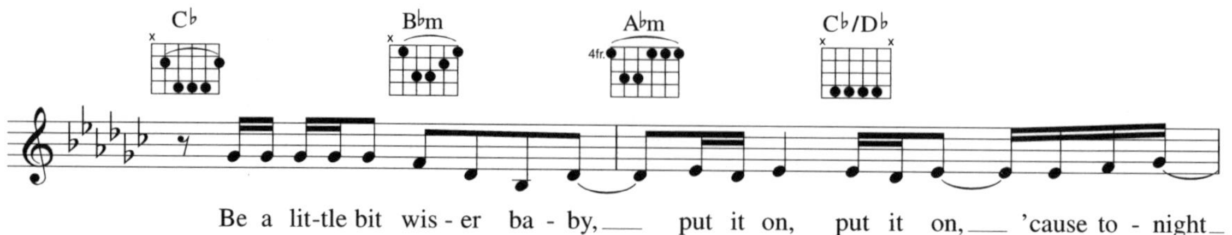
C♭
B♭m
A♭m
C♭/D♭
4fr.
Be a lit-tle bit wis - er ba - by, put it on, put it on, 'cause to - night

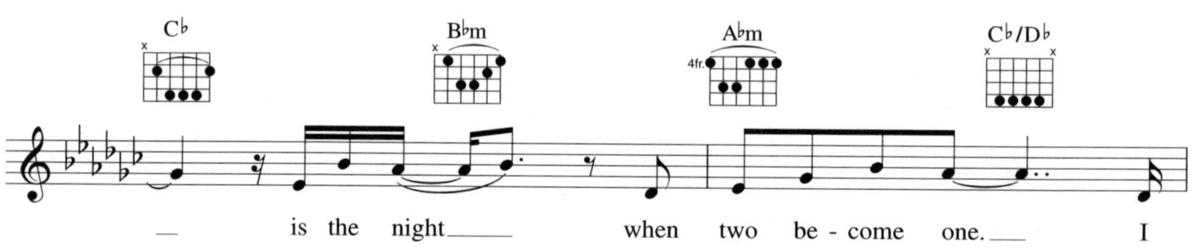
C♭
B♭m
A♭m
C♭/D♭
4fr.
is the night when two be - come one. I

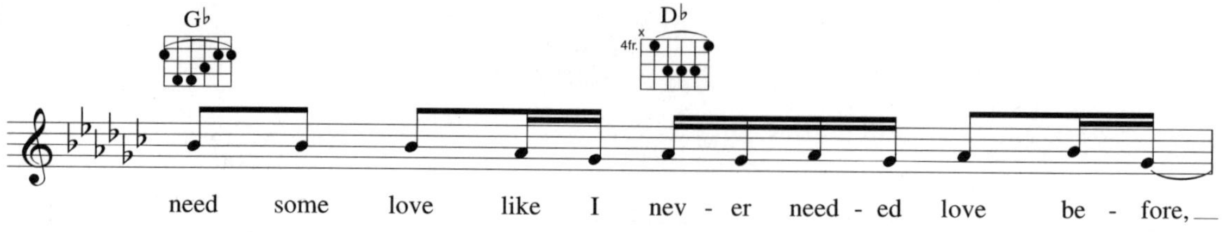
G♭
D♭
4fr.
need some love like I nev - er need - ed love be - fore,

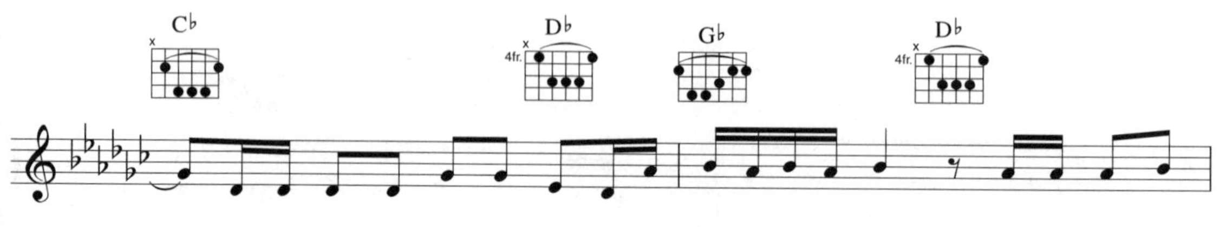
C♭
D♭
G♭
D♭
4fr.
(wan-na make love to you ba - by.) I had a lit - tle love, now I'm back for

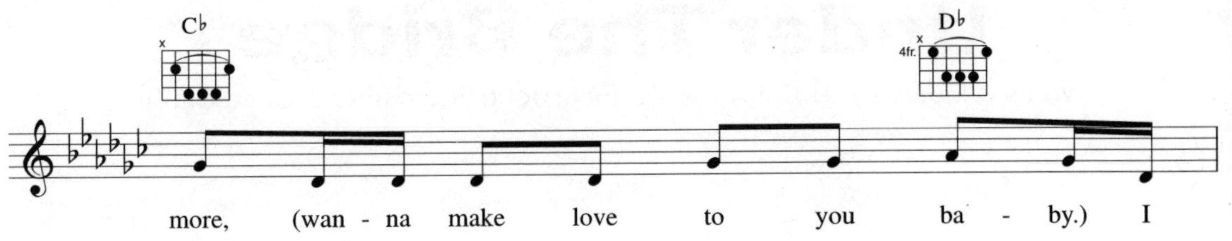

C♭
D♭
4fr.
more, (wan - na make love to you ba - by.) I

G♭
D♭
4fr.
need some love - like I nev - er need - ed love be - fore,

C♭
D♭
4fr.
G♭
D♭
4fr.
(wan-na make love to you ba - by.) I had a lit - tle love, now I'm back for

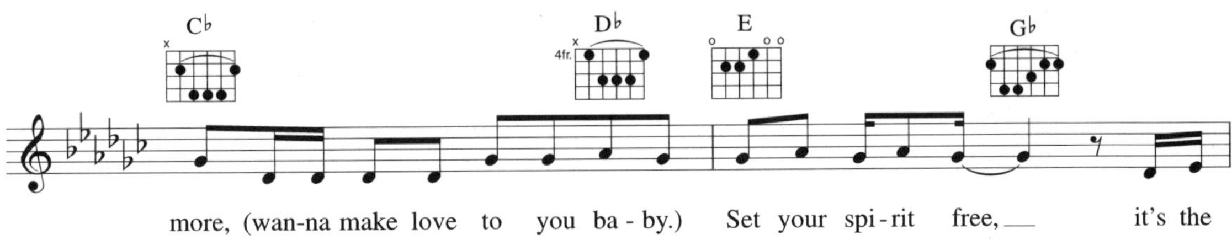

C♭
D♭
4fr.
E
G♭
more, (wan-na make love to you ba - by.) Set your spi - rit free, it's the

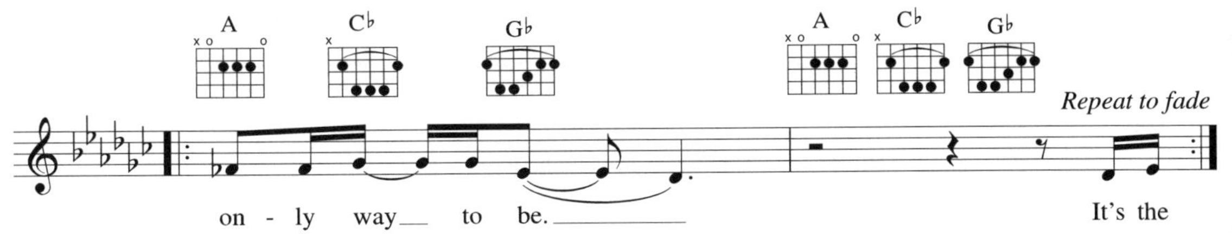

A
C♭
G♭
A
C♭
G♭
Repeat to fade
on - ly way to be. It's the

Under The Bridge

Words & Music by Anthony Kiedis, Flea, John Frusciante & Chad Smith

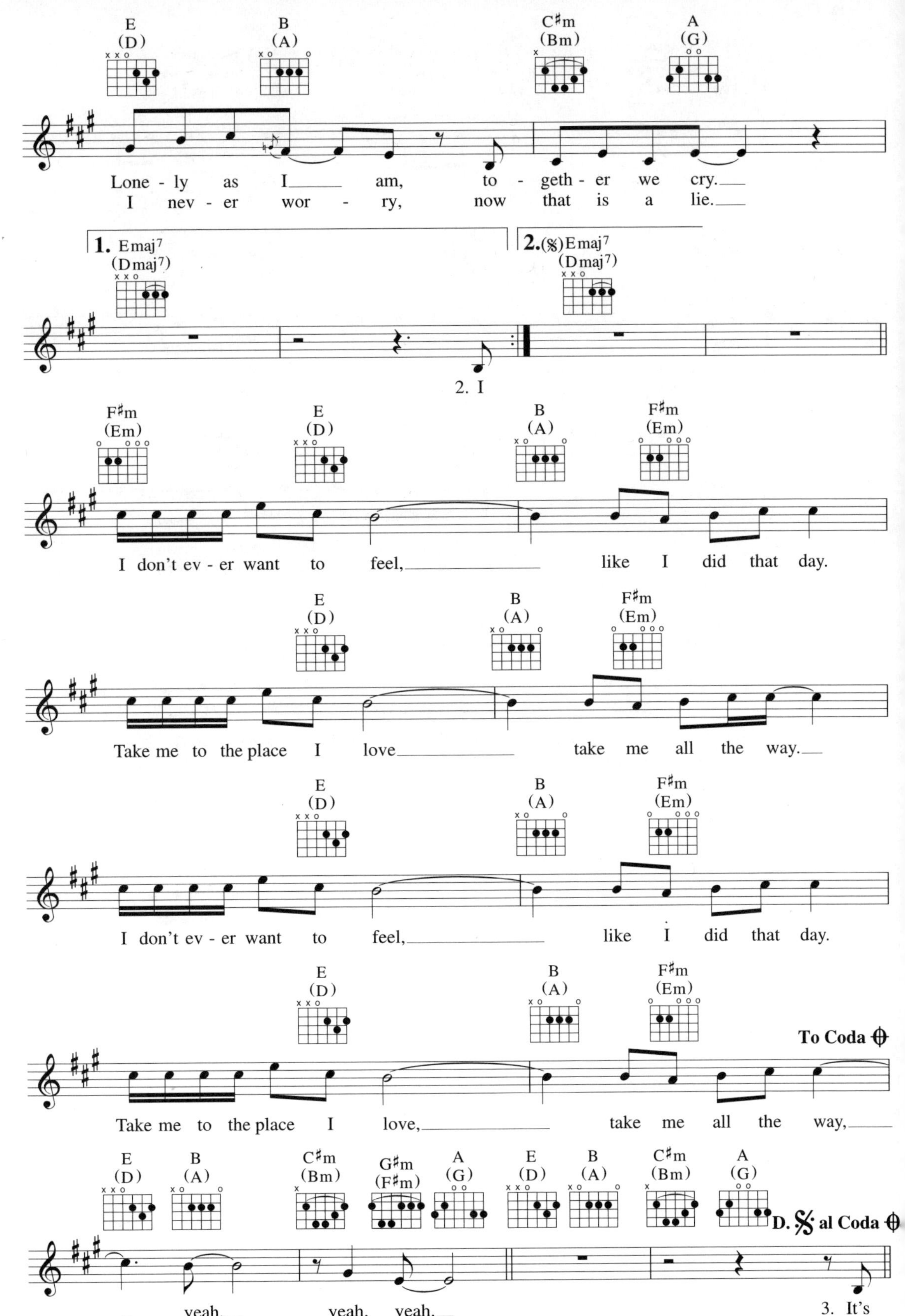
E (D) B (A) C♯m (Bm) A (G)
Lone - ly as I am, to - geth - er we cry.
I nev - er wor - ry, now that is a lie.
1. Emaj7 (Dmaj7)
2. (𝄋) Emaj7 (Dmaj7)
2. I
F♯m (Em) E (D) B (A) F♯m (Em)
I don't ev - er want to feel, like I did that day.
E (D) B (A) F♯m (Em)
Take me to the place I love take me all the way.
E (D) B (A) F♯m (Em)
I don't ev - er want to feel, like I did that day.
E (D) B (A) F♯m (Em)
To Coda ⊕
Take me to the place I love, take me all the way,
E (D) B (A) C♯m (Bm) G♯m (F♯m) A (G) E (D) B (A) C♯m (Bm) A (G)
D.𝄋 al Coda ⊕
yeah, yeah, yeah.
3. It's

Verse 3: It's hard to believe
There is nobody out there
It's hard to believe
That I'm all alone
At least I have her love
The city she loves me
Lonely as I am
Together we cry.

What Can I Do

Words & Music by Andrea Corr, Caroline Corr, Sharon Corr & Jim Corr

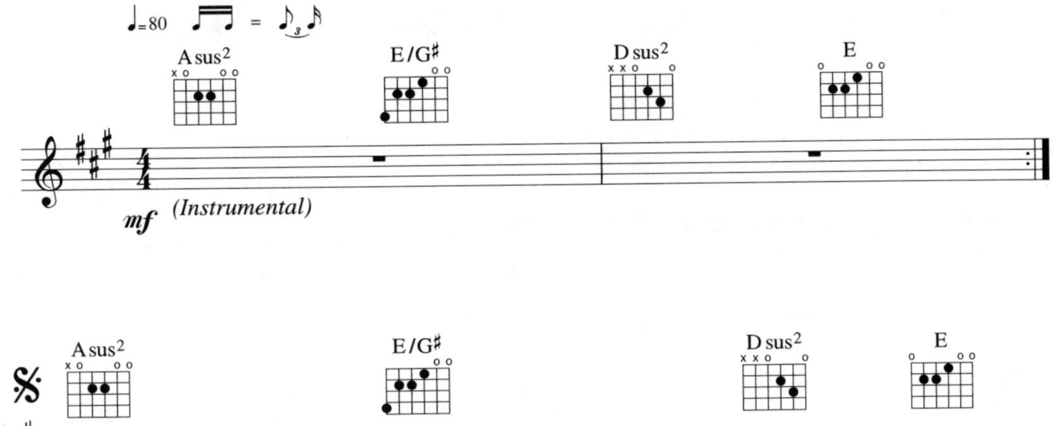

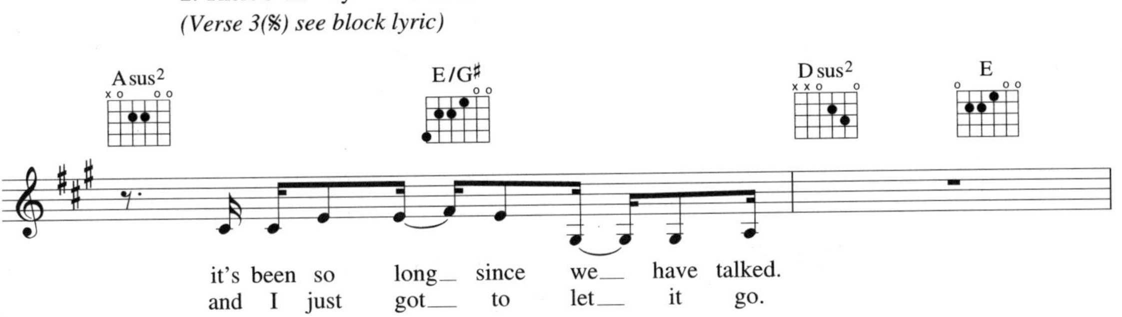

Asus2 E/G♯ Dsus2 E

I just don't know what I'm do - ing wrong.
If I don't try and I don't hope.

A
E/G♯
D
E
What can I do to make you love me?
A
E
Bm7
E
What can I do to make you care?
A
E
D
E
What can I say to make you feel this?
A
E
Bm7
E
To Coda
What can I do to get you there?
F♯m
D
E
D
E
No more wait - ing, no more ach - ing.
F♯m
D
E
D
E
D.S. al Coda
No more fight - ing, no more try - ing.

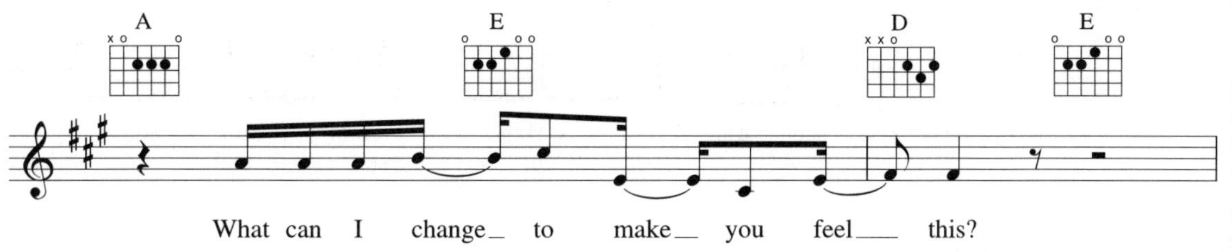

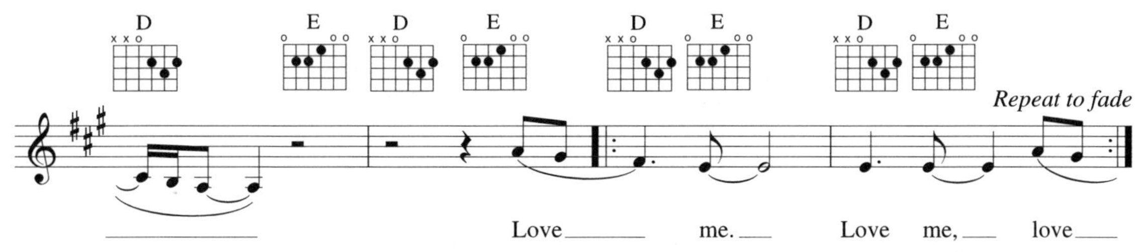

Verse 3:
Maybe there's nothing more to say
And in a funny way I'm calm
Because the power is not mine
I'm just gonna let it fly.

When You're Gone

Words & Music by Bryan Adams & Eliot Kennedy

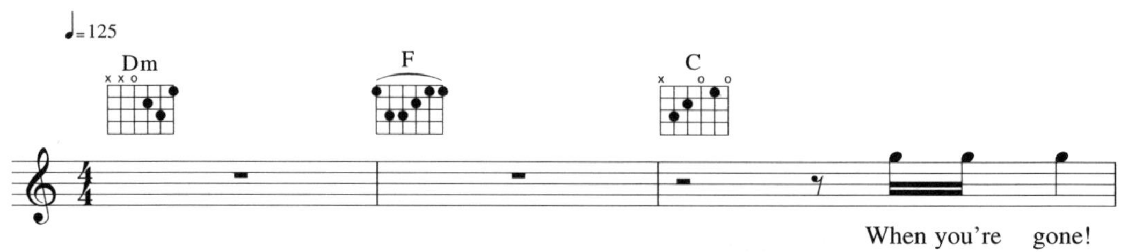

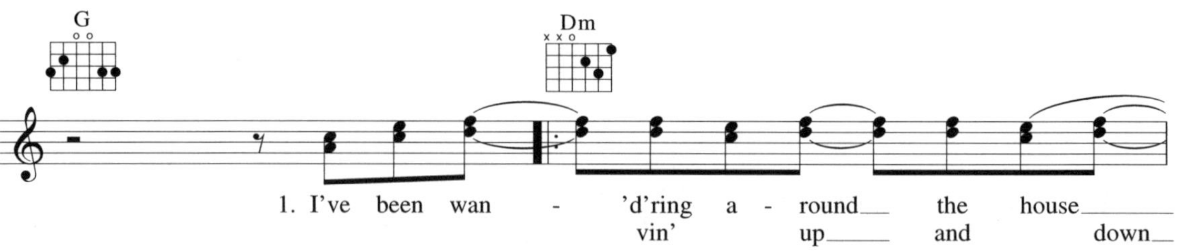

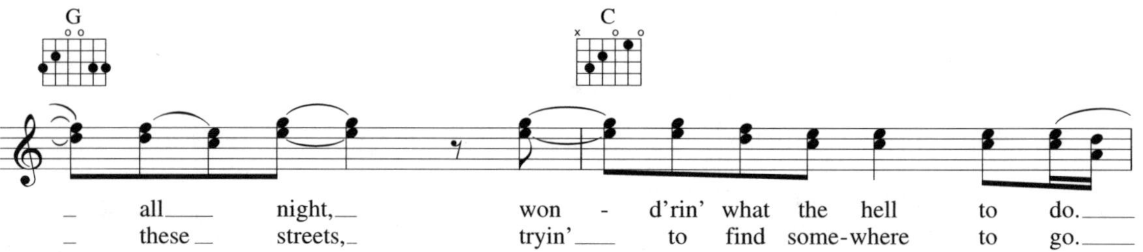

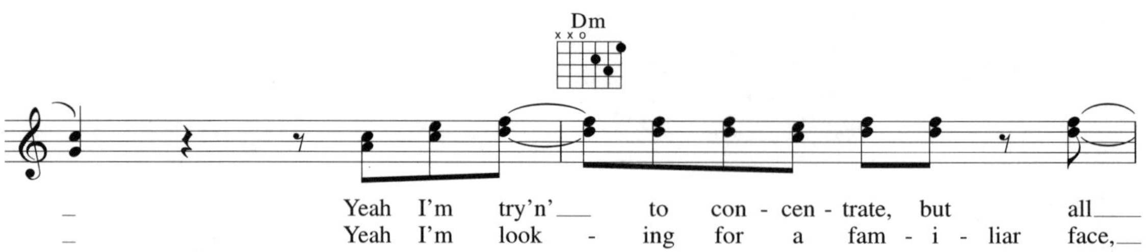

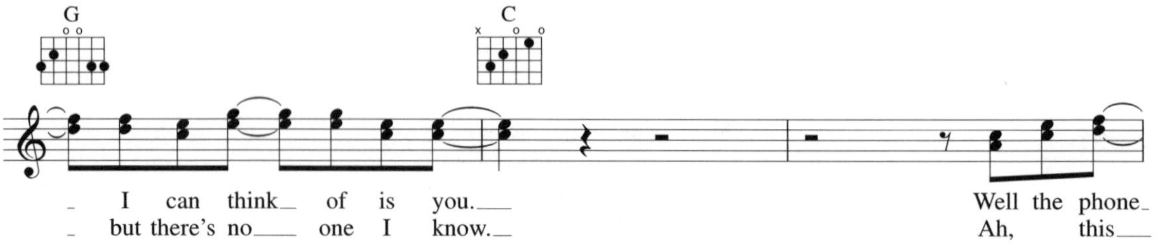

Dm
G
__ don't__ ring,__ 'cause my friends__ ain't__ home,__ I'm tired__
__ is____ tor - ture this____ is____ pain,__ it feels__
C
__ of be - in' all a - lone.______ Got the T.____
__ like I'm gon - na go__ in - sane. I hope__
Dm
B♭
__ V.____ on,____ 'cause the ra - dio's__ play - in'
__ you're__ com - in' back____ real__ soon 'cause I don't
G
songs that re - mind me of you.____
know what to do.____
Ba - by when you're
Dm
F
C
G
gone. I real-ise I'm in love.____ Days__ go on and
Dm
F
C
on, and the nights__ just seem so________________ long,

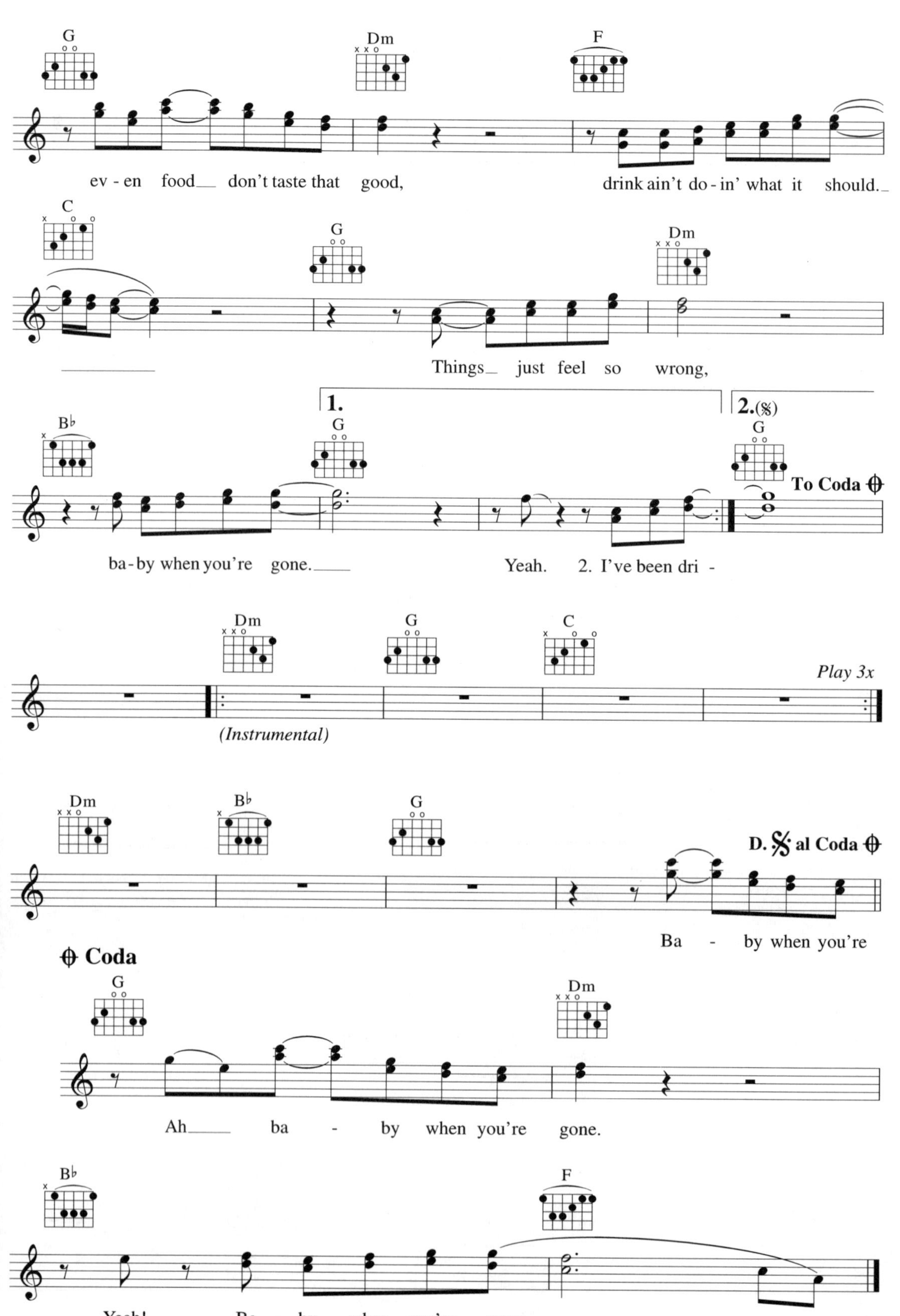
G
Dm
F
ev - en food don't taste that good,
drink ain't do - in' what it should.
C
G
Dm
Things just feel so wrong,
B♭
1.
G
2.(𝄋)
G
To Coda 𝄌
ba - by when you're gone.
Yeah. 2. I've been dri -
Dm
G
C
Play 3x
(Instrumental)
Dm
B♭
G
D.𝄋 al Coda 𝄌
Ba - by when you're
𝄌 Coda
G
Dm
Ah ba - by when you're gone.
B♭
F
Yeah! Ba - by when you're gone.

Why Does It Always Rain On Me?

Words & Music by Fran Healy

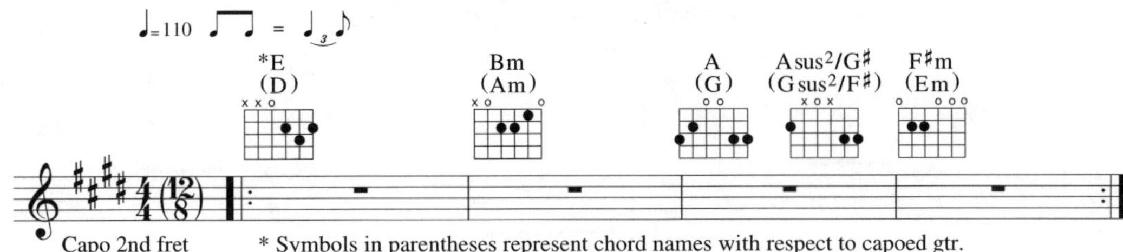

* Symbols in parentheses represent chord names with respect to capoed gtr.
Symbols above represent actual sounding chords.

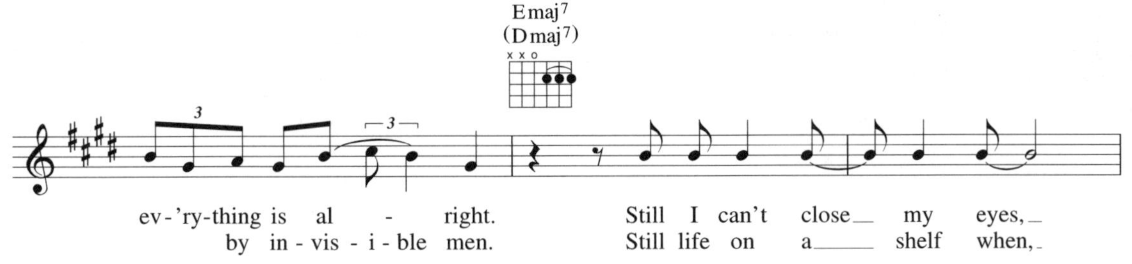

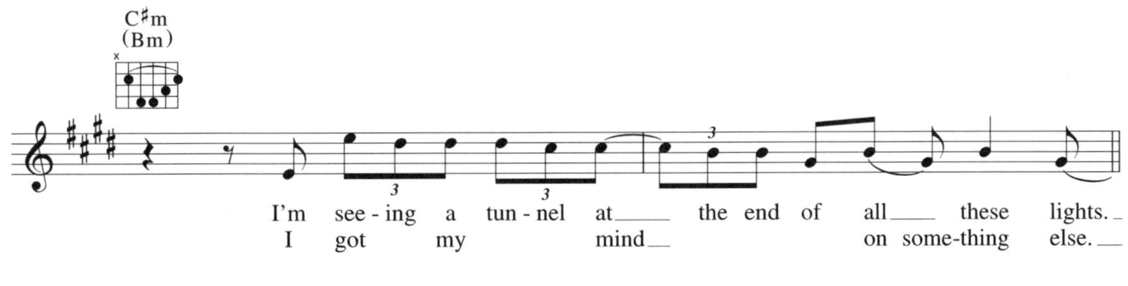

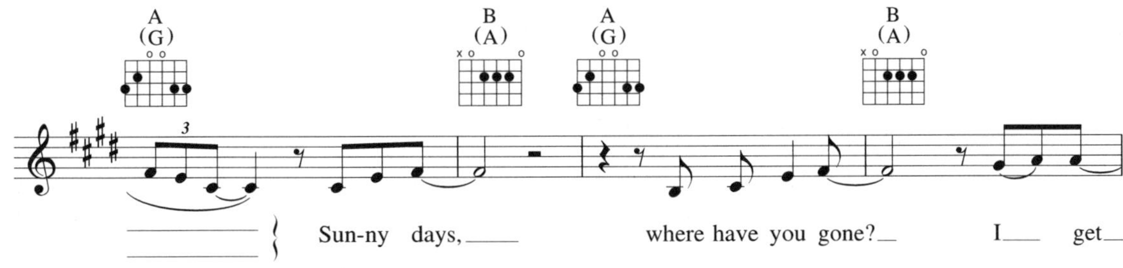

A (G)
Asus2/G♯ (Gsus2/F♯)
F♯m (Em)
B (A)
the strang - est feel - ing, you be - long.
E (D)
B (A)
A (G)
Asus2/G♯ (Gsus2/F♯)
Why does it al - ways rain on me?
Is it be - cause I lied
F♯m (Em)
E (D)
B (A)
when I was sev-en - teen?
Why does it al - ways rain on me?
A (G)
Asus2/G♯ (Gsus2/F♯)
1. F♯m (Em)
Ev - en when the sun is shin - ing,
I can't a - void the light - 'ning.
2. 3. F♯m (Em)
C♯m (Bm)
I can't a - void the light - 'ning. Oh
where did the blue
E (D)
C♯m (Bm)
E (D)
sky go?
Oh, and why is it rain - ing so?
D (C)
D/C♯ (C/B)
Bm7 (Am7)
Bm7/A (Am7/G)
Bsus4 (Asus4)
B (A)
It's so cold.

E (D)
B (A)
Why does it always rain on me?
A (G)
Asus2/G♯ (Gsus2/F♯)
F♯m (Em)
Is it because I lied when I was seventeen?
E (D)
B (A)
Why does it always rain on me?
A (G)
A/G♯ (G/F♯)
F♯m7 (Em7)
Even when the sun is shining, I can't avoid the lightning.
E (D)
B (A)
A (G)
Asus2/G♯ (Gsus2/F♯)
Why does it always rain on me?
F♯m7 (Em7)
E (D)
Why does it always rain
Bm (Am)
A (G)
Asus2/G♯ (Gsus2/F♯)
F♯m7 (Em7)
E (D)
on on.

Wicked Game

Words & Music by Chris Isaak

E
Bm
do.
I nev - er dreamed that I'd
A
E
meet some - bo - dy like you.
(𝄋) love
Bm
A
E
I nev - er dreamed that I'd lose some - bo - dy like you.
Bm
A
E
No I don't wan - na fall in love.
Bm
A
E
No I don't wan - na fall in love,
1.
To Coda
Bm
A
E
with you,
1. cont.
Bm
A
E
with you.

Verse 3:
What a wicked game we play
To make me feel this way
What a wicked thing to do
To let me dream of you
What a wicked thing to say
You never felt this way
What a wicked thing to do
To make me dream of you.

Wide Open Space

Words & Music by Paul Draper

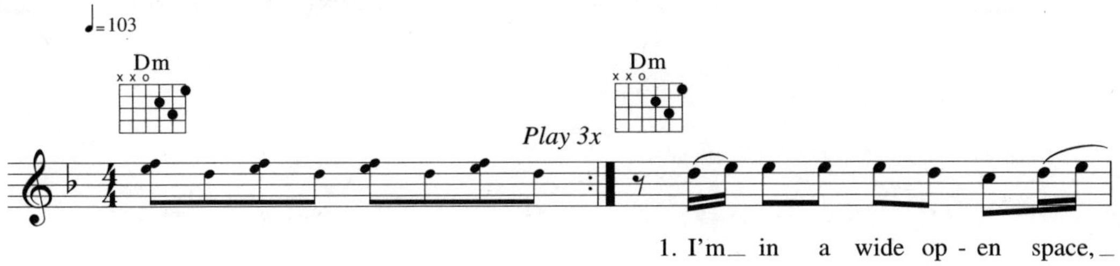

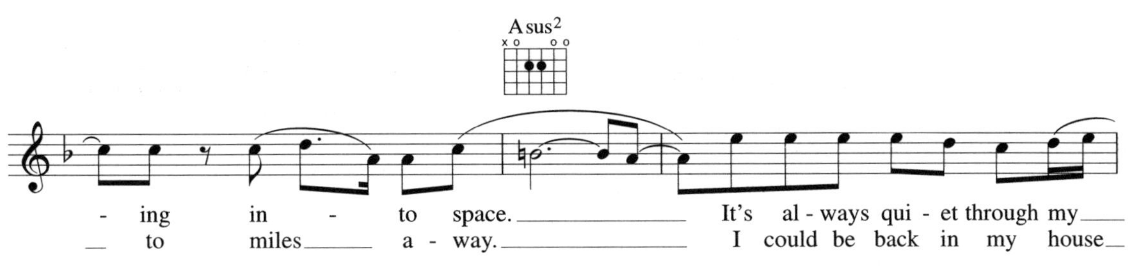

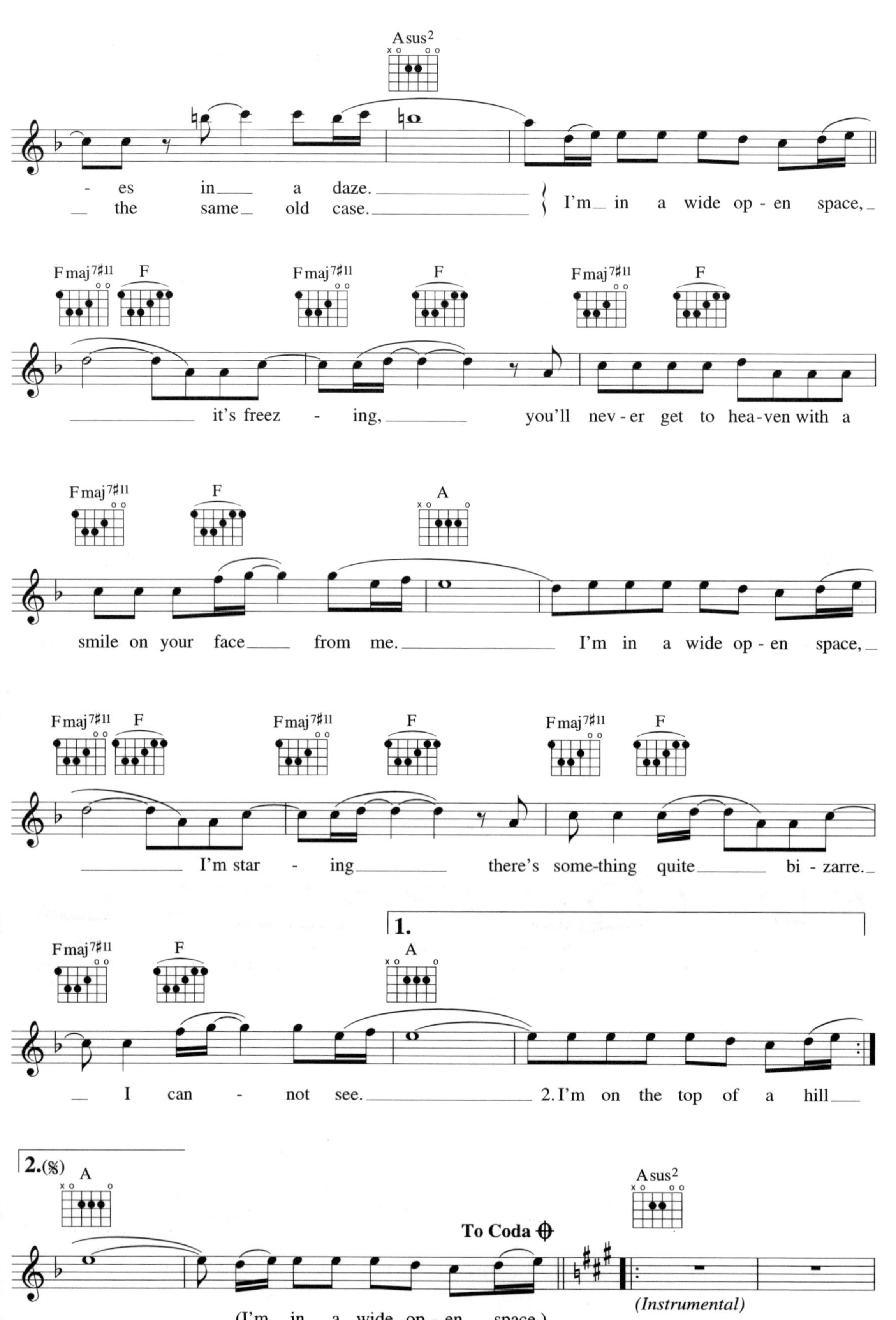
Asus2
- es in a daze.
the same old case.
I'm in a wide op - en space,
Fmaj7♯11 F Fmaj7♯11 F Fmaj7♯11 F
it's freez - ing, you'll nev - er get to hea - ven with a
Fmaj7♯11 F A
smile on your face from me. I'm in a wide op - en space,
Fmaj7♯11 F Fmaj7♯11 F Fmaj7♯11 F
I'm star - ing there's some - thing quite bi - zarre.
Fmaj7♯11 F
1.
A
I can - not see. 2. I'm on the top of a hill
2.(𝄋)
A
To Coda ⊕
Asus2
(I'm in a wide op - en space.)
on 𝄋 only
(Instrumental)

Em
Asus2
Play 4x
D.S. al Coda
3. Wide op - en space, _

Coda
Fmaj7♯11
F
_ it's freez - ing, _ you'll nev - er get to hea - ven with a

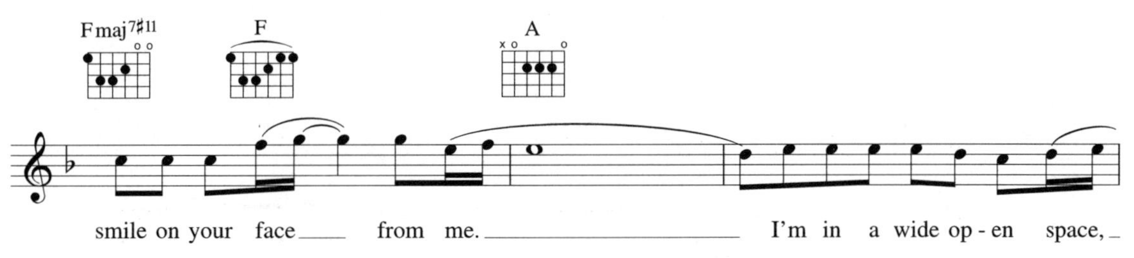
Fmaj7♯11
F
A
smile on your face _ from me. _ I'm in a wide op - en space, _

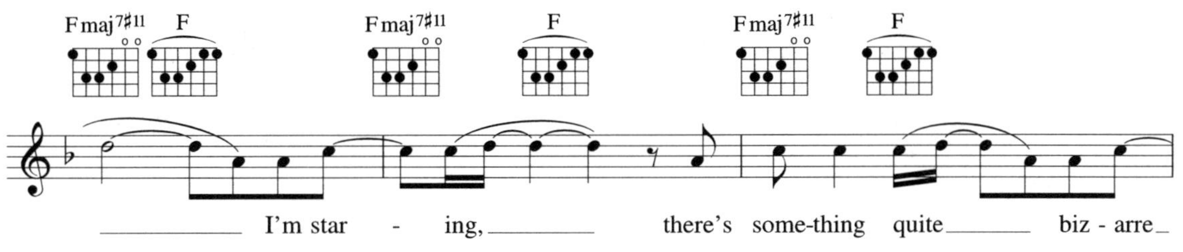
Fmaj7♯11
F
_ I'm star - ing, _ there's some-thing quite _ biz - arre _

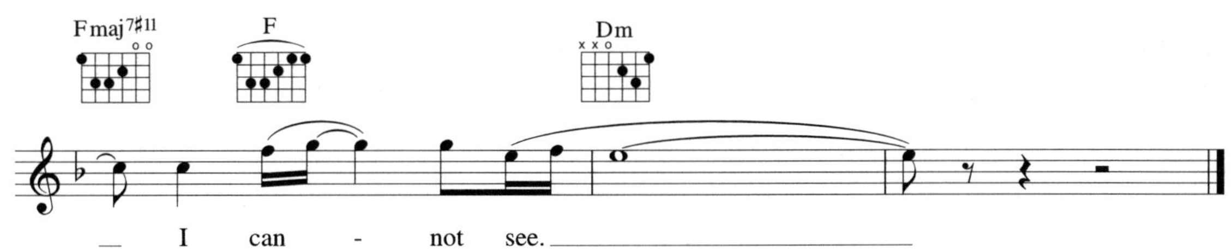
Fmaj7♯11
F
Dm
_ I can - not see. _

You're Gorgeous

Words & Music by Steven Jones

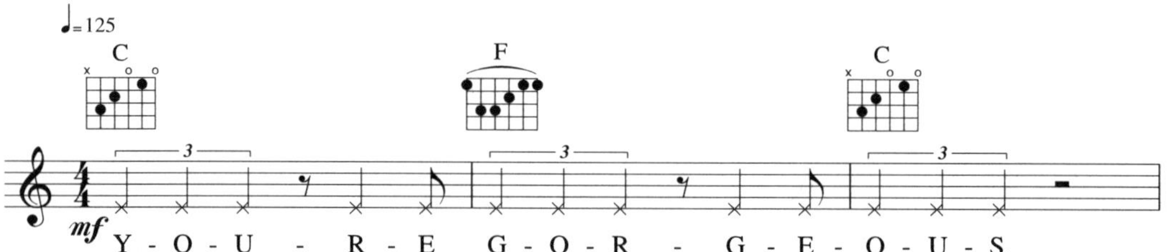

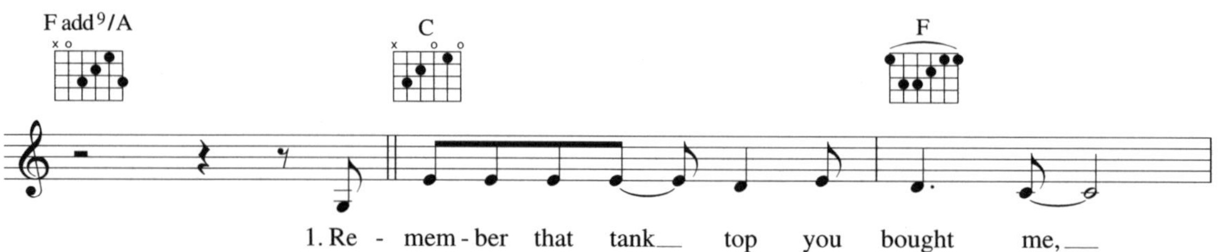

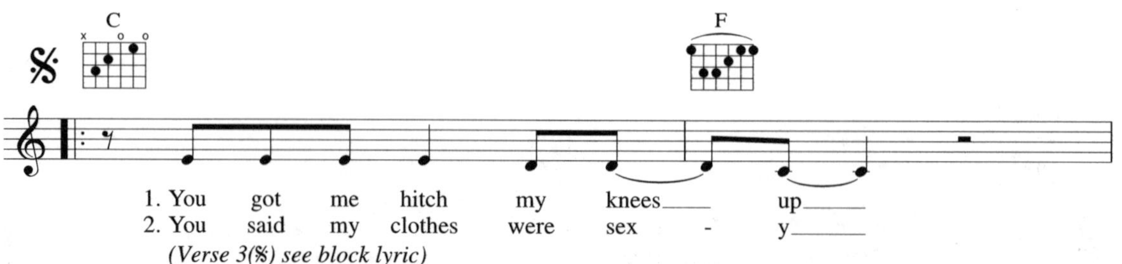

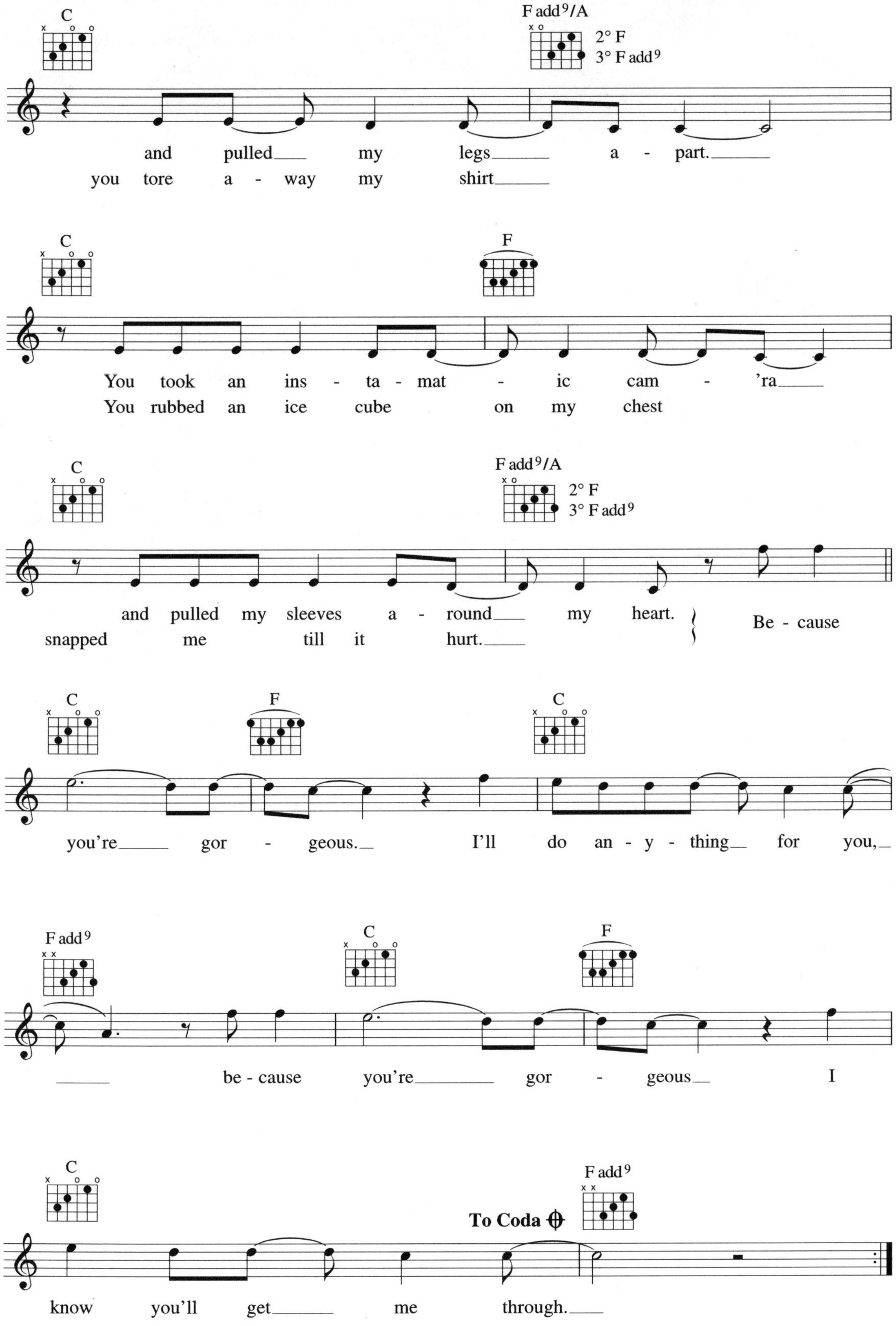

C F add9/A 2° F 3° F add9

and pulled my legs a - part.
you tore a - way my shirt

C F

You took an ins - ta - mat - ic cam - 'ra
You rubbed an ice cube on my chest

C F add9/A 2° F 3° F add9

and pulled my sleeves a - round my heart.
snapped me till it hurt.
Be - cause

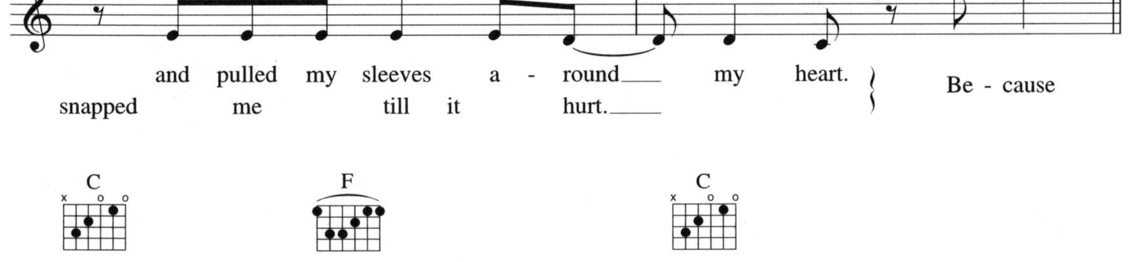

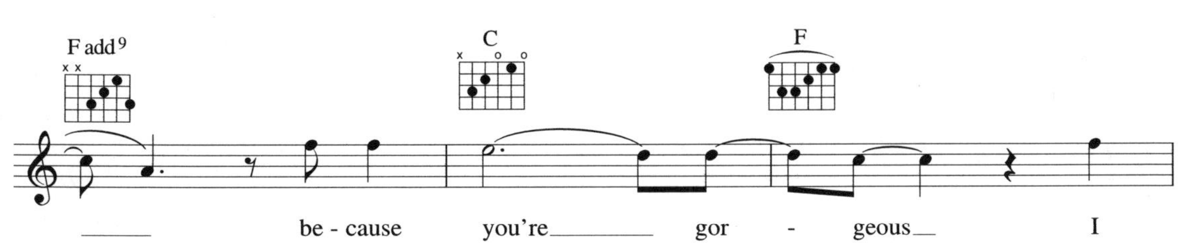

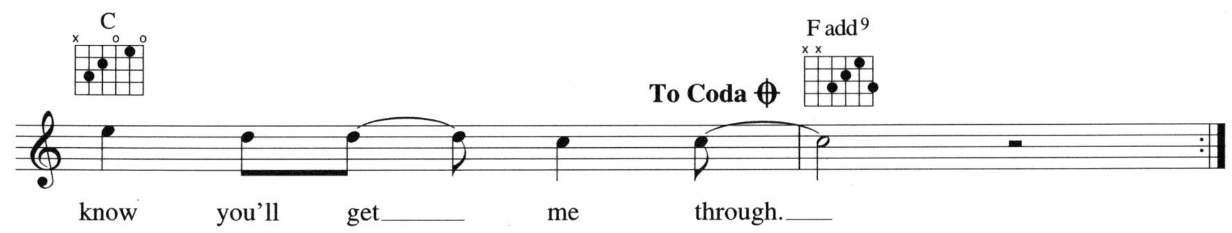

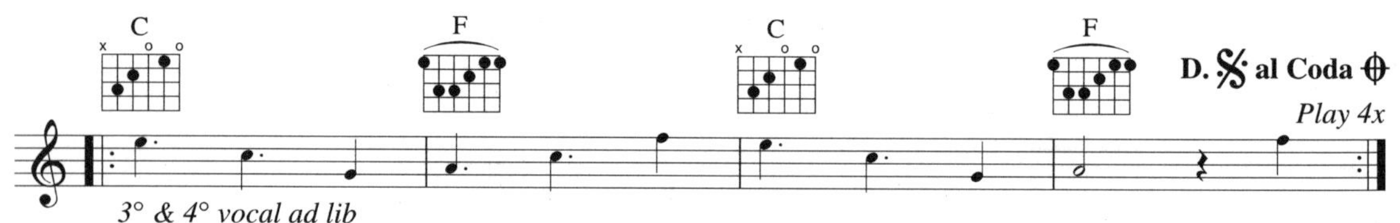

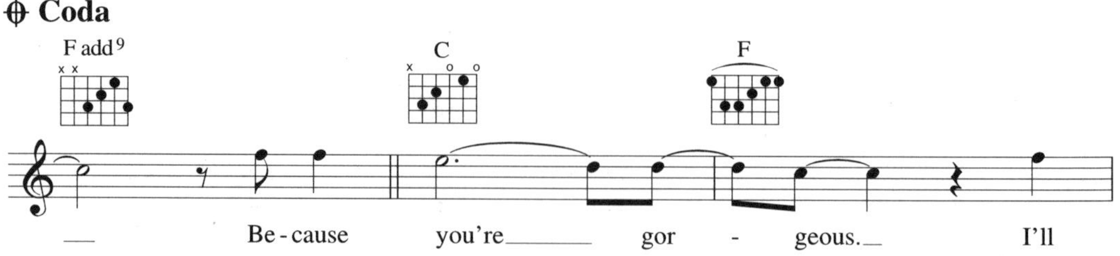

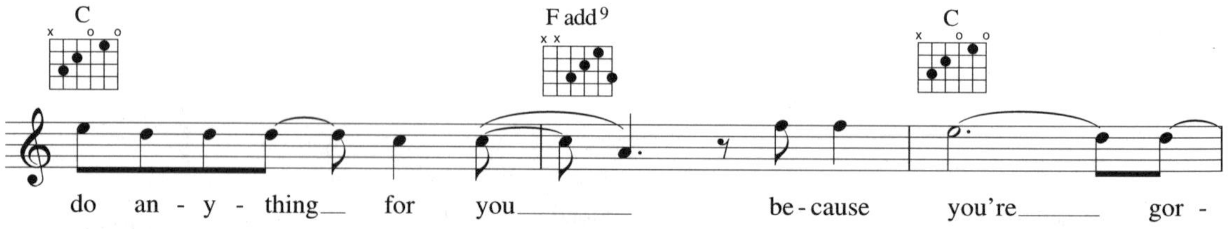

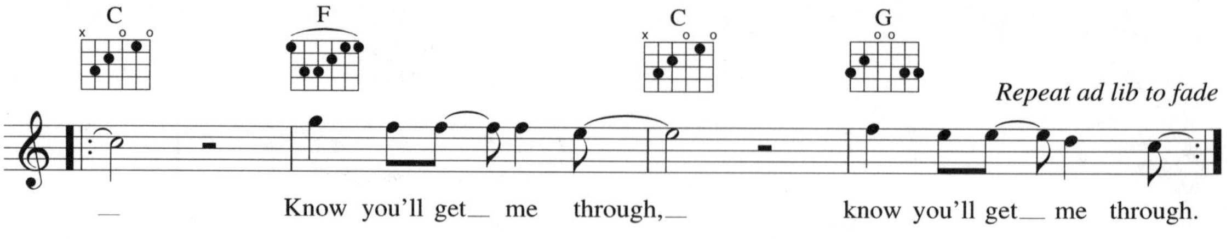

Verse 3:
You said I wasn't cheap
You paid me twenty pounds
You promised to put me in a magazine
On every table in every lounge.